Souls of Iron

James Polczynski

Published by James Polczynski, 2022.

Souls of Iron

James Polczynski

Published by James Polczynski, 2022.

SOULS OF IRON

First edition. January 3, 2022.

Copyright © 2022 James Polczynski.

ISBN: 979-8-9857998-2-8

Written by James Polczynski.

In memory of my grandfather, James Aites, the greatest man
I ever knew

In memory of my grandfather, James Aites, the greatest man I ever knew

"In the labor of engines and trades and the labor of fields I find the developments,

And find the eternal meanings. ...

Iron-works, forge-fires in the mountains or by river-banks, men around feeling the melt with huge crowbars, lumps of ore, the due combining of ore, limestone, coal,

The blast-furnace and the puddling-furnace, the loup-lump at the bottom of the melt at last, the rolling-mill, the stumpy bars of pig-iron, ..." – A Song for Occupations, Walt Whitman

"I thank you very much for your portrait and that of your little boy who has a fine, intelligent face ... let there be something of iron in his soul and in his body". - Robert Coleman, in Paris, to his brother George Dawson Coleman,

"I have always found Cornwall and its history intensely interesting and romantic. Perhaps not so romantic as the history of Salem [Derby ancestral home] ... With such a large Irish family inheriting parts of the same property it can well be imagined that there were innumerable fights that led to serious misunderstandings if not to feuds. I know they existed. I have no idea what caused them nor does anybody else of my generation. I once met a cousin, Miss Fanny Coleman, now dead, on a ship coming back from Japan. I had never seen nor heard of her before. She told me that she had been very fond of my mother when they were girls but as her branch of the family and mine were at war, they had to resort to a sort of bootleg friendship conducted on long horseback rides unbeknownst to their parents. ... My cousin, Mrs. Buckingham, who lives at Cornwall on the edge of the mine pit, bought out the family's interest a few years ago and presented it to the State ... I understand that their [Bethlehem Steel] explorations at a depth have developed more ore than my family mined in 150 years". – Personal correspondence of Roger Alden Derby

Table of Contents

Front cover: North Lebanon Furnace.

Introduction

I grew up twenty miles north-east of Pittsburgh along the Allegheny River, one of the "Three Rivers" for which Pittsburgh is famous. The rivers were dotted with steel and aluminum mills, which provided tens of thousands of jobs. My paternal grandfather was a miner. My father was an engineer for various steel companies, including U. S. Steel. My uncles worked in different capacities in other mills. My maternal grandfather was a metallurgist for Alcoa. I spent over ten years working as a contractor for many steel and aluminum companies, including Wheeling-Pittsburgh, Dofasco, Lukens, and Bethlehem. I caught the tail-end of the great steel age in America.

The industrial history of America is one of the great stories of our rise as a country to a world power. The manufacturing of iron and steel is one of the most fascinating subsets of that history. The science of extracting iron from ore to create products ranging from stove plates to I-beams is magical. The feeling of the heat and the visual play of chemical interactions can leave one speechless, requiring no knowledge of the processes to appreciate the beauty.

The genesis of this book began when I purchased what had been the Cornwall Store in Cornwall, Pennsylvania. It had served many functions throughout the years. Miners and iron workers would buy clothes, supplies, and even meat and groceries there. In fact, the last Coleman descendant to live in the Cornwall Mansion, Margaret Buckingham, would send to the store for fresh ground meat when she was expecting guests. The meat was then tossed into the fishpond at the mansion to the delight of the visitors as the fish streamed to the surface. There was a jail cell in the lower level of the store and the local Post Office on the first floor. There are two outbuildings still standing, a carriage house and barn. The icehouse, octagonal gas house, two-room outhouse, and cupola are long gone. The building sits in the shadow of an iron trestle bridge, which was built to carry the Cornwall and Lebanon Railroad from Lebanon, Pennsylvania to nearby Mount Gretna, created as a recreational retreat and Chautauqua spiritual center.

I visited the Lebanon County Courthouse and started following the title chain on the property and eventually found myself looking at hand-written deeds from the 1800s. I came to understand that the land on which the store was built was once part of a much larger property called the Cornwall Plantation. Altogether, around 10,000 acres were stitched together to support the need for charcoal for the furnace and homes for the owners and the workers at the mines and the furnace. The first iron in Cornwall was made before the Revolutionary War, and by 1800, the operations were owned by Robert Coleman. His descendants continued making iron in Cornwall and other locations for over a century.

There is a good amount of archival information available on the Coleman families and the Pennsylvania iron industry. I have spent hundreds of hours sifting through personal family letters, business letters, corporate minutes and logs, newspaper articles, and other related documents. The bulk of the material, though, was available in Pennsylvania, in Lebanon, Lancaster, Philadelphia, and Harrisburg.

I strongly recommend reading the Notes as you make your way through the text. There is good information in the Notes, but it made sense to isolate them from the main narrative. It may also be helpful to refer to the genealogy at the back of the book when you find yourself trying to sort out which Robert, William, or Anne is being discussed.

Like other multi-generational family dynasties, there were disputes and fractures in the branches of the Coleman families as they evolved their businesses. My focus in this book is to explore what caused the divisions in the family as well as what held branches together. There were disagreements among family members, and some of those led to lawsuits, but there were also partnerships formed that brought members together across different branches of the family. The main narrative begins prior to the Revolutionary War and extends to shortly after World War I. At that time, the combined wealth of the family members was in the tens of millions. In over 140 years, only one member of the family lost his fortune.

The Coleman iron dynasty came to an end with the purchase by Bethlehem Steel of the Cornwall ore body and the various furnaces, mills, and other holdings in Lebanon County. I have tried to avoid using secondary sources as much as possible. I have tried to make sure everything is accurate and avoided adding my interpretation of people's actions and motivations, allowing the events and facts to speak for themselves. Any mistakes are entirely of my own making. I hope that this book will provide a good summary of the Coleman families and their ironmaking and mining activities in Central Pennsylvania during the last half of the 18th Century to the early 20th Century. I also hope it serves as a representative window of the evolution of an industrial family-run dynasty over a roughly 150-year period. Finally, I hope you find the Coleman story interesting.

Prologue: Last Cast

On a mild January 13th, 1949, James Lloyd Derby and his wife[1] disembarked onto the platform of the Pennsylvania Railroad's Lebanon station. Their bags would be collected by a porter and delivered to the Weimer Hotel, the former Eagle Hotel – Lebanon's finest for over a century. They had plenty of time to unwind, have dinner, and retire early. In the morning, Frank Campbell would pick them up and take them to the Alden Villa, "Millwood", in nearby Cornwall, Pennsylvania. Derby had numerous childhood memories of visiting the mansion. This trip was imbued with sadness, though - James' cousin Jack, John Percy Coleman Alden, had passed away the day before Christmas, less than a month prior.

Jack Alden was descended from many prominent families. His mother, Mary Ida Warren, was named for her mother and for Mount Ida, in whose shadow the family's summer home sat near Troy, New York. Mary Ida's father, George Henry Warren, was prominent in many local businesses. His railroad, the Mohawk and Hudson, was purchased by Cornelius Vanderbilt and brought into the New York Central Railroad system. Mary Ida's brother, Whitney Warren, designed Grand Central Station, the showcase station for the New York Central. Jack's father, Robert Percy Alden, was descended from the proud Plymouth bloodline of John and Priscilla Alden. Jack's grandmother was the granddaughter of Robert Coleman, Pennsylvania's wealthiest and most powerful iron master at the time of his death in 1825.

Jack's Aunt Sarah married Dr. Richard Derby, of the powerful and very wealthy Derby shipping empire of Salem, Massachusetts. The Derby family intermarried with the Lloyd family of New England

and Long Island and settled around Lloyd's Neck, just north of Oyster Bay, Long Island.

Jack's will left the Alden property, including all farmland, animals, and buildings, to his Derby cousins, James, his sister Anne, and brothers Richard and Roger Alden, in equal parts.[2] As a lawyer, James took the lead to figure out how to handle the disposition of the property. He and his siblings had decided "the only solution to our problem [was to sell the property], what with so many people to be on the title, etc". This initial visit was to conduct an inventory of the estate, the contents, and the condition. The mansion was very much a classic Gilded Age country "cottage", kept year-round by employees, but only used by the family during the summer months. The mansion had been constructed in the 1880s, and Jack Alden was the second generation to inhabit it. It had been built as a wedding present for Jack's father and mother, Robert Percy and May Ida Warren Alden.

Jack Alden, unmarried, was the last to carry the Alden name along his grandfather's branch, that of Bradford Ripley Alden. Jack's brother, George Henry Warren Alden, had died of meningitis in 1912 at the age of 29. Their father, R. Percy Alden, had left the bulk of his estate to his two sons. Both sons had also received bequests from their mother's side of the family, the Warrens. When George died, his estate passed to Jack. The New York Times reported on March 13, 1951, that the entire estate was valued at $3,357,438 net, with $2,726,910 in investments and $430,000 in real estate. There was a belief among the Derby cousins that the money was mostly "Warren money", but, in truth, the estate represented a mixture of money from the Coleman and the Warren sides of the family.

James' second cousin, William C. Freeman, Jr., the last remaining descendant of Robert Coleman to still have active, tangible ties to

Cornwall and Lebanon, suggested Frank Campbell as the right person to assist James. Frank Campbell worked for Freeman and had proven indispensable in the transfer of other family property. Tall and slender, Frank was good-natured and disciplined. He was thorough and efficient. After one meeting with Campbell, James asked his cousin if he could part with Campbell for a bit while the estate was liquidated. And so, from the first day, Frank Campbell would help with the sale of the estate.

Campbell picked up the Derbys at 10:00 am on Friday. They drove the six miles to Cornwall and had lunch at the Quentin Riding Academy (later the Quentin Riding Club). The Quentin Riding Academy property had previously belonged to William C. Freeman's father, William C. Freeman, Sr. Derby was convinced the Alden property was salable, but it would be best to separate the sale of the livestock and other farm-related assets from the sale of the mansion. There were already a few parties interested in the property. Harry Harkins and nine fellow investors, who represented the Riding Academy, offered to purchase the entire property for $50,000. This proposal was rejected by Derby, believing it to be too low. An interest was also expressed by Ed Russell, who married a niece of Winston Churchill, and was the new owner of the Harrisburg Patriot newspaper (purchased from the vast estate of the very wealthy and successful Vance McCormick). He was looking to "find a country estate where there would be room to expand". He had seen the exterior of the mansion in early December, but not the interior. James and his brother, Roger, anticipated a sale price of close to $100,000, and it would appear this figure was too high for Russell.

Derby's optimism for the sale of the property remained steady as he told Campbell, "If the property were not such a fundamentally good one it would be a discouraging prospect. But I feel we will be moderately successful." Indeed, the property was remarkable. Set on over 200 acres of slightly rolling hills with uncut timber, its own water supply, various outbuildings, a stable, another 200-plus acres of farmland, and, of course, the mansion itself. The Alden Villa was Stanford White's first single-family home design. White's fellow partner, Charles Follen McKim (of the architectural firm of McKim, Mead and White), had rented an apartment in Manhattan from Derby's father, Dr. Richard Derby, and designed a home for Derby's grandmother, Anne Alden, in Lloyd's Neck, New York.

The westward wing of the mansion juts out, displaying a bank of eight stained glass panels atop a central door flanked by two additional stained-glass panels and two lower clear panels, which could be opened for air flow. The total height of the windows stands two large stories. The windows, with six similar windows to match along the southern exposure, are each composed of over 200 small sections of glass, most of them clear, but many of various pastel blues, oranges, greens, yellows, and reds. Each window has a central square, circle, or diamond with tree and floral shapes. Two of the panels include the date the home was finished, 1881, in Roman Numerals. Each window by itself is brilliant, but the combined effect is mesmerizing. The date in the windows is echoed on the currently exposed plaster in the formal dining room, with the writing, "Garfield [President Chester A. Garfield] dead November 19, 1881".

To the south extends a porte-cochere, and along the wall between the porte-cochere and the west bank of windows are embedded White's signature star-shaped bottle bottoms. The massive red split door at the side entry, with oversized floral wrought iron hinges, opens to the foyer. The woodwork is wonderfully rich and detailed with carved beading and sculpted beams. The grand barrel ceiling of the ballroom meets the top of the music room's fireplace, whose marble mantle holds a glass-fired brick front. The library contains heavily paneled wood and a curved wall seat. The adjoining office includes a recessed fireplace with marble seating. The Dining Room contains a built-in buffet similar to those in other mansions, such as Kingscote in Newport, Rhode Island. Each panel of the buffet sports a different tooled design. The woven wicker Dining Room ceiling is the only one still extant in the country. The total cost of construction was $30,000.

Campbell was the first point of contact with interested parties. He handled all inquiries about the property, managed the completion of insurance maps, estimated the value of the timber, and generally executed any necessary task. Despite the efforts made to find a buyer, no interested party, which now included nearby Elizabethtown College, would agree to the asking price. It was decided that the best path was to hold an auction. The announcement was published in numerous newspapers in August.

> Auction of "Millwood". the Alden Estate. consisting of about 520 Acres of fine farming and well-watered Pasture Lands with the following Improvements: Large English Type main 'residence', 2 complete farms with homes. and 1 more than ample farm bldg., one farm having 265 acres. Four manager and tenant homes: natural spring reservoir: large swimming pool: choice greenhouses. etc. Above tracts will be sold separately or as a whole. Siegrist. Koller and Siegrist. Attys. Lebanon. Pa. James Lloyd Derby. Atty., New York City.

On September 16, 1949, the Alden Villa and all 520 acres were purchased at auction for $88,000 by Mrs. D. J. Monas of Bangor, Pennsylvania. She represented the Amalgamated Clothing Workers of America (ACWA), an original member of the Congress for Industrial Organization (CIO) in the 1930s. Mrs. Monas was a central organizer of the CIO in Pennsylvania. She led strikes and protests against the clothing "sweatshops" of the day. She was an uncompromising union member, a shrewd businesswoman, and a champion of workers' rights. Along with her husband, David, she had long envisioned an educational and recreational center for the union membership.

Mrs. Monas had considered expanding the center beyond the Alden estate, but was unable to acquire any connecting land. She had written William C. Freeman on October 6, 1950, asking if the land across the road from the Alden property was for sale. Freeman explained the property was "occupied by employees or former employees ... it would be impossible to convey any of these properties without doing an injustice in some cases and adversely affecting lives and circumstances in others", but added his encouragement and support, "The Alden estate, however is a fine property with great possibilities for development, and I am sure you will be able to accomplish many of your objectives on those premises. If any local details with which you are unfamiliar should arise at any time, our Mr. Frank W. Campbell will, I know, be glad to be helpful".

When opened in 1955, the *New York Times* reported,

> Down in the Cornwall Mountains of Pennsylvania the Amalgamated Clothing Workers, C. I. O., has opened a vacation resort and education center for 18,000 shirt workers in the area. The union's theme for the magnificent estate, which was built seventy-five years ago to meet the requirements of a millionaire, is "Bread and Roses".

> That is a pretty descriptive slogan, to our way of thinking, and a desirable one. Bread and butter matters are obviously the concern – and properly so – of unions. Roses – meaning the things of the mind and spirit – are

too, and it is good to see increasing union recognition of that fact, although most of us have come to expect that kind of broad-visioned approach from the Amalgamated.

There is one other intriguing aspect to the union's Pennsylvania project. In a sense, the passing of that 520-acre estate with its mansion house designed by Stanford White and its paneled stable from a single man to 18,000 shirt workers is a rather incisive commentary of the social and economic changes that have been wrought, under our free society, by time and taxes.

We are happy to see that the Amalgamated has gathered roses. We hope they bloom beautifully and steadily.

Five days following the auction, in a letter to Freeman, James Lloyd Derby reflected on the results of the auction,

I had hoped against hope that some individual of the Country Squire type, would be the ultimate purchaser of the Alden property. In this day and generation that result does not appear to be in the cards, and while the successful purchaser may not be entirely desirable, I believe that for the sake of Cornwall it will be more advantageous than if the property had gone to other would-be purchasers whom I observed at the sale.

Mrs. Monas and others worked for six years without pay to bring the property to life, which became known in Cornwall as the Union Center. Derby's impression that the CIO might do what was best for the property was close to the truth – the ACWA kept much of the mansion as they found it. Union funds began to decline in the 1970s, and the entire property was sold in 1983. The new owners hoped to transform the property into a bible college but were unable to secure the funding.

In the early 2000s, a local developer purchased the property, sold off the mansion and carriage house, and created a 55+ retirement community on the remaining land. The carriage house was moved closer to the mansion and restored, but restoration of the mansion stalled due to legal disputes among the owners. The mansion, added to the National Register of Historic Places in 2011, had sat in need of significant repair and restoration for decades. Along with a multitude of problems, the roof was in dire need of repair, the inside wood was drying out, and the eastern bank of stained-glass windows were bowed. The mansion, along with the restored carriage house, changed hands in December 2021, and the new owner quickly addressed the multiple needs. It is now open for events and overnight stays.

When the Alden Villa was built, there were three separate branches of the family making iron in Lebanon County. Individual family members were worth between a million and a few million dollars. Together, the family members' combined wealth ranked them among the highest in the country. By the time the Alden estate was sold, the wealth, at least for some descendants, was greatly diminished. Roger Alden Derby's son reported that at the time of Jack Alden's death, his parents were living on $10,000 a year. The roughly $200,000 inherited from Jack Alden and the sale of the Millwood property were timely. Many other descendants, though, still held significant wealth, and many to this day still benefit from the dynasty that started in the 1700s.

The story of the Alden Villa is part of the fabric of a larger tale. It is a tale of a sixteen-year-old immigrant and his descendants, of their construction of an iron empire and their challenges in maintaining it. The empire weathered great recessions and one great depression, five wars, radical changes in technology, and changes to corporate governance and tax law. It is a tale of ambition and sacrifice, of family division and close-knit bonds of love and devotion, of industrial growth and catastrophic loss, of great joys and unbearable pain.

Chapter 1: The Hills

The range of hills along the southern boundary of Lebanon County in Pennsylvania is part of the Kittatinny range. These hills, called the Endless Hills by Native Americans, were formed over 265 million years ago during the last period of the Paleozoic era of the Permian period. The forces of nature at work produced beds of limestone, mostly composed of calcium carbonate. Later during the Triassic period of the Mesozoic era, intrusions of magma formed the iron ore, which was most strongly concentrated in the Cornwall area. The ore would lie undisturbed until the 1730s.

The first inhabitants of the land had little use for the ore, aside from using the reddish oxide for paint. At the time of the early exploration by Europeans of what would later become the Lebanon and Cornwall area in Central Pennsylvania, the land belonged to the Leni-Lenape tribe, also known as the Delaware. They migrated from Canada and took control of a great deal of land from the Allegewi tribe. The Lenape lived primarily along the Delaware River and used the area of what is now Lebanon County as a hunting ground. The regular rhythm of the Lenape would be disrupted in the last quarter of the 17th century.

In 1677, William Penn was trying to secure the purchase of New Jersey from Lord Berkeley, and hoping for success, he dispatched 230 settlers to journey from London. The *Kent* left port in late spring and arrived at Sandy Hook many weeks later. The fare for passage was five pounds, but if a passenger could not afford it, they could sail as an indentured servant for a pledge of three years' service. New Jersey was under the jurisdiction of New York and the rule of Major Fenwick.

Anticipating problems, Penn had instructed the settlers to settle as far away from Fenwick as possible. The concerns were not unwarranted, and by 1678, many of the settlers migrated to other regions. Penn switched his focus and, in 1681, was granted a charter for Pennsylvania, or Penn's Woods. The next year, he sailed on the *Welcome* and on October 24, 1682, arrived at the Delaware River. He also purchased Delaware from the Duke of York. By March of the next year, he made his home in Philadelphia. Penn could make his own laws, set up his own government, and build towns. He was not allowed to correspond with any authority at odds with England. Penn was under obligation to pay an annual homage of two beaver skins to the King and required to send one-fifth of any gold or silver mined to the Crown. Penn created government and laws, as well as guidelines, for the construction and jurisdiction of this new land. Among the guidelines was a call for just and fair treatment of the Native Americans.

In 1684, he returned to England. He did not visit his colony again until 1699. He died in England in 1718, fifteen years before the Native Americans officially and finally traded away their hunting grounds, which contained what later became Lebanon County, Pennsylvania. Chester County initially comprised all land west of the Schuylkill River. Until settlements migrated west, there was no need to subdivide the vast unknown land, but as settlements did progress and interests became competitive, new counties were created. In 1729, Lancaster County was formed from Chester County. It would take until after the Revolutionary War, in 1785, for Dauphin County to be split off from Lancaster, and not until 1813 for Lebanon to be carved out of Dauphin and a small northern portion of Lancaster County.

William Penn authorized agents to negotiate for the purchase of the land from the Native Americans on his behalf. It was not until September 7, 1732, many years after the buildup of the colony, that Conrad Weiser, on behalf of the sons of Penn, finalized agreements for "all those tracts of land or lands lying on or near the river Schuylkill in the said Province or any of the branches, streams, fountains, or springs, thereof eastward or westward, and all lands lying in or near any swamps, marshes, fens or meadows, the waters or streams of which flow into or toward the said Schuylkill river, situate, lying and being between these hills called Lechay hills and those called Kitochtinny hills, which cross said river Schuylkill about thirty miles above (west of) the Lechay hills, and all lands whatsoever lying within the said bounds and between the branches of the Delaware river on the eastern side of the said land, and the branches or streams running into the river Susquehanna on the western side of the said land". [1]

Brothers John and Henry Grubb sailed from England on the *Kent* to the New Jersey colony. Henry was listed as an indentured servant. In November 1679, John Grubb and Richard Buffington, two of the settlers from the original New Jersey settlement, migrated south and purchased 340 acres at Upland Creek near the modern border of Delaware and Pennsylvania. There were rumors that William Penn would establish the area as a new colony, founded as a bastion of Quaker principles. This appealed to John Grubb, who gradually became a significant landowner. Among his purchases was a third ownership in a 600-acre property at Naaman's Creek along the Delaware River. This would become the Grubb homestead for future generations.

John Grubb died in 1708. His widow married Grubb's former partner, Richard Buffington, and moved with at least her youngest son, Peter, to East Bradford, near modern-day Coatesville. After completing an apprenticeship as a stone mason, Peter began contracting local work. He became acquainted with numerous stone deposits, including some in the Lancaster area. On April 4, 1737, Peter purchased 171 acres along the Hammer Creek, as it came to be known, borrowing its name from the eventual forge hammer he would install, which would pound and reshape iron. Later that year, in November, he purchased 300 acres six miles west of the creek from William Allen for £135. The tract of land contained an abundant supply of iron ore.

Allen, a wealthy Philadelphia businessman, partner of Joseph Turner, future Chief Justice of the province, and founder of Allentown, purchased 5,000 acres of land in the "wilderness" of Pennsylvania from Turner in 1734. Turner had purchased the land from John, Thomas, and Richard Penn two years earlier at the price of 100 acres of land for fifteen pounds and ten shillings. Turner and Allen were involved in the iron industry in Pennsylvania and may have been aware of the ore deposit, especially given the very specific location of Grubb's initial purchase. Turner and Allen were already invested in the Durham Furnace in Bucks County and started New Jersey's Union Iron Works in 1742. They likely knew there was ore in the property, but just as likely, they may not have been interested in investing more capital ninety miles from their base of operations.

The initial 300 acres Grubb purchased, just south of what is now the city of Lebanon, Pennsylvania, included three hills which became known as the Big Hill, the Middle Hill, and the Grassy Hill. Each hill contained quantities of iron ore of varying degrees of quality. In 1901, Henry C. Grittinger reported on a site a mile east of the Cornwall Iron Furnace at which evidence of slag and white iron was found. The site was shown to him by J. Taylor Boyd, who was made aware of the site from a long-term resident of Cornwall when Boyd first came to work as Superintendent at the mines in 1853, in charge of overseeing the openings of George Dawson and Robert Coleman. Boyd believed that a small bloomery furnace was installed at the site to "test" the iron. He further concluded that the site was never thought of as a permanent location for a furnace since the site was in a small ravine insufficient to power a water wheel.

It is often stated that Peter Grubb built this first bloomery furnace, but Grittinger believed it was more likely Peter's brother, Samuel, who may have built the bloomery. The site discovered by Boyd and Grittinger had been on land leased to Samuel and Joseph Taylor, adjacent to Peter's land. Peter contracted Samuel to build a furnace on the land he already owned. It seemed more likely to Grittinger that Peter would have tested the ore in a bloomery furnace he built on the Hammer Creek, "which was the largest stream in the neighborhood". There were two "Hopewell Forges" built, an "upper" and a "lower". The exact dates when these forges were built are not known, but it is believed the first one built was a bloomery to reduce the ore directly, and the second was a more traditional forge used to rework pig iron from the furnace.

Peter's furnace was the first iron furnace constructed in the area. The ore was of such high quality that Peter believed the operations would be successful. It was a risk, but one which Peter was willing to take. He named the furnace and the area Cornwall after his father's ancestral home in England. The furnace was completed and fired into blast by 1742. Grubb gradually acquired more of the surrounding land and actively operated the furnace and forges for two years, but in 1744, he placed an advertisement in the Pennsylvania Gazette seeking to lease the iron works.

> To be LET, A Furnace, Sawmill and Forge, within 13
> Miles of the City of Lancaster, for 20 years, or otherwise
> as may be agreed upon giving good Security if required;
> all of them being almost new, with good Water and
> Timber, with an unquestionable Quantity of good Iron
> Ore, laying near so that three men and two Horse has
> and can supply her with Ore every Day, when she is in
> Blast. Pigmetal is proved to be very good, Hearth-stones
> handy, Limestone Sand and Twere Clay on the Premises,
> a Quantity of Coals housed, some Wood cut: She may be
> put in Blast early this Summer if required. There are 80
> Acres of Land within Fence, 20 Acres of Meadow cleared,
> 50 ore may be easily made, 7000 Rails ready mauled, with
> other Conveniences, to accommodate an Iron-Work. If
> any Person hath a Mind to lease the said Works, let him or
> them repair to the said Place and treat with Peter Grubb
> on Conditions.

A group of twelve men signed a lease for £250 a year for twenty years beginning in 1745. This group included Peter's brother, Samuel, and others, all Quaker businessmen. The group struggled to make a profit, and shares changed hands. George Churchman, one of the original twelve investors, persuaded Jacob Giles of Maryland to invest. Giles had experience with iron works, and the hope was that he could bring some organization and profit to the works, which included the furnace and forges. Giles brought in Amos Garrett, who had managed the Bush River Iron Works in Maryland. There were many issues between the two that lingered six years after the end of the twenty-year lease. As late as December 1771, Giles and Garrett were still in the courts to settle their disputes.

Having leased the Cornwall Furnace, Grubb removed to Delaware and collected the annual income while buying and selling land until he died in 1754. Peter's sons, Curtis[2] and Peter, inherited the furnace, forges, and remaining land according to Pennsylvania intestate law since their father had not left a will. Curtis, in his early twenties, received two-thirds of the furnace and forges, and Peter, a teenager, inherited the remaining third. The lease on the furnace and forges would not expire for a little over a decade, until June 1765.

Chapter 2: Possessed of But a Small Capital

It was a two-day carriage ride from Salford Forge (near present-day Norristown, Pennsylvania) to Elizabeth Furnace. Robert and Ann Old Coleman made the journey with their two-year-old daughter, Margaret, and six-month-old son, William. A great deal had happened since the sixteen-year-old Robert Coleman first stepped onto the docks of Philadelphia.

That was 1764. Philadelphia was a busy city full of life, hope, and much activity. It was a young city that was convinced of its importance. At one time a solid bastion of Quakers, the city had begun attracting adventurers such as Benjamin Franklin. "The crown jewel of British North America. Its people and institutions, rather than its physical characteristics, allowed the Quaker metropolis to surpass Boston as the colonies' leading city".[1] Stepping onto the Philadelphia streets was a great relief after the long, crowded voyage across the Atlantic. The city was in sharp contrast to the thinly populated, rural country village Robert Coleman had called home for his first sixteen years.

He had sailed on the *Betsey* bound for the American Colonies. His older brother, William, had embarked on a similar voyage earlier in the year to British North America.

It can be assumed that Coleman was consumed with a mixture of excitement and concern. It was fall, and the sail across the Atlantic Ocean would likely have been a rough one. He possessed three guineas (the basic equivalent of a month's salary for a hard laborer at an iron furnace in the Colonies) and letters of introduction to Philadelphia merchants. Perhaps the strongest element in his possession was his will and determination.

Robert Coleman was born on November 4, 1748, and grew up in the Northern Ireland town of Castelfinn in the parish of Donaghmore in the county of Donegal. Situated on the river Finn, Castlefinn, called Castle-Fynyn in the reign of Elizabeth, was a little less than 120 miles north-west of Dublin. His mother died when he was young, and his father, Thomas, had remarried - a union which produced more children.[2] Robert displayed fluency with numbers and had a quick mind. With the growing size of his father's household, and since he was of the age when he would have left home anyway, it was decided he would map his fortunes in the Colonies.

Arriving in Philadelphia, he presented his letters of introduction. One of the letters was delivered to Mark Biddle, who offered Coleman a clerkship in his Philadelphia store. Coleman proved himself worthy of more responsibility. As part of his duties, one of Coleman's tasks was to take minutes of conversations between prominent businessmen, allowing him to become acquainted with how local affairs were conducted. Blair McLenahan, to whom Coleman had also presented a letter of introduction, informed Biddle that the Reading Prothonotary needed a full-time clerk. The Prothonotary's office in Reading, about sixty miles north-west of Philadelphia, was conducted by James Reed. Coleman and Biddle agreed it was a sound opportunity.

Under Reed's supervision, Coleman continued his education, recording wills, contracts, deeds, and other transactions. All the records were handwritten. There was much value in an easy-to-decipher record, especially when disputes would arise. It also demonstrated attention to detail, critical to a successful record of business transactions. Some of the contracts Coleman had to copy were for material purchases by Peter Grubb, Jr. in nearby Lancaster County. When Peter took a look at the carefully penned contracts written for him by Reed's office, he asked who had written them.

Grubb asked for and was granted permission to hire Robert Coleman. At the age of seventeen, in the spring of 1766, Robert Coleman became the head clerk for Peter Grubb's Hopewell Forge, at £100 per year, over thirty times the amount he had arrived with in the Colonies.

The iron industry in the area had grown significantly since the elder Peter Grubb built the Cornwall Furnace and the Hopewell Forges. Curtis and Peter Grubb took possession of the furnace and forges at the end of the twenty-year lease on the properties. Curtis, despite inheriting a larger portion of the properties, ran the less profitable furnace since he was not as experienced as his younger brother. Peter, Jr., lived in the mansion built by his father near the forges while Curtis built a new mansion in Cornwall overlooking the furnace.

Just east of the Hopewell forges, John Huber had built Elizabeth Furnace in 1750, the same year England issued the Iron Act restricting the erection of new forges and furnaces. Elizabeth Furnace was further expanded by Huber's son-in-law, Henry William Stiegel, after he purchased the furnace in 1757. Stiegel had married Huber's daughter Elizabeth in 1752. Roughly a mile downstream from the Hopewell Forges sat the Speedwell Forge. The Speedwell was built by James Old in 1760. Old had arrived in the Colonies a decade earlier from Wales. He married Margaretta Davies the daughter of a Welshman. Old was a prominent citizen of the Lancaster area and an accomplished iron master. Young Coleman caught the eye of Old, and he hired Coleman away from the employ of the Grubbs, eventually installing Coleman as head clerk of all of Old's operations.

Old had leased a forge along the Quittapahilla Creek several miles north-west of Cornwall and first stationed Coleman there. When Old moved his family into the mansion home at Speedwell,

Coleman moved with the family and then, finally, when Old leased the Reading Furnace, Coleman again moved with the family. The Reading Furnace, alternatively spelled Redding, located east of Reading, Pennsylvania, was built by one of Pennsylvania's iron pioneers, Samuel Nutt. He built two furnaces of the same name, and both were situated along the French Creek. The first was built in 1720. Sixteen years later, it was dismantled and replaced with a newer, slightly larger furnace. Shortly after the second furnace's construction in 1739, Nutt died, leaving the property to his wife and his son. They sold the furnace to William Branson in 1760. Branson leased the furnace to Old.

On October 4, 1773, at the Reading Furnace, Robert Coleman married James Old's 18-year-old daughter Ann (also, as was common, called Nancy).[3] They were married by the Rev. Thomas Barton. Many years later, the Coleman family flush with success, Johann Frederick Stoever, Jr., recounted an anecdote from a visit to Elizabeth Furnace. Stoever visited Coleman to discuss land purchases that may have interested Coleman. Before business, the family and guests sat down to dinner – fine food served with fine china. The mood was jovial, and all were at ease. Coleman commented on his courtship of Ann, "But nothing delayed my marrying my employer's daughter, Ann Old, except her own shilly-shallying for a space to take the conceit out of me".

The couple started their journey at Salford Forge, north of the Reading Furnace. The forge was built by John Krider as early as 1767 on land inherited from his father, a blacksmith. Salford was described as a "Forge for making of Bar Iron". Krider ran the forge himself, but in 1773, he leased the operations to Coleman for £250 per year for a period of three years – pretty much the going rate at the time.

While at Salford Forge, Coleman volunteered for the Colonies in the Revolutionary War, and Ann Coleman helped manage the forge. Ann wrote to Robert in September 1776 while he was stationed at Amboy, New Jersey, informing him, "Kellings sent an order here you left with him for iron on which we sent one lode". Later in the letter, she added, "I shall take every particular care of in your absence which I pray God may not be long. I conclude with my love to you as I remain your ever loving wife". Her wish was granted because Robert returned quickly. He requested from the Philadelphia Council that his workers be spared service in the war effort so he could work up the inventory he had on hand. He would be moving on. In October, he and his father-in-law signed a seven-year lease for Elizabeth Furnace for £450 a year - only a few miles east from where he began his iron career at Hopewell Forge. As the carriage wound down the dirt road and Coleman caught sight of the furnace, he embraced the opportunity to run his first furnace.

Chapter 3. Success However Crowned My Endeavors

Henry William Stiegel, who was commonly known as Baron Stiegel, due in large part to his grand style of living, greeted the Colemans when they arrived at Elizabeth Furnace. Stiegel, a previous owner of the furnace, had overextended himself in his purchases and operations, adding a glass manufacturing factory to his iron making. He had heavily mortgaged his properties to support his expansion. When he could not make payments on his debt, he was placed in debtor's prison in Philadelphia in 1774. When he was released from prison, he returned to Elizabeth Furnace, but not as the owner. Stiegel worked for Robert Coleman as a foreman (Stiegel and Coleman were family in a way since the Baron's daughter married one of James Old's sons). Stiegel's intimate knowledge of the operations and his fluency in German would prove useful.

The furnace was owned in equal parts by Charles Stedman, John Dickinson, and Daniel Benezet. Stiegel had been in partnership with brothers Alexander and Charles Stedman, both of Philadelphia. Alexander became financially strained and was forced to either sell or surrender many of his holdings. He lost his share in Elizabeth Furnace through a sheriff's sale, purchased by Dickinson in 1770. Charles held onto his share while Stiegel had mortgaged his to Benezet for £300.

As Coleman settled in, he began to get a hold on the operations. Later in life, he commented,

> In the year 1776, possessed of but a small capital, and recently married, I took a lease for the Elizabeth Furnace estate for the term of seven years, not anticipating at that

time that before the expiration of the lease I should have it in my power to become owner in fee simple of the whole or a greater part of the estate. Success however crowned my endeavors. A new and regular system was adopted, by which the business of ironwork was made to resemble more a well-conducted manufactory than the scenes of confusion and disorder which had before that time prevailed in that business. During the continuance of the lease I made several purchases of lands contiguous to the estate, ...

Coleman worked hard to improve the furnace operations. He determined it cost £4,660 to break even on the manufacture of 1,000 tons of pig iron. He recorded the breakdown of costs as:

2,500 loads of coal at £2,500

1,500 loads of ore at £107

2 tiller wages for 10 months at £90

2 mine founders at £80

1 mine setter at £40

1 banksman at £40

1 gutterman at £40

1 carpenter at £45

Founder's Wages at £225 and £150

Potters Wages at £125

Managers, Clerks and House Keepers at £250

Travelling Expense at £30

Puddling in hearth and other expenses at £150

An entire plantation existed to service the operations and the needs of the workers. The furnace was the core around which the remainder of the plantation revolved. Homes for the workers were built, crops were planted, livestock were raised, facilities for church and school were provided, and a store was maintained to supply other needs. Coleman, along with his father-in-law and Peter Grubb, paid for an educator for the children of the workers. The school was a cooperative undertaking of separate iron works in the immediate area. Likewise, itinerant ministers would circulate among the different works. Iron plantations needed to be self-sufficient because they were often located in remote areas. Furnaces were built where there was easy access to water, iron ore, and timber.

A water wheel powered the blast of air required to keep the furnace burning at the appropriate temperature to melt iron ore. The wheel provided the force to operate two large bellows, which directed air into the rear of the furnace (the bellows used at Cornwall were 20 feet 7 inches long, 5 feet 10 inches wide across the breech, and 14 inches wide at the point at which the nozzle was inserted into the furnace). It took an acre of trees a day to keep a furnace running with a good supply of charcoal. Colliers would spend months in the woods chopping down trees, building charcoal mounds, and tending the mounds until the wood was baked into charcoal. Furnaces ran nonstop. A supply of charcoal was stored in nearby barns where it could be easily wheeled to the top of the furnace, where it would be dumped into the stack. It took three days to load a furnace with charcoal to achieve the required heat, usually between 2300 degrees and 2600 degrees Fahrenheit. At that point, the furnace would be charged every hour with carefully measured alternating quantities of charcoal, ore, and limestone. The limestone acted like a sponge to hold the impurities which were released from the ore, allowing the molten iron to percolate to the bottom of the furnace, where every twelve hours the furnace was tapped to make bars of pig iron, each one weighing around 100 pounds, or cast products, such as pots, pans, furnace plates, and other products.

Coleman continually purchased land. He eventually cobbled together 10,000 acres. Coleman himself purchased numerous farms and land, and his sons, when they became active in the business, continued to purchase additional land. It was critical to have a healthy supply of timber and required careful management. Some furnaces went permanently out of blast for want of timber for charcoal. In general, the preferred woods were hardwoods such as chestnut, oak, hickory, and walnut, but some softwoods were used, such as pine and ash.

The workforce on the plantation included a combination of free and enslaved workers.[1] Both the Grubbs and Colemans owned slaves. In 1786, Coleman owned 17 slaves (he later acquired additional enslaved workers when he became the owner of the Cornwall Furnace). Most of the enslaved workers were stationed in the household or the fields, but some worked as Colliers and a few in the furnace. Some were actually paid a small salary for their work, but they still were not free. In 1780, Pennsylvania, recognizing the inhumanity of the slavery system, passed an act for the gradual elimination of slavery. The act, though, did not call for the immediate elimination of slavery, but allowed the system of slavery to continue under limited restrictions. Only those born after the act's passage were freed, but not until they turned 28. Pennsylvanians were prohibited from importing new enslaved workers into the state. To help enforce this law, slave owners were required to register their enslaved workers every year. They could still be sold, but only if they were already enslaved in the state. Coleman was careful to abide by the act. He demanded proof of registration before purchasing any enslaved worker. A further amendment to the act, in 1788, forbade any enslaved female who was pregnant from being transported out of the state. It would take decades from the passage of the act before there were no enslaved workers in Pennsylvania.

It took about 35 men to staff the furnace. Workers worked two twelve-hour shifts per day. Once a furnace was in blast, it stayed in blast unless there was a problem or the water source froze due to cold periods. While Coleman used very few indentured servants, he did take advantage of using captured Hessian soldiers to expand the workforce. General George Washington's triumph on Christmas 1776, at Trenton, resulted in the capture of hundreds of Hessian soldiers. The soldiers were re-purposed; some of them were hired out to both the Cornwall and Elizabeth furnaces. They were leased for 32 to 45 shillings per month, usually paid in iron.[2] Coleman purchased the freedom of many of the Hessians for thirty pounds each. A separate barracks was built for the prisoners with iron bars over the windows. Stiegel, from Germany as well, was put in charge of their work. They dug a mile-long canal seven feet deep and seven feet wide, today known as the "Hessian Ditch", which increased the flow of the water over the water wheel. A steady flow of water controlled the pressure of the air blown into the furnace. This, in turn, increased production.

The primary product of Elizabeth Furnace was iron, but it also provided steel to forge muskets, delivered to Carlisle, one of the major stores for the war.[3] The furnace supplied shot and shell and was one of the furnaces, along with Cornwall, selected by Captain Daniel Joy to produce cannons.[4] There are better records for the Cornwall Furnace's production of cannons than for Elizabeth.

Captain Joy provided an update on September 10, 1776, that he had just proved two cannons at Cornwall and that 27 cannons were cast by that time. There was concern that the cannons were overweight. It took an entire 12-hour pour to produce one cannon, so mistakes were costly. The cannons were then further processed with a boring machine that was powered by a water wheel. In Joy's letter, he noted delays due to repairs on the water wheel at Cornwall. Furnaces such as Elizabeth and Cornwall were critical to the revolutionary cause, especially since loyalists (which included Turner and Allen) refused to put their furnaces into blast.

John Dickinson, a Founding Father, and his wife, Mary Norris Dickinson, sold their third to Coleman.

> ... and in the year 1780, I purchased from John Dickinson, Esq., the one undivided third part of the Elizabeth Furnace and lands thereunto belonging, he having before that time become the owner of all the estate and interest which Alexander Stedman held in the same. In the year 1784, I purchased out Mr. Charles Stedman, who also held an undivided third part of the estate. The remaining third part of the original estate was not purchased by me from Daniel Benezet until the year 1794, he either not being inclined to sell or asking more than I thought it expedient to give.

Colman agreed to pay Dickinson 375 ounces of gold, or the equivalent amount, based on the standard value of an ounce of gold of Portugal. The entire amount was finally paid by 1785. Many of Coleman's agreements were made with the provision that payments would be made over a period of years. Inflation was high, and deals could be struck with somewhat flexible terms if both parties were trustworthy.

In 1784, shortly after signing rent extensions, Coleman bought out Charles Stedman's third. He also purchased the Speedwell Forge from his brother-in-law, William Old. This was the start of an almost twenty-year push in building one of the most valuable iron empires in Pennsylvania.

Through careful planning and patience, Coleman established relationships of trust with those he did business with and associated with. He was also shrewd enough to act on a deal when it knocked on his door. He managed his business well and built steady profits. One of the more critical relationships he had was with his previous employers, the Grubbs. There was a supply of ore on the Elizabeth property, but it was not as rich, nor as abundant as the Cornwall ore. (Between August 1960 and October 1962, Bethlehem Steel removed 161,501 tons of iron ore from the mine, yielding ore that averaged about 40% iron, which, while the percentage was higher than the ore being mined in Cornwall in the 1960s, was a lower percentage of iron than was in present in the Cornwall iron ore in the 1780s.) Coleman supplemented his own ore by purchasing the higher-quality Cornwall ore. With a higher-grade ore, a higher quality pig iron could be produced and realize a higher price in the marketplace.

On February 23, 1774, Peter Grubb's wife, Mary, died from complications following the birth of their second son, Henry Bates. Peter was devastated, and as time progressed, he started drinking more. In 1776, he was drinking heavily at a tavern in Lancaster and raised a toast of "Success to King George". While the charge of "crimes committed against the State" was dismissed, his reputation as a drunk continued to grow. On another occasion in early 1777, believing a powder mill was connected to someone he had a grudge against, he declared, "Damn the Powder Mill, let us blow it to hell". Almost two weeks later, there was an actual explosion at the mill. After investigation, the Council of Safety acquitted Peter of any charges, concluding Peter "behaved in his usual mad way ... the effects of Liquor". From this point forward, Peter's relationship with Curtis began to swiftly deteriorate.

Curtis' third marriage to Ann Grubb, his Uncle Samuel's daughter, further complicated matters in the minds of both Curtis' son, Peter III, and Peter, Jr. Peter III became concerned about the future portion of his inheritance and was afraid of the impact of the growing feud between his father and his uncle. He requested an early distribution of his inheritance. Curtis agreed to the request and papers were drawn up in 1783 granting Peter III one-sixth of the ore banks and Cornwall Furnace and one-third of the Hopewell Forge.

To avoid any future disruption of the supply of pig iron for the forge, Peter began construction of his own furnace, Mount Hope. Distrust between Curtis and Peter grew, and threats were made by both brothers. Peter III grew concerned about the value of his ownership in the properties and sold his shares to Coleman on September 26, 1785, for 8,500 pounds, arranged over seven years.

Provision was made in the agreement[5] to allow for "the liberty of digging, raising, and hauling away a sufficient quantity of iron ore to supply the furnace which he purchased of John Patton, or any other furnace which he may erect elsewhere, provided there is not more than one furnace blowing at the same time".

Peter, Jr., also considered selling his shares to Coleman, but could never commit to the decision. In January 1785, Coleman agreed to pay Grubb a yearly sum of 200 pounds of gold or silver or pig iron in equivalent value for seven years in exchange for the rights to extract ore belonging to Peter Grubb. The agreement required

Coleman to provide an immediate delivery of thirty tons of pig iron valued at twelve pounds per pig to be delivered "upon request" and the following summer to deliver one hundred tons at market price. Coleman suggested, now that they were partners, he and Peter meet to "see that the works are carried on in the most advantageous manner and put on such a footing that each owner may know how and when to draw out his particular or proportionable share of the profits". He also made it clear he would not tolerate any actions by which he would not "reap a benefit from the estate without enjoying the share I am entitled to". As the year proceeded, Peter's behavior became more erratic and both Coleman and Curtis Grubb grew concerned about their partnerships with Peter. On December 8, 1785, Coleman and the Grubb brothers signed an "agreement of amicable proceedings" to protect all three parties.

Peter's mental health worsened, and only three days into 1786, he sat down and wrote a note saying, "my head has been keen for business but now it is squash" and then attempted to shoot himself, but a workman stopped him. On the 17th, though, at Hopewell, he shot himself in the head and died. This left Curtis Grubb and Robert Coleman partners with Peter's eleven-year-old son, Henry Bates, and his thirteen-year-old son, Alan Burd. There was considerable activity in aligning existing agreements with the changing circumstances. One consideration involved Coleman leasing the forge. Jasper Yeates, one of the children's guardians, met with Robert Coleman and his brother William (reunited and working with Robert) to discuss options. Coleman worked with the guardians, as well as Curtis, to try to straighten things out. Finally, an agreement was reached, but not until 1787. The Cornwall Furnace would belong to Curtis and Coleman

(¾ owned by Curtis and ¼ by Coleman) and the Hopewell Forges to Alan Burd and Henry Bates Grubb. The Ore Banks would remain three-sixths to Curtis, two-sixths to the Grubb boys, and one-sixth to Robert Coleman.

Two years later, on January 27, 1789, Curtis Grubb passed away, leaving his share to his son, Curtis, Jr., who only survived his father another year. Coleman leased the share of the Cornwall Furnace, which had belonged to Curtis following Curtis' death. When Curtis, Jr. died, the properties transferred to Curtis' daughter, Elizabeth. When she turned twenty-one, she sold the three-quarters share of the Cornwall Furnace and three-sixths of the Ore Banks she inherited to Coleman, who installed Rudolph Kelker as manager of the furnace. When Kelker died in 1801, Coleman appointed his twenty-five-year-old son, William, as manager. Grubb descendants would later write about Curtis Jr., "through this unfortunate boy the greater part of the Cornwall ore bank was lost and passed into the hands of Robert Coleman".

Under Coleman's ownership, production steadily increased at the Cornwall Furnace, more than doubling the output during the last decade of the 1700s. Given the demand for quality iron and the availability of the Cornwall ore, Coleman built his only furnace in 1791 in Colebrook along the Conewago Creek, a few miles west of Cornwall. The cost of constructing a new furnace was about $30,000, but in addition to this cost, there was the cost of building an entire plantation, including a furnace master's home, a mill, and homes for workers. The furnace was initially run by Samuel (Squire) Jacobs, the brother of Cyrus Jacobs, Coleman's brother-in-law (a famous poem titled The Legend of the Hounds is said to have been written about Samuel Jacobs). He also signed his first lease on Spring Forge in York County in 1793 for two-hundred pounds per year and started buying shares in the Martic Forge operations in southern Lancaster County in the 1790s, for which he eventually acquired outright ownership.

The Martic operations had included a furnace using a local supply of ore, but it ceased operations in the 1790s. In the 1800s, when the Coleman family operated the Martic Forge and Factory, they shipped pig iron from Elizabeth Furnace to Martic. The operations eventually included a nail factory, a rolling mill, two forge hammers and a slitting mill. Pig iron was first fined into bar iron which was run through rollers to produce flattened iron. This could be further processed through a slitter to produce iron rods. The rods were further processed to create nails. Since the rollers turned in opposite directions, each roller required its own water wheel for power. A roller was a little over a foot in diameter and between three and four feet long. The complete ironworks were spread throughout several separate buildings, but the rolling and slitting stands were connected in series by a common shaft.

It is difficult to ascertain when the first nails were produced at Martic, or when the rolling and slitting mills were first introduced. Sources credit the addition of the Colemanville (as the area became known) rolling and slitting mills to Edward Coleman in 1828. That is the date given for the creation of the mills in a publication of *Documents Relating to the Manufacture of Iron in Pennsylvania* published in 1850. It is hard to understand the motivation Edward Coleman had, if he was the force behind building the mills, since he sold his interest in April of 1828.

The conversion of iron to steel was introduced at Martic, likely during the partnership of James and Thomas Bird Coleman. In 1850, there were only 13 iron works in Pennsylvania making steel. Martic and Castle Finn were two of those. In 1850, Martic produced 400 tons of steel, and Castle Finn produced 100 tons.

With all the expansion Coleman engineered, he still was leasing a third of Elizabeth Furnace in the early 1790s. When Benezet drafted the lease extension in 1791, it was for five tons of iron per year instead of the previously agreed six tons. Realizing the mistake, Benezet appealed to Coleman to revert to the six tons and to do so in secret, so as not to be embarrassed. Coleman agreed. Benezet sold his third in 1794. Coleman was reasonable, fair, and patient. He acquired a good portion of his empire through partnerships, many of which spanned a decade or more.

Alan Burd Grubb decided to pursue a medical career and agreed to sell his portion of the ore and iron interests to his brother, Henry Bates Grubb, who was short of the necessary funds to pay his brother. This opened a significant opportunity for Coleman. Starting in 1798, Henry began a partnership with Robert Coleman. Henry sold half ownership in Hopewell and the Mount Hope furnace. This made Coleman an equal partner. They also became partners in one-third of the Ore Banks. In 1802, the partnership was dissolved, with Coleman ending up owning an additional one-sixth control of the Ore Banks and complete control of the Hopewell Forges. In 1803, Coleman closed the upper (bloomery) forge at Hopewell.

The iron market was strong enough to support the multiple furnaces and forges Coleman owned. He moved to Lancaster in 1809, leaving his son, James, in charge of Elizabeth Furnace. His final expansion, in 1811, was the purchase of a trade vessel, the *General Hand*, to ship iron to the Caribbean and England. After over thirty years of planning and building his industrial empire, he retired. He went from working as a clerk at the Hopewell Forges to owning most of what Curtis and Peter Grubb had owned (except for one-sixth of the Cornwall ore rights). His retirement mansion was just east of the current square on King Street in Lancaster. He also purchased surrounding plots. The Coleman children received the best education available. As Coleman's sons completed their education, they became involved in the management of the iron properties. In 1810, he had seven living sons; the oldest, William, was in his thirties, and the youngest, Thomas Bird, was 16. In between were James, Robert, Edward, Stephen Chambers, and George. [6]

Chapter 4. Full of Age and Honor

During Robert Coleman's career, he purchased two furnaces, built another, purchased additional forges and iron works, acquired five-sixths of the largest iron ore deposit ever discovered in the eastern United States, and bought a merchant vessel. Yet, with all that activity, he was active in politics and public service. He won a narrow victory in 1783 to the Pennsylvania General Assembly, but served only one term, losing his bid for a second term. In 1787, he was elected as a delegate to ratify the Federal Constitution and represented Lancaster County to formulate and pass Pennsylvania's state constitution. Politically, he was a Federalist. He served as a Presidential Elector in both 1792 and 1796. In 1792, there was no question of the results – Washington received an overwhelming majority, but in 1796, the election was close. Jefferson lost to Adams by three votes, one of which was Coleman's vote for Adams.

He was appointed Associate Judge of Lancaster County in 1791, a position he held until his retirement. He ran for a vacant United States Senate seat, for which he lost to James Ross, a prominent politician in western Pennsylvania, by ten votes. He also served as a Trustee of Dickinson College and a warden in Lancaster's St. James Episcopal Church.

In 1794, he was commissioned as Captain and marched with Washington to western Pennsylvania to put an end to the Whiskey Rebellion, which started as a tax imposed in 1791. Later descendants took pride in Coleman's association with Washington. Family members coveted the "privilege" to inherit the Gilbert Stuart portrait of Washington, which Coleman had commissioned.

Robert and Ann Old Coleman had fourteen children born over a twenty-five-year time span. All but Margaret and William were born at Elizabeth furnace. In the years between buying Stedman's third and Benezet's third, Coleman built an addition to the Elizabeth mansion, more than doubling the footprint. He also added an extensive porch on three sides of the mansion. There were never fewer than four children living at the mansion at any point during their residence at Elizabeth. Sadly, a son, Peter[1], named for Coleman's grandfather, did not survive his first year, and Thomas, named for Coleman's father, died in the second year after his birth. A daughter, Harriet, born in 1799, died in 1810. There were seven sons and four daughters who survived to adulthood.

Four sons survived Robert Coleman. Twenty-three-year-old Robert, Jr. died in 1811, Stephen Chambers in 1816 at Speedwell Forge, and George in 1821, also at Speedwell. William was twenty-five when he became manager of Cornwall Furnace and moved into the mansion built by Curtis Grubb, overlooking the furnace. James Coleman lived at Elizabeth Furnace after his father retired to Lancaster. Thomas Bird moved to York and managed Spring Forge (Coleman sold the forge to his brother-in-law, John Brien, which passed to Coleman's nephew, David Eaton, in 1807, and then was re-purchased by Coleman in 1815 for 5,500 pounds). Edward married Mary Jane Ross in 1816, the daughter of James Ross, who had defeated Robert Coleman for the United States Senate.

Elizabeth, the first of Robert and Ann Coleman's daughters to marry, fell in love with Charles Hall. They married just before her eighteenth birthday in 1796. Hall, who had some business dealings in Lancaster, was from a prominent Maryland family and established a legal practice in the newly created Lycoming County, Pennsylvania. In 1806, Robert Coleman purchased the home and property of Samuel Wallis in what is now present-day Muncy (years later, it would be discovered that Wallis had been a Tory spy during the Revolution). Charles and Elizabeth took up residence on the property, and Charles added to it with additional purchases. It was renamed Muncy Farms and is still in the possession of descendants.

The only other daughter to marry was Margaret. She married in her early thirties, but she was not without suitors. In fact, Charles Hall's brother, Elisha, twice asked for Margaret's hand and was twice denied, being informed by Coleman, "a match of that kind will never take place with my consent". At least one other young man declared she "was beautiful enough to make men a little breathless when they saw her enter a room". She eventually married Judge Joseph Hemphill of Philadelphia, who was acquainted with his future father-in-law – Hemphill and Coleman were both staunch Federalists. The Judge and Margaret married in 1806 and were given a townhouse in Philadelphia. It is likely no coincidence that Margaret received her gift in the same year as Elizabeth received the Muncy property. In 1819, Joseph and Margaret also purchased a summer home in Fairmont Park, then known as Somerton and today known as Strawberry Mansion.

James Coleman, likewise, did not marry until his thirties. On the eighteenth of September 1822, he married Harriet Dawson of Philadelphia, eighteen years his junior. Harriet was quite beautiful, well-poised, and confident.

Thomas Bird Coleman met Hannah Cassatt shortly after moving to York. He was twenty-two when they married on April 14, 1817. The Cassatts were a prominent family in York. Her father, David, was President of the York Bank and had helped organize the York Water Company. [1] Etched in her grave monument are words of love and deep appreciation, "she practiced every virtue and displayed every quality which could adorn her sex and give grace and dignity to Human Nature. / Lovely in person, mild in manner, ...".

Perhaps more than any of Robert and Ann Coleman's children, their third daughter, Ann Caroline, has received the most attention. Born at Elizabeth Furnace on October 18, 1796, Ann, like the other Coleman children, grew up with the advantages of wealth. She was educated at a finishing school in Lititz run by the Moravian Sisters. When the family moved to Lancaster, she made quite the impression on several young men. One of these young men was Henry F. Pleasants. He was smitten with Ann and made numerous references to Ann in his diary (1815) - she "looked heavenly - was cheerful ... sat in Pew with G Hubley directly facing Coleman's where I was gratified in seeing the beautiful Miss Coleman. About 12 called to see the Angelic A C. She was out ... went to Cotillion party. Ann Coleman looked divine. I danced with her the first dance, and twice afterwards ... her manners are so modest - retiring. Her countenance so sweet and engaging - so irresistibly winning, it is impossible not to admire her".

Another young man, a rising star (or "young buck") in Lancaster society and a future President of the United States, James Buchanan, was a friend of Ann's brother George. There is some discrepancy in how James and Ann met. The most popular account reports they met at a dance at the White Swan Inn, but another account holds they met at a picnic. Regardless of where they met, Ann was quite taken by Bucannon. They became engaged in 1919. Robert Coleman has been much maligned as a cruel and controlling father, but it is important to recognize that he did consent to the engagement, despite whatever misgivings he may have had regarding Buchanan (Robert Coleman was a trustee at Dickinson College in Carlisle, Pennsylvania, when Buchanan was expelled for a brief term, while on the way to graduating).

Ann broke her engagement with Buchanan. It is thought she was concerned that Buchanan was not paying her the attention she desired. A decisive event led her to break the engagement. After returning from a litigating trip to Philadelphia, Buchanan stopped to visit William Jenkins. Jenkins was not home, but his wife and her unmarried sister, Grace Hubley (the same mentioned in Pleasant's diary), were. Grace was a "pretty and charming young lady". Ann became jealous and hurt and sent an angry note to Buchanan. It was reported that he "turn[ed] pale when he read it".

Buchanan never saw Ann again.[2] She retreated to Philadelphia to visit her sister Margaret. She died there on December 9th. Judge Thomas Kittera noted seeing her the day before, "At noon yesterday I met the young lady on the street, in the vigor of health". Later that day, she started having convulsions. Physicians were called to her sister's townhouse, but could not save her. She died shortly after midnight of what Dr. Physick described as "hysteria".

She had been given laudanum, a drug which was not well understood. It was prescribed to calm nerves, to relieve the stress of menstruation, and even given to children to quiet them. Thousands of deaths were attributed to it. Johann Frederick Stoever, Jr. reported, "she was dressed ready for a ball and had suddenly fallen in a faint". During that time, some suspected suicide just as today, but it is perhaps more likely that she suffered a pharmacological reaction to the drug. Ann had been so full of joy. Her death was a hard blow to the entire family and especially to Robert Coleman, who adored Ann.

Coleman also provided opportunities for his extended family. His brother William joined him at Elizabeth Furnace, but the reunion was short-lived as William passed away in the 1780s. John Brien, and later Coleman's nephew, David Eaton, both, at different times, owned Spring Forge (as previously noted). Coleman also started buying shares of the Martic Forge operations in southern Lancaster County in the 1790s, which he eventually owned outright. He placed his nephew, Edward Brien, who married General Edward Hand's daughter, Dorothy, in charge in 1799. Coleman brought Brien into equal partnership at Martic in 1804. The contract written with his nephew included a clause that allowed Coleman to re-purchase the one-half of Martic, which he did upon the untimely death of Brien in 1816. Coleman offered $60,000 for the buyout, but curiously, the family sold the shares for $10,000.

Robert Coleman died on the fourteenth of August 1825, two months shy of his seventy-seventh birthday. He had given much to the cause of Independence. He contributed greatly to his community. He built a foundation for his heirs that would sustain their future security. He lived past the normal life span for industrialists of his era. He stood over six feet tall, but his shadow was longer. The Lancaster Journal noted, "Thus has departed from us, full of age and honor, a man who stood first among those who must ever rank as the most valuable members of society, and the most revered examples of mankind".

Coleman's will more than provided for his beloved wife, who would survive him until October 1844. He left her in sole possession of the Lancaster mansion and gardens on King Street, together with all furnishings, carriages, horses, and milk cows.[2] In addition, his four surviving sons would each contribute $1,500 annually in quarterly payments to their mother for the remainder of her life (at the time of her passing, all her sons had died).

Coleman's oldest daughter, Margaret, received $70,000 and the townhouse in Philadelphia on Chestnut Street. Elizabeth received $50,000 and the Muncy property (1825 was an exceptionally hard year for Elizabeth - her husband died in January, her son, Charles Henry, born in 1798, died in April, her father in August, and her sister Sarah in November). $5,000 was left to his niece, Ann Eaton, who was living with the Colemans at the time of Robert's death

Sarah Hand, born in 1802, received a new mansion house, next to Edward's mansion, plus two lots purchased from the Lancaster painter, Jacob Eichholtz. The will further stipulated her brothers William and James, and brother-in-law Joseph Hemphill were assigned to manage the inheritance to "... guard against possible difficulties from which none can flatter themselves, that they may certainly be exempted, and without any other motive, she being now unmarred ...". Sarah Hand Coleman was engaged to Reverend William Augustus Muhlenberg of St. James Episcopal in Lancaster, a union her father had not been in favor of. Her brothers obviously shared the feeling and threatened to limit her access to her inheritance if she insisted on the marriage. She broke the engagement off. Brokenhearted, she, like her sister Ann, sought refuge with her older sister, Margaret, in Philadelphia, and tragically also died from an overdose of Laudanum. The official cause of death was a pulmonary affection. Muhlenberg left Lancaster and was never married. He made a significant contribution to the field of education during his lifetime.

To his four surviving sons, William, James, Edward, and Thomas Bird, he left equal ownership in the Ore Banks, but the remainder of the iron properties were split. William, James, and Edward were given Cornwall Furnace, Elizabeth Furnace, Hopewell Forge, Speedwell Forge, Matric Forge, 300 acres in the Blue Mountains purchased from James Old, and over 700 acres near Mount Hope and other locations, including the mansion Edward lived in. The three brothers operated their shared properties as William Coleman and Co. Thomas Bird was given the Colebrook Furnace and Spring

Forge. William and Edward lived in Lancaster, James lived at Elizabeth Furnace, and Thomas Bird lived in the York area. There was no explanation provided for the division, but it is presumed that the value Robert Coleman placed on each of his sons' respective shares was equal.

Chapter 5. Division

William Coleman was fifty when his father died, eight years older than James and over fifteen years older than Edward and Thomas Bird. William and Edward, despite their age difference, were close and eventually would pursue joint ventures outside of the iron business, including development and investment in navigation projects. On April 23, 1828, in separate agreements, they sold their holdings in the furnaces, forges, and ore hills. Edward sold his holdings equally split between James and Thomas for $210,000, while William sold his holdings to Thomas for $180,000. This left Thomas the majority owner of the shares in the ore banks, while being equal partners in Elizabeth Furnace, Cornwall Furnace, Martic, Hopewell, and Speedwell forges. Also, included in the agreements were various parcels of land. James and Thomas Bird operated their joint holdings as James Coleman and Company (retiring William Coleman and Company, which William, Edward, and James operated).

The partnership was short-lived. James Coleman died on September 9, 1831. It was clear Thomas Bird did not wish to be in business with his brother's children and maybe more directly, his widow – he sued for partition later that year and in February the following year the partition was approved. [1] The shared properties were split into two parcels (purports), No. 1 and No. 2, valued respectively at $280,000 and $270,000. Purport No. 1, which was awarded to Thomas Bird consisted of the Cornwall Furnace, the Speedwell and Hopewell Forges, and various other land holdings, while Purport No. 2, awarded to the heirs of James (his children), consisted of Elizabeth Furnace, the Martic Forge ironworks, and other land holdings. Thomas Bird paid the $10,000 difference to the heirs of his brother and later paid an additional $5,000 "to preserve the peace and harmony of the farm and prevent litigation" (Harriet had complained the settlement agreement was insufficient). From this point forward, the descendants of the two brothers operated independently of each other and mined ore based on their respective shares in the Ore Banks.

William and Edward were "brought out of retirement" to help with the operations at Elizabeth and Martic. They oversaw operations and handled various legal proceedings. This is illustrated in a dispute with Rebecca Lukens, who, following the death of her husband, took over the Coatesville iron business, becoming the first female head of an industrial company. Lukens claimed iron supplied from Elizabeth Furnace was inferior and refused to pay for it. William filed suit to retrieve the money. Before the suit could be settled, William passed away. Edward assumed handling the legal proceedings. Despite an agreement made on March 1, 1837, in which Lukens agreed to pay William Coleman, guardian, $7,023.50, Lukens claimed the iron quality was below grade. A panel of referees was assigned to review the dispute. The referees determined Lukens did not need to pay the full amount, but only $1,824.54 for the little over 21 tons used. On appeal, it was determined that the referees "misbehaved", and, since the iron was used and the manufactured product was sold by Lukens using the iron, the judgment was upheld for the Colemans. A settlement of $5,000 would be paid to Harriet Coleman in five payments. The last payment was made on October 6, 1843.[2]

At the time of the partition, James' sons, Robert and George, were only nine and seven, respectively. Robert was born July 16, 1823, and George was born January 13, 1825. Managers and clerks were hired to keep Elizabeth Furnace operating until the boys were of age to assume control. Some of these individuals would enjoy employment with the Colemans for their entire careers. Robert Kelton "had the charge of Elizabeth furnace as superintendent of James Coleman's estate [and] also managed Martic Forge". Charles B. Forney, born in Lancaster on July 18, 1820, supervised the estate operations at Elizabeth and then later the furnace. J. Taylor Boyd served as an Assistant Superintendent at Elizabeth Furnace (until he was transferred to the Ore Banks). Nathaniel Ferguson started as a clerk at Elizabeth Furnace and later became Superintendent. Altogether, he spent nine and a half years at Elizabeth, serving as Superintendent for seven years.

In addition to the two boys, James and Harriet had three daughters. Ann, also known as Anna, was born on February 21, 1826, Sarah Hand on November 27, 1828 (the middle name was given in honor of her grandfather's good friend General Edward Hand), and Harriet, known as Hallie, on June 4, 1830. James' widow, Harriet, maintained a townhouse in Philadelphia and spent a good amount of time there, active in Philadelphia society. The children were very close and shared a deep love and devotion. There is a wonderful portrait by Thomas Sully, painted in 1846, of sisters Anna and Harriet.[3] Their heads leaning into each other and their left hands touching, the sisters express a dreamlike stare. Harriet's right-hand rests gently on Anna's shoulder. She looks very much like her mother, her blond hair in curls, in contrast to Anna's darker hair. Sully also executed a portrait of Sarah by herself.

Anna was the first to marry. In 1847, she married Dr. Charles Parker, who had been a classmate of Anna's brother, Robert, at Yale. Parker first met the Coleman family at Elizabeth Furnace in 1843. Writing to a friend, he noted, "The Coleman place is a perfect barony the house is the castle and all the other buildings are its tributaries. The Iron furnace is near the house and in plain view, it is a miniature Etna in constant eruption running floods of metal and vomiting forth by day a cloud and by night a pillar of fire, furnishing a continual moonlight for our evening promenades. There are here all the resources for pleasure that one can desire, Books, Horses, Guns, Music, Dancing ... Miss Coleman [Anna would have been 17] is beautiful ... Their younger sister is still more beautiful". Parker was sensitive to Anna's status. Before they were married, he signed an agreement relinquishing any right to Anna's property or money. Before the marriage, he wrote to Harriet Coleman putting her mind at ease, "In looking forward to my union with Anna with anticipation of almost perfect happiness, there is still one circumstance which has given me some embarrassment and I respectively ask your aid to remove it ... I am aware that your daughter has some property of her own".

The union was a happy one. They settled in Philadelphia, where Charles had established his medical practice, but he had also inherited large parcels of land in the Midwest. He and Anna toured the properties in the summer of 1847, including a stop at Niagara Falls. Anna kept a diary of the journey and, despite experiencing bouts of sickness, recorded many pleasurable experiences. Her entries share a deep affection for her husband. The couple also toyed with the idea of settling on one of the nicer properties. The next year, Charles again undertook an inspection tour by himself as Anna was pregnant. During the tour, he developed a severe cold. The illness lingered after returning to Philadelphia, and tragically, he died at the end of the year. Anna gave birth to a daughter, Charlette, on March 30, 1849, and remained in Philadelphia raising Charlette as a single mother, which caused concern from Harriet. Anna wrote her mother in 1852 regarding this decision, "I know that I am fulfilling my dear Charles' wish to maintaining my own establishment, as I am left in it ... I trust you do not feel hurt at my decision. It would be unspeakable for me to leave it. Let me therefore beg you dear Mother to look upon this as a settled thing".

George Dawson Coleman, known to the family as "Daws", attended preparatory school in Princeton, followed by enrollment at the University of Pennsylvania, where he received a Bachelor of Arts in 1843 and a Master's in 1846 with a focus in engineering. Between degrees, he toured furnaces and forges in both the United States and Europe, taking notes on the latest technology and processes being used. Upon graduation in 1846, George Dawson and Robert began construction of Lebanon County's first anthracite furnace. The technology may have been new to Lebanon, but there were over 40 anthracite furnaces built across Pennsylvania and New Jersey at that time. The brothers selected a location in West Lebanon along the Union Canal. They used ore from Cornwall and anthracite coal from Pennsylvania, arriving mainly via the Union Canal, which connected the Susquehanna River at Harrisburg with the Schuylkill River at Reading, and passed directly just south of the new furnaces.

Their first furnace, appropriately named No. 1, was blown in February 1847, and No. 2 in early 1848. The furnaces were 35 feet tall and banked into the side of a hill. It took a while to get the furnaces operating smoothly, but after improvements to the charging and other processes were introduced, the furnaces started producing between 6 and 8 tons of pig iron per day. Charles B. Forney assisted with their construction and was transferred from Elizabeth Furnace to the North Lebanon Furnaces as manager. A large pipe manufactory was added as well. Robert and George Dawson lived just above and north of the furnace in a "farmhouse" they built, so their time in Philadelphia was less frequent.

In 1849, the brothers agreed to purchase their sisters' shares in the Elizabeth Furnace, the Martic Iron Works, and the Ore Banks for $244,000. George Dawson remained heavily involved with the new furnaces while Robert shifted his focus from the making of iron to the selling of ore. Beginning in 1848, Robert started selling ore on the open market. He formed a partnership with Robert Kelton, a longtime employee who had worked at both the Elizabeth Furnace and at Martic. The firm Coleman, Kelton and Campbell operated in Philadelphia and remained active until 1858. Ore from Cornwall had been sold to operators outside the immediate owners of the Ore Bank for many years, but only in small quantities. Robert became the first owner to aggressively sell ore.

On January 13, 1852, George Dawson married Deborah Brown, who was descended from well-established Philadelphia families. Her father, William Brown, came to America from Ireland and married Deborah Norris in 1823. Deborah was descended from Isaac Norris, for whom Norristown, Pennsylvania, is named, and married Thomas Lloyd's daughter, Mary. Isaac and Mary's son Joseph Parker Norris married Elizabeth Hill Fox, and their daughter Deborah married William Brown. George Dawson's mother welcomed her new daughter-in-law with hopeful words, that her son and his bride would make the "wilderness of the iron works blossom as a rose ...". Anna wrote to Deborah, "My Dear Miss Brown, I can only regret that I was not acquainted with the fact [George Dawson's engagement to Debbie] before leaving the city so that I might have had the pleasure of a personal introduction to my future sister instead of the formality of a written one ... Dawson is so kind and good a brother ... Look upon me as Dawson's very affectionate sister, Anna C Parker".

The partnership between George Dawson and Robert officially dissolved in 1854. While visiting Paris, Robert fell in love with a French native, Rosalie Parant. They married, and Robert moved to Paris. Robert sold his one-half holdings in the new furnaces and existing iron works to his brother, but retained his shares in the Ore Banks, "... to George Dawson Coleman of Lebanon County—all estate, title claim, interest lands, furnace, iron works, etc. held as tenants in common RESERVING HOWEVER mines & banks of Ore Hills for the sum of $40,000 ...". This was further qualified, "... does grant, barter, sell and convey the equal undivided or 1/2 part, right, and interest in Elizabeth Furnace, Matric Works, est. Colemanville Est. works and lands etc. ...".

With the North Lebanon Furnaces in full production, George Dawson shut down the Elizabeth Furnace in 1856 and made plans to sell the Martic operations. According to the Lancaster New Era, in 1856, R. W. Coleman wrote to Maris Hoopes, who had come to the Martic works at Colemanville in 1829, asking him to meet in Lancaster to discuss a proposal. They met at the Hubley Hotel just off the central square. Coleman asked Hoopes to move to Cornwall and take on the management there. He also indicated there would be positions for Hoopes' two sons. Hoopes reviewed the offer with George Dawson Coleman, who was alarmed at the prospect of losing Hoopes, and indicated he was looking to "sell Colemanville". Coleman made a deal with Hoopes. If Hoopes sold enough of the land and property to realize a profit of $53,765 for Coleman (which included $20,000 for Dorothy Brien's estate), the remainder of the real estate and property would belong to Hoopes. The last visit of George Dawson Coleman to Colemanville occurred just before the deed was conveyed to Hoopes. Coleman acknowledged Hoopes for "his judicious management of affairs [that] tided the concern safely over breakers" of the panics of 1837, 1853, and 1860. Coleman added, "he felt under deep obligations to Mr. Hoopes for his devotion to the interests of his family and to himself". It is unclear how reliable this account is. The above account was written in 1906, based on the recollections of local residents, as all the principal parties were no longer living. Formal records indicate the heirs of James Coleman sold the operations to George Steele.

Sarah and Harriet Coleman were active in Philadelphia society, and it was natural that they found romantic matches there. Coincidentally, they married brothers. Harriet married William Heyward Drayton on October 31, 1850, and Sarah married William's brother, Henry Edward Drayton, on June 4, 1851. The Drayton family was one of the earlier families to settle South Carolina, first arriving there in the late 1600s. Over the course of multiple generations, the Draytons established numerous plantations, including Drayton Hall and Middleton, or Magnolia Place, along the Ashley River on the outskirts of Charleston. William and Henry's grandfather, William Drayton, Sr., sold his share in the plantations to his uncle John Drayton before beginning service as the Justice of the Provenance of St. Augustine. He lost his job in 1780 after displaying sympathies with the colonial revolutionaries and returned to Charleston. His son, William Drayton, became influential in South Carolina politics, but, as a staunch Unionist, moved to Philadelphia in 1833 in response to South Carolina's stance during the Nullification Crisis. He became the second President of the Bank of the United States and a prominent attorney in Philadelphia.

William Heyward Drayton worked as a civil engineer up until the panic of 1837, at which time he switched to the law. He was 13 years older than Harriet, but the family seemed pleased with the match. Along with a report on the impact of storms on Colemanville, George Dawson wrote to his mother in July 1850, "It certainly has occurred at a very unfortunate time for us as our engagements are large & our means of meeting them are thus diminished. We had just received some large orders which we are obliged to abandon - & the loss in time & the cost of repairs will be very heavy—... Robert is still here having been delayed by that accident [Robert was injured in a carriage accident just before his departure for France] & his movements are as yet uncertain. ... I am very much pleased with Harriets engagement with Mr. Drayton ... We all know Harriets disposition - She has heretofore had very much her own way in everything & every wish & desire gratified ... we have lately had so many examples of unhappy unions ... Dr. Peace & Wife ...".

Henry Edward Drayton attended Bolmar's Academy in West Chester and then studied medicine under Dr. Casper Morris. He graduated from the University of Pennsylvania in 1845 and visited hospitals in Europe before beginning a practice at the Episcopal Hospital in Philadelphia. He and Sarah had one child, James Coleman Drayton, born June 4, 1852. Sadly, Sarah died thirteen days later due to complications from the birth.

The family suffered through the death of a beloved sister, the death of the husband of another, and the separation of a partnership, although an amicable one, between brothers. A new drama began to play out in 1852 and 1853, which would result in a permanent rift in the bonds of the family. Anna had been under the care of Dr. Edward Peace, and their relationship blossomed into a romance. This was alarming to the family since Dr. Peace was divorced, a separation he initiated. Divorces were rare during this time, and when a divorce was granted, it was considered standard etiquette that divorced parties would not remarry while both parties were living. Dr. Peace's ex-wife, Caroline Willing[4,] sent a letter to Dr. Peace denouncing his courtship of Anna and later sued for, and was granted, a decree to change her legal name, and those of her children (Ella Moore, Charles Maxwell, and Richard Lloyd) to Willing. Caroline Willing's letter was shared by George Dawson in a letter to his mother, Harriet, regarding his sister Harriet's engagement.

Dr. Peace graduated from the University of Pennsylvania in 1833 and joined the medical staff there in 1840. He was a well-respected physician and very involved in Philadelphia society, being a member of the Philadelphia Medical Society, the Academy of Natural Sciences, and the Philadelphia County Medical Society. He had been a colleague of Charles Parker and was well known to the Coleman family for years. When Anna first expressed her intentions toward Dr. Peace, it created a serious uproar not just in the Coleman family but in the larger Philadelphia society.

As rumors first started to circulate, a close friend of the Colemans, Mary Lippincott, wrote to Harriet, "Anna left home yesterday afternoon with little Charley [Charlette]. Dr. Peace and Anna were engaged. Her friends disbelieve it and contradicted it ... a gross insult to her ... how can I tell you of my horror, and grief to learn she acknowledged an interest in him, but at the same time saying she was not engaged to him". Anna's siblings voiced their concerns and comments to their mother. George Dawson reported on Robert's visit to Anna urging her to give up "that man", "I told her that in the event of any connection between her and that man she must give up all her family and true friends ... she admitted him into her house. He proposed and she accepted him ... she [Anna] ordered them [Robert and Mary Lippincott] out of her home ... She has been told plainly what she may expect and she has chosen. At present we can do nothing more now. And I fear that no one can". Anna's sister Harriet wrote to their mother, "I could not have believed that a child of yours could ever have done such a thing. I have not seen her since this dreadful news. It is hard to think I have no sister [Sarah had passed away], for if she does commit this sin [marrying Dr. Peace] she can be nothing to any of us". Robert wrote [Dr. Peace had gone to Robert to inform him of his intentions], "All that you have so feared and dreaded has come to pass. Anna has disgraced herself and all connected with her. Blinded and mad, the miserable [?] has in the face of all the prayers ... that wretched man Peace ... that to marry a man, who had a wife living, was to make herself in the eyes of the world nothing but a prostitute". George Dawson added, "I would

with far pleasanter feeling inform you of the death of any one near &
dear to us all than be obligated to communicate to you this loss to us
of our once dear sister Anna".

Anna was heartbroken. She wrote to her mother,

> This engagement probably has brought about several
> months sooner than it would otherwise have been taken
> place by the vehemence of Robert and Dawson ... Dr.
> Peace as well entitled to address me as any other
> gentleman of my acquaintance ... I had as high a regard
> and esteem for the man whom they affected to despise. I
> have been treated in such an inhuman and brutal manner
> by both these persons [her brothers] that nothing but
> the humblest apologies can later induce me to hold any
> relations with them. Robert informed me that I should
> not enter your house nor should my child either. That
> the noble character and angelic disposition of the man
> whom I shall marry will reconcile you to any change in
> our relations. I consider myself of an age and in a position
> to consult only my own conscience. One thing you must
> feel dear Mother that I am the child who loves you most
> and will cherish you most kindly if you will allow me
> and no matter what course you may see proper to pursue
> you know that my feeling toward you will never change
> that I shall be ever as now your affectionate daughter. ...
> I could not have thought it possible that a brother and
> sister could have treated me in such a cruel inhuman
> manner. Dawson was most kind in his manner though his
> words were as hard to bear. May God bless him this for
> such kindness to one who sorely needed it. ... wherever
> he [Dr. Peace] wishes to go. As my own family have

renounced all interest in me, it is of little consequence where I am if with him I love.

Anna did, through time, visit her mother, but Harriet never again warmed her heart to Anna. She placed all of Anna's letters in a folder marked "My Poor Anna's Letters".

After one visit, she reported to Heyward Drayton, from Harrows Gate, New Jersey, "My poor unfortunate child came to see me twice and brought her child. I was able thank God to stay calm and collected and even when her piteous face was looking up at me ... although my head was almost bursting". Harriet could never forgive Anna. In Harriet's will, she left Charlette Collins Parker[5], "a bracket and broach of tortoise shell with bunches of corral leaves on each that I bought her from Naples but never gave her". There was only one member of the family who remained close to Anna, and that was her brother-in-law, Henry Edward Drayton. He, himself, experienced alienation from his brother William. When their mother died, it was discovered she had altered her will more in favor of Henry. William disputed this and threatened legal action, believing Henry's second wife unduly influenced their mother before she died. Henry, not well during this period, agreed to settle the inheritance favorable to William's grievance.

There were further issues raised when Henry died in April 1862. He had appointed three guardians for his and Sarah's only son, James Coleman, who was nine-years old at the time of his father's death. The proposed guardians were Henry's second wife, Mary, his brother Percival, and, much to the concern of the Coleman family, Anna Parker Peace. None of the three was overly pleasing to the Coleman family, but especially so was the concern with Anna. Her brother, George Dawson, wrote to William Heyward, "Dr. Drayton's will read in my presence is of such a character as to require legal advice and perhaps some prompt action". This concern was increased when both Mary Drayton and Percival, a bachelor, declined guardianship. The courts upheld Anna Peace's guardianship for James Coleman Drayton.

James Coleman Drayton grew up with the Peace family, which included Charlette and the Peaces' five children. Drayton married Charlotte Augusta Astor in 1879. (Charlotte's sister, Hellen, married James Roosevelt, Franklin Delano Roosevelt's older brother.) As the years passed, Charlotte grew restless and became involved in an affair with Hallett Burrowe, the son of a director of the Equitable Insurance Company, who lived next door to Drayton's mansion, Stronghold, in Bernardsville, New Jersey. When Charlotte's father, William Backhouse Astor, Jr., found out about the dalliance he threatened to cut Charlotte out of his will, which left her $850,000 upon his death, if she did not put an end to the affair, but Charlotte was too infatuated with Burrowe and fled to Europe with her lover leaving Drayton with an annual amount of $12,000 to support the children.

Drayton was enraged and followed his wife to Europe. He challenged Burrowe to a duel in Paris, which was never realized, but the scandal was publicized in New York's Town Topics and other newspapers. James Coleman Drayton and Charlotte were divorced in 1892. William Astor died in April while he and Charlotte were in Paris. Town Topics reported, "some of his tendencies were inherited by Mrs. Coleman Drayton whose troubles caused her parents no little uneasiness ". William Astor had cut Charlotte from his will.

After the divorce, Drayton retained custody of their children. His oldest child, Caroline Astor, had a distant relationship with her mother, and when she married diplomat William Phillips in 1910, Charlotte was not in attendance. Caroline did visit with her

Charlotte just prior to the wedding, though. William Phillips worked closely with the Roosevelt administration during World War II and he and Caroline were close friends with Franklin and Elanor Roosevelt.

Drayton and the children fell ill with typhoid in 1902 while summering in Dark Harbor, Maine. One of the cooks was Mary Mallon, famously known as Typhoid Mary, who was an asymptomatic carrier of the fever. Fortunately, there were no deaths in the Drayton household. Drayton moved to Newport, Rhode Island, in the 1920s and spent his final years living there at "Boxcroft". He died in Newport on November 11, 1934, following a lingering illness.

Charlette Parker married her second cousin, James Rawle, on November 29, 1871. James was the son of Louisa Hall, daughter of Elizabeth and Charles Hall, and Francis William Rawle. The Rawle family of Philadelphia traced their American origin to their arrival in 1686 from England to escape persecution for their Quaker faith. James became a partner in J. G. Brill and Company in 1872, which manufactured streetcars, trolleybuses, and railroad cars. He was well respected for his superior financial leadership. The couple built "Castlefinn" in Bryn Mawr, Pennsylvania, to honor their common great-grandfather. The home was near the Peace's "Annasdale", where Charlette grew up as a teenager.

Chapter 6. New Life in Cornwall

In 1827, Thomas Bird Coleman purchased the Palmyra Forge south-east of York, just off the Susquehanna River, and renamed it Castle Finn Forge in honor of his father's homeland in Ireland. In addition to the regular wrought iron products, he manufactured blister steel. He and his wife, Hannah, lived at the forge until she died in her early thirties in 1830. Left to care for their six children, Anne (also known as Ann), Margaret, Isabella, Sarah Hand, Robert, and William, Thomas Bird moved the family to Lancaster. He survived his wife by only six years, dying at his mother's home on September 10, 1836. This left his iron properties in much the same state as when James had died. Robert was just barely a teen, and William was ten years old. Again, William and Edward lent assistance, but John Reynolds of Lancaster, appointed as guardian for the children, assumed much of the responsibility for operating the estate. Ann Old Coleman assumed an active role in her grandchildren's upbringing.

William Coleman was designated the administrator of the estate. A notice, dated October 25, 1836, was placed for a period of time in the York Gazette and other papers that all debts owed to furnaces and forges previously owned by Thomas should be directed to the managers of the different operations, and all other debts should be paid to John Reynolds, who was authorized as William's agent and attorney. William declared all debts owed to and by Thomas Bird Coleman be settled by April 1, 1837, and any debts not paid by that time would be sent to collections.

Anne was the oldest of Thomas Bird Coleman's children, born in 1817. When the girls reached an appropriate age, they all received a similar, privileged schooling. Anne attended the Mercer School in Baltimore. Roger Alden Derby, Anne's grandchild, discovered, through a chance meeting with a woman on a train in 1947, the existence of two journals which Anne had kept. The journals contained her letters and poems in which she noted visits from family and friends. In those letters, she kept the family up to date and often requested news and updates. There were also letters from suitors. She would at times stay with her Cassatt relatives in York, where she received the following letter in 1837 from I. R. Irwin, an officer from Charleston, "Permit me to send you the enclosed earrings and bracelets, which were taken from a squaw who was unfortunately [?] in one of our skirmishes ... maybe I should not offer them, lest your delicacy should be alarmed ... evidences of the pleasure with which I remember our acquaintance". Another suitor, just noted as E.T. sent her a poem when she was 19, "Say not thy heart is cold/When thy own beaming eyes/Kindle this love that's told/In burning sighs ...".

The man who captured Anne's heart was Bradford Ripley Alden, whom she married in York on June 9, 1842. Alden was a 1st Lieutenant in the Army, a career military man, and a fifth generation of John and Priscilla Alden. Alden's father, General Roger Alden, went to Yale, Class of 1773, taught school in New Haven, Connecticut, joined Arnold's Expedition to Quebec in 1775, was commissioned as a lieutenant in January 1777, fought at Germantown, and spent the winter at Valley Forge. He resigned from the military in 1781 and studied law at Stratford, Connecticut. After 1784, he moved to Meadville, Pennsylvania, and became an agent of the Holland Land Company. He stayed in Meadville until 1825, when he was appointed Ordinance Storekeeper at West Point. Bradford graduated from West Point in 1831. He and Anne had two children, Robert Percy, born in 1848, and Sarah, born in 1850. Bradford did have assignments which took him away from home, but from 1845 to 1852, he was an instructor of Mathematics and Military Tactics at West Point. There is an intimate painting (now owned by the Detroit Institute of Art) by Alden's good friend, Robert Walter Weir[1], who taught Art at West Point. It shows Anne, then 35, and her two young children in 1852, in their quarters at West Point.

Following 1852, Bradford was stationed at Fort Vancouver and Fort Jones, where he was injured in 1853. While at Fort Jones in Northern California, he took part in an operation during a conflict with Native Americans along the Rouge River in southern Oregon. He was shot during the fighting which permanently disabled him and led to his eventual retirement in 1854. The family travelled through Europe hoping for a curative restoration, but he never found relief from his injury. In the late 1850s, he did involve himself in oil drilling not far from his boyhood home in Meadville, Pennsylvania. He died September 10, 1870, at the Atlantic Hotel, Newport, Rhode Island. His grandson, Roger Alden Derby, reflected on this part of his family history, "He [Bradford Alden] and my grandmother travelled in Europe from 1854 till 1857 and collected a number of fairly valuable works of art. This was a period of recuperation for him and by 1859 he appears to have been able to do some exploration work for oil in Western Pennsylvania. Forty-six Artesian wells were bored under his direction to a depth of 600 to 700 ft. and he was among the first to appreciate and develop this important natural resource. He was an invalid for the balance of his life".

Thomas Sully painted Margaret, Sarah, and Isabel Coleman in 1844. Anne was not included in the portrait as she was already married. As the oldest of the unmarried sisters, Margaret is shown seated. Sarah is standing far left, and Isabel is framed in the center. Margaret stares at the viewer with a soft, inquiring gaze. She married William Grisby Freeman who graduated from West Point three years behind Alden.

Freeman was also a career officer in the Army. He and Margaret were married in Philadelphia in January 1845. He had fought in Florida and received several promotions during his career, his final promotion to Brevetted Lieutenant Colonel in 1848 for "meritorious conduct, particularly in the performance of his duty in the prosecution of the War with Mexico". Freeman retired in 1856, and the couple built a mansion in Cornwall where Freeman participated in the family business. Isabella, named after her mother's sister, and Sarah never married. Isabella became ill and died while visiting Anne in West Point in 1849.

Sarah purchased a mansion at 1525 H. Street N. W. at Lafayette Square in Washington, D.C., in 1853, known as the Ashburton House, so named for the British Diplomat Lord Ashburton, the British representative involved in resolving the northwest border dispute between the United States and Canada. The treaty was signed in the house. A year after purchasing the house, Sarah deeded one-half ownership to Margaret. The house became the winter home for the Freemans and was where William Grisby and Margaret Freeman's children were born. When in Cornwall, Sarah, along with her brother Robert, lived in the Cornwall Mansion. Margaret and William Grisby Freeman built their own home in Cornwall but may have lived for a period in the Cornwall Mansion as well. Sarah commissioned a greenhouse built in 1881 and supervised many improvements to the property and the gardens. William and Sue Ellen Coleman had their own residence, usually referred to as "The Cottage", in Cornwall.

Robert, perhaps from the influence of his brothers-in-law, entered West Point in 1842, but rather than pursue a career in the Army, he assumed control of the iron works which his father had managed. He was, though, good friends with Generals Scott and McClellan and served as a volunteer Aide to the latter during the Civil War in the Peninsula Campaign of 1862, for which he was given the title of Colonel. Robert W. Coleman never married, but William C. Freeman, Jr.'s grandson, Theodore Clattenburg, Jr., showed John and Marjorie Feitig an undated letter addressed to Coleman, noting they were glad to hear that Coleman's engagement to one of John Reynold's daughters was broken off. The author of the letter further declares that Coleman should marry and recommends two ladies to consider, one of whom was Elizabeth Brooke, whose family was also involved in the Pennsylvania iron industry.

An amicable suit for partition was filed in 1848, in which Robert purchased the shares in the ironworks and the ore shares from his siblings. Later, William became a full partner with his brother, and the two operated under R. W. and W. Coleman Company. A full accounting of the terms of partition has not been located. There was one transaction, though, in which William Coleman of Colebrook paid $17,500 to Robert W. Coleman of Cornwall for the undivided half interest in the Castle Finn Forge estate in York County, which consisted of 20 tracts, 263 acres, and 106 perches. There is also a separate, earlier transaction noted at the York Historical Society of a payment of $190,000 Robert made to the other heirs of Thomas Bird Coleman. It seems Robert first purchased the shares of his siblings and later, when William came of age, allowed William to purchase half of the ownership of the ore rights, forges, and furnaces. When Robert W. died, he divided his estate equally between his surviving sisters and William's daughter and son. Interestingly, a portion of the estate that Robert W. purchased from his sisters returned to them through inheritance.

During the period following the death of Thomas Bird Coleman until his sons took over, John Reynolds and others were critical to the continued operation of all the properties. For example, the Colebrook Furnace was managed by Henry P. Robeson from 1834 to 1843. From 1844, until Colebrook closed, the furnace was managed by John Benson. Many individuals who worked at Colebrook continued their careers with the Coleman businesses. Colonel David Steitz Hammond, who was the great-grandson of Lebanon's founder George Steitz, started as a clerk at Colebrook in 1844 and later managed the Cornwall Furnace.

Robert, three years older than his brother, was the leader in their partnership. Both were thin and not physically overwhelming, but Robert, especially, was bold and strong-willed, possessing a solid vision of what he wanted to accomplish. There is an interesting anecdote relayed by Charles B. Forney in his testimony during the Coleman v. Coleman lawsuit. Curious as to what his cousins, George Dawson and Robert, were up to in North Lebanon, he took a ride on his horse out to North Lebanon during the construction of the anthracite furnaces. Forney reported, "Mr Robert Coleman came along shortly after we got underway and in speaking of the experiment, said that he would not have ventured what his cousin did, and rather ridiculed the experiment". Perhaps the ridicule was a ruse because Robert W. and William purchased land just north and east of the Ore Banks from Peter Smith and in 1849, began construction on their own anthracite furnace, with much the same design as the North Lebanon furnaces.

Chapter 7. Rise of the Hot-Blast

By the end of the 1850s, there was only one of the original charcoal-burning furnaces operating - the Cornwall Charcoal Furnace. The furnace was referred to as the Cornwall Furnace, while the new hot-blast furnace built by R. W. and William Coleman was referred to as the Cornwall Anthracite. Elizabeth Furnace ceased operations in 1856. By then, the North Lebanon Furnaces were running efficiently. The Colebrook Furnace was dismantled by 1860, after lying idle for a few years.

The Cornwall Furnace continued producing superior iron during this time and still made a profit. To keep it operating smoothly, many modernizations were installed around the middle of the 19th century. According to Henry C. Grittinger, the stack itself was rebuilt in 1856, measuring 32 feet high, 21 ½ feet square at the base, and 11 feet square at the top. At the time the furnace was put out of blast to make ready for the improvements, it measured 28 feet square at the base, 23 feet square at the top, and 31 feet 8 inches in height. The original furnace opening faced north, but as improvements were made during the 1800s, the cast house was rebuilt, and the furnace opening was re-oriented to the west.

Alternating air tubes were installed as well as a steam engine to drive a large wheel, 24 feet in diameter, which moved the pistons pushing air into a central collection box, which then directed the air to the furnace. Two additional side tuyeres (A tuyere, or tuyere, is a tube, nozzle, or pipe through which air is blown into a furnace or hearth) were added to deliver a more consistent air pressure to the furnace. The first steam engine was installed as early as 1841, and, for over a decade, operations alternated between powering the air by steam and water – often operating the water wheel in warmer weather.

Waterpower was used for the last time in 1857. A replacement steam engine was installed in 1859. A brick arch was built on top of the stack to deflect the furnace gases to heat two single-cylinder boilers at the top of the furnace and to the side.

The original hot-blast furnaces built in North Lebanon were constructed with limestone in much the same way as the cold-blast furnaces were constructed, just slightly taller at 35 feet. The familiar look had a couple of additions. The hot air was heated in a cast-iron stove, which stood alongside the furnace and rose to about the same height as the furnace. They also included boilers and blowing engines. R. W. and William Coleman more or less copied the same design as their cousins used. As the furnaces were improved, the furnace stacks were replaced with cast iron and rose to heights above 50 feet. The furnace capacity increased significantly. The square shape of the charcoal furnace became rounded, encircled at the bottom with a tubular skirt for the air blast (refer to the cover photo). In the early 1850s, the new furnaces produced 6 to 8 tons a day, three to four times the yield from cold blast furnaces. Production continued to rise with each improvement. The hot blast furnaces were producing in weeks what was previously produced in a year. It was also true that what could be accomplished with twenty workers now required seventy or more (the extra workforce was more than justified by the increased productivity).

During the 1840s, the cost of making iron in America was almost double the cost in England. A significant part of the difference was due to higher labor costs in America. It became even more important to continue production improvements, widening the gap between profitability and labor costs. Maintaining and increasing profitability demanded a commitment to technological growth.

Moving from charcoal to anthracite coal reduced fuel costs by at least twenty percent, but the furnaces filled the air with smoke and ash.[1] Charcoal fuel burned "cleaner" than coal. Burning anthracite coal and reducing the iron ore to molten iron was dirty. The smoke was so thick at times that it was impossible to see the furnace stacks and boilers. At night, the plants were dotted with flares of fire escaping from the operations. Railroad tracks surrounded the furnaces and wove through the operations. Equipment was scattered throughout the property. The cast iron furnace stacks and boilers, with pipes and tubes extending from their bodies and wrapped around them, rose into the air in stark contrast to the surrounding hills and town. The supporting cast house, engine house, and other buildings were more familiar, made from stone and brick, but the overall impression of the furnaces was mystifying to the average citizen. Everyone knew, though, when in operation, there would be jobs and money to pay for their needs.

While George Dawson Coleman continued to expand the North Lebanon furnaces, R. W. Coleman increased his capacity with the purchase, in 1857, of the Dudley Furnace for $85,000 and renamed it Donaghmore (in honor of the land from which his grandfather immigrated). The furnace was built in 1853 by Simeon Guilford, John Krause, Levi Kline, John Weidman, and Jefferson Shirk. They never quite got the furnace running smoothly and may have been relieved to sell. Robert W. made sufficient improvements to the furnace that it started to produce reasonable results, although it was the least productive furnace owned by R. W. Coleman Heirs and, later, by the Cornwall Iron Company.

Before 1850, the owners of the Ore Bank generally consumed the ore they mined in their respective furnaces, with limited sales of ore to local manufacturers such as Pennsylvania Steel or on the open market in Philadelphia and Baltimore. There were sales to Western

Pennsylvania, but as that region's industry grew, sales declined (still as late as 1859, 6,500 tons of Cornwall pig iron were sold to furnaces at Pittsburgh). The anthracite hot-blast furnaces consumed increasingly significant tons of iron ore.

During the 1850s, the proprietors of the Ore Bank increased their sales of ore to other furnaces. It was noted during later lawsuits, "By the policy of Mr George Dawson Coleman in selling such large quantities of ore to be (?) out of Lebanon County he had done our County more harm than any other man that ever lived in it". George Dawson and his brother, though, were encouraged by the profit they could make from selling ore on the open market. Proprietors were charged $1.65 per ton and sold to other parties at $3.65. It was suggested that if a proprietor sold ore to market, the difference should belong to the Ore Bank, but the preference was to reduce ore sales to the outside. R. W. and William Coleman believed Robert and George Dawson were taking more ore out the ore bank than what was reflected in the mining reports, "It is pretty evident that George Dawson Coleman and Robert Coleman made these sales for their own convenience, sold at low prices to raise money, have had all the advantages thereof, and have been charged no interest on the money received".

It was also noted as early as 1845 by John Reynolds, working for Robert W. and William Coleman, that the volume of ore being removed by the Grubbs, the minority owners of the Ore Bank, exceeded the proportion of their ownership. These concerns led to an agreement in 1848 by the owners of the Ore Bank to keep track of their consumption and provide reports of how much ore they were mining. The agreement proved inadequate. During the winter months at the start of 1851, Robert W. begged his cousin George Dawson to resolve the discrepancies, but his appeals went unanswered. Robert W. wrote to George Dawson, "Mr. Shirk brought me some documents this evening that show a most hopeless case if ever arranging to our mutual satisfaction the ore account between us. The whole matter is so involved that I can make nothing of it as far as your statements are concerned... Will and I, after thinking the matter over to let the settlement of that year [Spring 1850] stand as it was made and yield our claim of [?], though we believe ourselves entitled to it. This account should have been settled six months ago and every hour makes this kind of thing more unsatisfactory, to all concerned ... Oblige me by sending your check". To oversee their interests, George Dawson and Robert Coleman moved their Superintendent at Elizabeth Furnace, J. Taylor Boyd, to manage their mining operations in Cornwall. To further complicate matters, Robert and George Dawson Coleman had filed for partition in 1851 (it was denied in 1852). Exasperated, Robert W. and William sued the other shareholders of the Ore Bank[2], claiming the other owners had withdrawn more than their share of ore and failed to compensate the disadvantaged partners. An existing agreement between the common tenants of the Ore Bank was being violated, which specified that if any party took more ore than they were proportioned, they would be required to settle for the overage at 50 cents per ton.

The dispute over the ore may explain the delay in plans to construct a railroad between Cornwall and the Union Canal. The North Lebanon furnaces needed to transport ore from the Ore Bank to the furnaces, and the Cornwall Anthracite would need to transport coal and charcoal from the canal to Cornwall. The Cornwall Lebanon turnpike road required constant repair. Further, it was slow and expensive to haul ore and fuel manually between Cornwall and North Lebanon. Brothers George Dawson and Robert Coleman partnered with their Coleman cousins, Robert W. and William, to construct the North Lebanon Railroad. They incorporated the short line in 1850, but construction did not begin until 1853. The first ore was transported over the completed railroad in 1855.

William Coleman died in 1861. He had developed pneumonia and never recovered his full strength. Surviving William were his wife, Sue Ellen Habersham Coleman, and his two young children, Robert Habersham, born March 27, 1856, and Anne Caroline, born October 27, 1858. William had met Sue Ellen in Savannah, Georgia, and it was there that they were married in 1855. The Habersham family in America dates to 1738 when James Habersham arrived with the evangelist George Whitefield in Savanah. James Habersham was the first to grow and export cotton in Georgia. His sons were leaders during the Revolutionary War. His son, Joseph, who was Sue Ellen's grandfather, served as Postmaster General from 1795 to 1801. Her father, Robert, ran an export and import business and expanded the family's agricultural pursuits to include growing and selling rice. It was quite difficult for Sue Ellen during the Civil War as her brother-in-law, Robert W., and other Coleman family members either fought on the side of or supported the North, while many of her relatives in the South fought for or were sympathetic to the Confederacy.

Samuel Small was appointed guardian for the children of William and Sue Ellen Coleman. Small had married Hannah Cassatt Coleman's sister, Isabel, and was a very successful businessman in York. Before William's death, Small acted as an advisor to his nephews regarding their iron business. After William's death, he became more active in Cornwall's affairs. He was responsible for investing the distributions from the iron-making properties on behalf of William's children as well as making decisions on their behalf. As an example, Small recommended that Robert and Anne contribute to the capital stock of the Peach Bottom Railway, "not particularly as an investment but to aid in building the road which will greatly enhance the value of the Castle Finn lands". He would stay involved with the family business until Anne reached her age of maturity.

Robert and Anne were also very close to their maternal uncle, John Rae Habersham. He visited Cornwall frequently, usually staying at Sue Ellen's "Cottage". John Rae became a father figure to Robert, and the two shared almost weekly letters throughout Robert's teenage years and early adulthood. The letters were usually more personal, rarely touching on business concerns.

R. W. Coleman had relied on the support of his brother William but always remained the leader of the business. Along with the help of men like Reynolds and Small, he hired many Superintendents and managers to take on various roles within the operations. One of the more significant of these men was Artemus Wilhelm. Born in Baltimore in 1822, his family moved to York when he was six years old. He learned the trade of brick laying and assisted his father in erecting the Ashland Furnace in York County. He was contracted by R. W. Coleman in 1849 to erect a replacement furnace for the Cornwall Anthracite. The existing furnace was failing, and Wilhelm built a successful furnace for $30,000 less than the original cost. He was contracted to build a second furnace and by 1854 was in full employment with the Colemans. He became a superintendent of Speedwell in 1854 and Manager of the Anthracite Furnace in 1857. When William Coleman died, Wilhelm assumed Power of Attorney for William's estate. Wilhelm became a central figure in the operations for the next two decades, residing in a home on the eastern side of the old Cornwall Turnpike, across from William and Sue Ellen Coleman's home.

The lawsuit brought by R. W. and William Coleman against the other shareholders of the Ore Bank continued to languish in counterclaims and appeals, but the abuses of ore removal continued. To help resolve the issues, the Cornwall Ore Bank Company was incorporated on January 14, 1864. The first formal meeting of

proprietors occurred on February 1st in the office of the North Lebanon Railroad Company. Present were Robert W. Coleman, Samuel Small (representing William Coleman's children as guardian), George Dawson Coleman, Richard C. McMurtrie representing Robert Coleman, Edward Burd Grubb, and Artemus Wilhelm. George Dawson Coleman was elected President, and R. W. Coleman Secretary. A salary of $1,500 a year was set for the General Superintendent of Mines, J. Taylor Boyd. The price of ore

was set until July 1st at $2 per ton (a long ton established as 2,240 pounds) and $2.50 for "Sundries", which were sold to third parties. Removal limits were set based on the percentage of ownership. For every 1,661 tons allocated to Cornwall Anthracite, there were 200 for Cornwall Furnace, 736 for Donaghmore, 918 for North Lebanon Furnaces, 178 for Mount Hope, 7,829 for Others (Sundries), 2,242 for C. B. Grubb, and 543 for White and Ferguson of Robesonia, for a total of 11,544 tons. Mr. W. Lorenz was engaged in a survey of mines, with assistants Jacob Weidle and Adam Grittinger. This survey was meant to clear up confusion from a previous survey, known as the Clark Survey.

Grubb descendants still held a 1/6 interest in the Ore Banks. Henry Bates Grubb died in 1823, intestate, leaving five children, Edward Burd, Clement Brooke, Mary Shippen, Sarah Elizabeth, and Alfred Bates Grubb, all under the age of fourteen. In February 1836, Edward Grubb, the oldest, born in 1810, brought suit (it is unclear whether this was amicable or hostile) against his siblings, resulting in Edward and Clement securing all 16/96 shares in the Ore Bank. The two brothers restored the properties their father had built, including the Mount Vernon Furnace, erected in 1800, 17 miles from

Cornwall. It had been idle from 1814 to 1821. The brothers also had furnaces at nearby Mount Hope and Manada. They were running multiple furnaces with the least number of shares in the Ore Bank."

Clement Brooke Grubb did not join the Cornwall Ore Bank Company. (Multiple sources incorrectly refer to Clement as Clement Bates Grubb. His maternal grandmother was Sarah Brooke, who was incidentally a great aunt to Mary Ann Brooke, who married Clement. The Brooke family had been owners of multiple iron furnaces, including Hopewell Furnace.) Years earlier, he had pulled out of the partnership formed with his brother, Edward, and was leasing his ore rights to two of his wife's uncles, Edward and George Brooke. This created extra work for J. Taylor Boyd, who kept separate books on the ore removed by the Brooke brothers. Boyd reported overages to Grubb for settlement, who, in turn, had to settle with the Brooke brothers. For one year, there were over 10,000 excess tons removed by the brothers. Whether Clement grew tired of the arrangement with the Brookes, or he wanted to remove ore for his own purposes, he joined the Ore Bank Company on April 20, 1869. The company back-dated Clement's membership to January 14, 1864, the date of the company's formation.

White and Ferguson, the owners of the Robesonia Furnace, also did not join the Cornwall Ore Bank Company. Robesonia had a controversial history in relation to the Ore Banks, which extended back to the purchase of Peter Grubb III's 1/6 interest in the Ore Bank by Robert Coleman. The agreement allowed Peter the right to mine ore, "... and also saving and excepting until the said Peter Grubb, Jr. the grantor, his heirs and assigns forever, the right, liberty and privilege, at all times thereafter, of entering upon the premises thereby granted and released, with his and their servants, horses, carts and carriages and of digging, raising and hauling away a sufficient quantity of iron ore for the supply of any one furnace".

This right was purchased by George Ege in 1788 for 3,000 pounds. Ege and Robert Coleman were well acquainted with each other, having partnered at one point in the Martic operations. After Ege's death, Henry Robeson, who had previously managed the Colebrook Furnace, purchased Robesonia and formed the firm of Robeson, Brook and Company. When Robeson passed away in 1858, Robesonia was managed by Robeson and White, White being his son-in-law. During this time, Nathaniel Ferguson, who had worked at Elizabeth Furnace, came to work at Robesonia, and when Robeson died, entered into partnership with White. All of these firms owned the right to haul ore from Cornwall to supply the operation of one furnace. In the 1840s, Robeson, Brook and Company built an anthracite furnace at Robesonia, which consumed a significantly greater quantity of ore than the previous charcoal-based furnace. They built a second anthracite furnace, but only ever had one in blast at a time, so they could never be accused of violating the terms of the rights for a supply of one furnace. Since Robesonia was not a member of the Ore Bank, they did not have to abide by the Articles of Association of The Cornwall Ore Bank Company. Robesonia's relationship with the Ore Bank would remain controversial for decades.

The newly formed Cornwall Ore Bank Company was challenged in April 1864 when the miners went on strike, demanding to be paid $1.50 per day instead of $33.60 per month. Based on the hours worked, they would make more under the proposed payment terms, but the additional expense to the company would be close to $200,000. The monthly wage the miners were being paid for their six-day work week roughly compensated them for a five-day work week at $1.50 a day. Apparently, there was enough concern that the Lebanon Sheriff was notified. A force of fifty men was raised, but by the time they arrived in Cornwall, the situation had quieted down. Three miners were charged with disturbing the peace and found guilty of "conspiracy to commit an illegal act". Each was fined ten dollars and released.

In December 1864, not a year into the formation of the Ore Bank Company, R. W. Coleman died in Cornwall. He had been the leader of his family in Cornwall and was generous to the community. Shortly before he passed, he anonymously gave 100 tons of coal to Cornwall and Lebanon residents. He divided his holdings equally among his three surviving sisters, Anne, Margaret, Sarah, and his nephew and niece, his brother's children. Together, Robert H. and Anne Caroline Coleman, not yet teenagers, became majority owners of the iron-making operations as well as the ore banks. They were only eight and six years old.

Over a decade after R. W. Coleman's death, the Pottsville Evening Chronicle published an article on June 21, 1877, "The Cornwall Ore Mines: New Claimants to This Immense Deposit of Iron Ore". It reported on two men who brought suit claiming to be children of "the late Robert W. Coleman, deceased, who, so far as the public knows, was a bachelor all his life". The two men, brothers from New York, sued to receive what they claimed was their rightful inheritance, claiming to be the two sons of R.W. Coleman and Eugenia Martin. Coleman did have a home in New York City, and Martin lived there during the same period. She married Andrew Jackson Lockwood in 1860. An additional article claimed, "Previous to the marriage ... she was delivered of two children, the father of whom was Mr. Robert W. Coleman, a wealthy gentleman, who died December 20, 1864. This gentleman allowed the sum of $1,200 per annum to Mrs. Lockwood for several years before and after her marriage; and two years afterward, purchased for her a farm in Pepin County, Wisconsin, containing 280 acres, with a handsome house, including the necessary quantity of furniture, cattle, etc. On this farm Mrs. Lockwood and her husband took up their abode. For some time, things kept on the [?] tenor of their way, and no ripple disturbed the soft current of their matrimonial existence. The two children born somewhat out of the lawful channel resided with the parties. How Mrs. Lockwood explained their existence to her husband does not appear. It may be that she disclosed the whole story to her lord, when he was perfectly content, and blamed her not. These children are now 13 and 16 years respectively. Soon after the purchase of the farm, Mr. Coleman purchased another piece of property for Mrs. Lockwood, on which there was a grist mill. $1,000 was spent on this purchase. There were some necessary repairs to be made to this property so that the deed of transfer was made to Lockwood with the intention that when those repairs were carried out, the whole property should be reconvened to the lady. The mill was then placed in proper working order and large profits realized". The story goes on to state that her husband became a drunkard, and trouble ensued, eventually sparking a lawsuit brought by Lockwood against Eugenia. She was able to prove that the property in question was, in fact, hers and that it was indeed gifted to her by R. W. Coleman. The case brought by her sons did not result in a favorable verdict. The true and exact nature of Coleman's relationship with Martin remains unknown.

R. W. Coleman Heirs was established to manage the Cornwall iron operations. Margaret Freeman started construction of a furnace in 1872 in North Cornwall, independent of the rest of the family. William C. Freeman, her oldest son, then in his twenties, oversaw the furnace, and Henry C. Grittinger, given a home next to the furnace's office, managed the day-to-day operations. There are plans and drawings at the Lebanon County Historical Society dated 1878 to 1879 for the manager's home prepared by Thomas Ustick Walter. The furnace, designed by Wilhelm, produced between 120 and 140 tons of iron per week. At the same time as the North Cornwall Furnace was built, the Bird Coleman Furnaces were built closer to the ore banks. They "tried to keep the 'new' furnaces out of sight from Cornwall Mansion, but not possible and remain cost effective". The name for the furnace was debated, "what we also want is a name for the new works to enable us to keep the accounts of the new furnace entirely separate. Mr. Freeman arrived here safely last evening and has suggested 'Thomas Bird Furnace', Mr. Small had wanted 'Cornwall' to be included. Mrs. Alden wanted 'West Cornwall' or 'Ironsides' ... already a problem in accounting with 'Cornwall' and 'Cornwall Anthracite'". They settled on Bird Coleman Furnaces. Money was borrowed from the Cornwall Anthracite to aid in construction. The new furnaces excluded Robert H. and Anne from ownership. There was an expressed intention to balance the ownership in the operations. The Bird Coleman furnaces, owned by Margaret Freeman, Ann Alden, and Sarah Hand Coleman, were designed by Wilhelm and mirrored the construction of the North Cornwall Furnace. J. P. Jackson was established as the manager and was provided with a spacious Beaus-arts style mansion close to the furnace.

The Ore Bank members progressively improved their furnaces, adding to the increased demand for ore. George Dawson Coleman erected an additional furnace at North Lebanon in 1864, intended to be run, curiously, with a cold-blast or a hot-blast. It never operated successfully, and the effort was abandoned. Instead, in 1872, he erected Furnace No. 3, strictly a hot-blast anthracite furnace. The furnace stood over fifty feet high and was constructed of cast iron plates instead of limestone. The once familiar stone stacks and accompanying water wheels were replaced by stark-looking metal stacks – symbols of a new generation of industrial power. When first put into blast, it was capable of producing 150 to 200 tons of iron per week. The operations were also the first in the country to use Gjers kilns (from a Swedish design) to roast the ore to remove its sulphur content.

Cornwall had multiple hot-blast furnaces and one cold-blast furnace. The family tried to keep the Bird Coleman Furnaces out of view from the Manor (in North Lebanon, a wall was constructed to shield one of the mansions from the glare of the furnaces at night). While the operations were the source of their wealth, they preferred not to see the daytime black smoke and the nighttime display of bright yellow and red flares of fire extending from the furnaces.

The post-Civil War period was subject to ups and downs in the iron industry. During the Panic of 1867, it was noted in the Coleman v. Coleman testimony, "Coleman [George Dawson] kept the furnaces running when there was a small market for his iron. He incurred heavy losses, but his men were kept at their jobs". Problems continued to persist in the 1870s. The Panic of 1873 arose as a result of many worldwide conditions. Even if the North Cornwall Furnace had been completed and blown in according to the original schedule, it is doubtful it would have been profitable. Sue Ellen Coleman wrote to Robert in October 1873, "thought the times were much too hard to send you candy. Perhaps all the furnaces will have to be stopped at Cornwall, and nobody will know where to get money. I will not have money enough to keep a carriage this winter [in New York] and only hope times will improve enough for me to do so in the Spring ... The 'Iron' people suffer almost more than anyone else now". The furnaces were put out of blast, but by early 1874, they were started back up. Still, in May, Sue Ellen reported to Robert, "I fear [you] will find everything quiet at Cornwall in the business line. I have a very discouraging letter from Mr. Wilhelm about the Iron business this morning. I fear there is no prospect for Willie's starting his furnace, which he hoped to do the last of May".

It took several years for the North Cornwall Furnace to work out issues in its operations. Freeman and Grittinger relied on Wilhelm for advice. Freeman instructed Grittinger, "Please consult Mr

Wilhelm in regard to the increase of men's wages and be governed by what he says in the matter. I am unwilling to do anything that would make trouble for him, and at the same time am aware the men will leave unless we increase their wages". Originally, there had been plans for a second furnace, but North Cornwall would only ever run with a single furnace. There also needed to be greater consistency in the iron produced. At the end of 1874, Wilhelm and Freeman visited with Mr. Felton of Pennsylvania Steel regarding a contract to supply iron from North Cornwall. The order was agreed on to supply iron for one year with a sample of 100 tons. At the time the price of iron was below the cost of production.

Despite economic conditions, the Cornwall furnaces continued to make progress on quality, but there were still issues in 1875 to be addressed as noted in a communication with Grittinger, "Mr. Wilhelm sent me a copy of the analysis of the last samples of iron sent to Steel Works. There is less copper in this lot than in any I have, but there is too much Sulphur. Can you not use more roasted ores? I hope the Roaster is now in good working order". By the end of 1875 Wilhelm wrote to Grittinger, "Enclosed I have your copy of letter and result of analysis received this PM from Major Bent containing the gratifying intelligence to commence shipments of iron at the rate of 5 cars daily which is in excess of the capacity of North Cornwall furnaces to produce. ... Great care should continue to be exercised in watching the copper in the ore closely and also to use uniformly at least 25 to 33% of well roasted ore". These instructions were the result of a letter from Bent, of Pennsylvania Steel, "I am most happy to report the marked improvement in copper and silicon. I wish I could also add Sulphur. You can, however, commence shipments of five cars per day". By the late 1870s, the furnace was considered in excellent condition, and shipments of iron were being sent as far as Pittsburgh.

The Bird Coleman Furnaces were considered the state of the art. The two furnaces were duplicated in their construction, including boilers, pumps, the engine rooms, and the stock and cast houses. Railroad tracks led into a 60-foot by 200-foot stone and iron stock house. Using pneumatic hoists, coal was dumped from the left side of the stock house, ore from the right, and limestone was stored at the far end of the house. A blast of hot air was used to remove sulphur from the ore, and then the ore was loaded into a pipe, which dropped the ore into waiting bins to be taken to the tunnel head to load the furnace.

The stacks were constructed from fire bricks and encased in an iron sheath. A winding iron staircase extended upwards on the outside of the furnace. Much of the iron used in the construction was produced at the Cornwall Anthracite furnace. An S-shaped tube connected the boilers with the furnace. External access to every part of the furnace was engineered to assist with repairs. The cast house engine used a 24-ton, 24-foot diameter flywheel. Water was sourced from a 62-foot well, which tapped the Furnace Creek. A 3 ½ foot tall tunnel, 1,025 feet long, directed the water from the creek to the well. Wastewater from the operations was recycled to the well.

The addition of the two Bird Coleman Furnaces brought the total of individual furnaces operated by the "Cornwall Colemans" to eight. Railroad tracks led to each furnace as well as to the ore banks. The ore banks themselves used a narrow-gauge track to move material around. The Cornwall Railroad (the North Lebanon Railroad was re-incorporated as the Cornwall Railroad Company), running from the Union Canal six miles away, brought coal and limestone to the furnaces and returned with ore. The traffic on this little length of road made it the highest-paying railroad in the country.

The growth in the local iron industry created additional jobs at both the furnaces and the ore banks. The work was hard, and while most laborers enjoyed steady employment, sometimes spanning multiple generations in a single family, the opportunity for advancement was limited.[3] The exception was for clerks, superintendents, and managers. For these positions, there was a significant opportunity to advance. Men such as Ferguson, Boyd, Grittinger, Wilhelm, and Forney all expanded their net worth and became community leaders. J. T. Boyd, for example, developed a "gated" community in Lebanon called Hawthorne Park in East Lebanon.

Stone, and eventually brick, housing was provided to miners and furnace workers. Each furnace had its own set of homes close by. The homes were mostly duplexes and included space for a garden behind the home. The rent for the workers was deducted from their pay. In contrast, Clerks, Managers, and Superintendents were usually provided stately homes as part of their employment agreements. These homes were always within view of the property they managed.

The various owners of the Ore Bank were mining ore from designated areas, but the quality of the ore varied by location and depth, furthering disputes among the owners. The greatest contention by some owners was that others were taking more ore out of the mines than their fair share. The lawsuit brought by R. W. Coleman and William Coleman against their cousins, George Dawson and Robert Coleman, and the Grubs, known as "Coleman v. Coleman", included a great amount of testimony and documents of the ore mined. During the case, William D. Fahnestock testified that the "opening made by Robert and George Dawson Coleman on the west side of Middle Hill, average was 72% [percentage iron in the ore]". George Dawson Coleman had no opening on the Grassy Hill, and John Reynolds commented, "I would judge the ore on Grassy Hill to be best ... I suppose R. W. and William Coleman have the finest and largest openings on Middle Hill". To get to the openings on the Big Hill where the mines of George Dawson Coleman were located, miners had to pass through the openings of R. W. and William Coleman. The various ores were classified. No. 1 was the highest grade. White iron was an inferior quality iron. The upper part of a hill was considered of more value than the lower depths, being more exposed (and generally of higher iron concentration). The further you got from the surface to a certain depth, the more sulphur was present in the ore. It was declared during testimony, "As you penetrate deeper into the hill the ore becomes harder, more sulphures, and probably somewhat mixed with copper, all of which diminishes the yield of iron, renders it harder to smelt and deteriorates the quality". Ore samples taken during this period revealed No. 1 for the Cornwall Anthracite to be 74% iron and No. 2 to be 64%. No. 1 taken from the Big Hill for the North Lebanon furnaces was 75%, No. 2 from the east side of Middle Hill 63%, and No. 3 from the west side at West 72%. Despite differences, according to Fahnestock, "below water level the ore is alike" and testimony was offered by Robert B. Cabeen, who sold ore for R. W. and William Coleman, judged "the iron made at the Lebanon furnaces to be identical with the Cornwall iron". Although George Dawson Coleman noted, "the ore in the different hills are of different qualities or kinds; and to make good iron it is necessary that these different kinds should be mingled in certain properties. The qualities of the iron ore in the same hill is also different, and a mixture of that also has been found beneficial".

Detailed records of the ore mined were submitted to the courts. George Dawson Coleman had at least 80 men working the mines at his three openings, and it has been estimated that he could have employed up to 150 to 200 men. Joseph Eckman, who worked at the mines on behalf of the Grubbs, estimated they would not reach the water level of R. W. and William Coleman in 20 years if they employed 500 men. The exact depth of the mines was not known.

> That in fact the three hills of iron and other ores within or partially within said lines are merely parts of a vast extensive bed of iron ore deposit, or a natural formation of said mineral, intermixed with other ores ... that this bed ... extends below the level of the adjacent land to an unknown depth, and under the soil of the adjacent land to an unknown distance. But that they do so extend is a well-known fact, and has been so known for a long space of time, at least as long ago as 1787 ... That though it is impossible to state with any degree of precision the quantity of iron and other ores ... can with certainty be stated to be an immense quantity, and not less than many millions of tons of iron ore ... the reason of which was that for all practical purposes the said mines were inexhaustible, and the owners thereof well knew that far more ore was left in the mines capable of being taken away and used by them than would suffice to equalize them.

Operations at the mines continued as the suit dragged on through years of complaints, counter complaints and appeals. The Grubbs answered the original complaint in 1851, and after a request for extension, Robert and George Dawson answered in 1852. Amendments were submitted in 1854, followed by additional answers and appeals. Communications between the parties were strained during this period. Responding on August 29, 1867, to a letter from Wilhelm, George Dawson wrote, "On my return from Phila this noon - I found an extraordinary letter dated Cornwall Anthracite Aug. 27, 1867, and signed A. Wilhelm and postmarked Lebanon - so that I judge it is genuine. I have forwarded it to Mr.

Small to ascertain whether you are authorized by your employers to write such a letter to me". A few days later, he followed up with Small, "Yours of 2nd inst. Is received. I am surprised to find that you cannot see any insolence in the letter [A. Wilhelm's]?".

By the time the ruling was handed down in 1868, it was decreed that Robert and George Dawson Coleman owed the estates of R. W. and William Coleman $146,957.59 and the estate of E. B. Grubb and C. B. Grubb $38,925.21. Further, the E. B. Grubb and C. B. Grubb estates owed the R. W. and William Coleman estates $24,766.69. The decree accounted for the reported quantities removed by the partners (mostly during the 1850s) and the respective shares of the partners – Robert and George Dawson Coleman holding 30/96, R. W. and William Coleman 50/96, and the Grubbs 16/96.

George Dawson Coleman seemed surprised when he heard the verdict. He had apparently not set aside sufficient funds to settle the dispute in the event of a decision against his interests. He wrote to Samuel Small, "I hear that we have lost our suit [Coleman v. Coleman] in the Supreme Court. I must acknowledge that I am very much disappointed, as our lawyers were very confident of success. The next matter now is to settle up, which I desire to do as soon as possible, if I can make arrangements with you and the administrators. I write to you because I know all parties will be guided very much by your advice. The sum I believe is $146,951.59 [off by six dollars] - with interest from Jan 1868 - say 2 years if settled by Jan 1870 - or about $146,585.82. ... I would like to give you a mortgage on my interest in the Ore Banks payable in 2 or 3 yrs for $50,000 or $100,000 or $150,000 ... I have also $28,000 in Lochiel Iron Co. bonds - also 12.5 shares of Tioga Improvement Co. stock - ... 300 tons No. 1 iron at $36 loaded in cars and 250 tons No. 2 at $34 - and 500 tons No. 3 at $32 a ton. ... it will take me some time to realize money [cash]. ... I will state that there is at present a mortgage of \$32,533.33 on my furnace property held by Mr. McMurtrie and my brother Robert which I will pay off if you take a mortgage of \$150,000 and want it secured by both Ore Bank & Furnace. This is the only encumbrance on my estates". George Dawson preferred to deal with Small over Wilhelm as he expressed, "I do not want Mr. Wilhelm's opinion - ... I will have nothing to do with Wilhelm ... I am ready and anxious to try to settle all matters if you will be the medium ... If it is decided that he is to take charge of the whole matter, the Courts will have to decide every point".

His true feelings were expressed to R. C. McMutrie, his brother's legal representative, "I have had some correspondence with Mr. Small about the payment of the award of the Court. He seems determined to demand the pound of flesh. I offered him securities which I felt assured he would accept, he declines. I have written to him that I intend to go to Georgia to attend the State Fair but that early in December I expect to hand him 'the pound of flesh' I hope you will be prepared to pay Roberts share ... I am willing to do anything to settle our dispute but I want to be met at least half way ...". The phrase "pound of flesh" obviously represented an unfair attitude toward his situation as he reiterates it to Small, "I cannot tell you how humiliated and mortified I am that I ever made any proposition to you. I see plainly that the 'pound of flesh' is demanded and you shall have it. ... I am anxious for peace but ready to fight". A little later he wrote again, "I hear with pleasure that you have consented to act in connection with Mr. Reynolds in endeavoring to settle amicably all matters in dispute and I sincerely hope that we may be able to avoid any further resort to lawyers and courts to decide between us ... It would aid me very materially if you or the administrators would take the \$28,000 bonds of the Lochiel Iron Co. I took these bonds at the time thinking that if the suit was decided against us you knowing their value would take them without hesitation ...".

In addition to the disputes between the Ore Bank partners, there were ongoing concerns regarding the quantity of ore being taken by Robesonia. As late as March 1880, Wilhelm wrote to Robert H Coleman, "I was in Philadelphia Saturday to consult Messrs Biddle and Johnson relative to a letter received from General E. Burd Grubb [Edward Bates Grubb's son]. Ore taken by Robesonia and by Grubb during 1879 took upwards of 41% of the 1/6 of all ore mined. Grubb took upwards of 22% of all ore shipped - an advantage of $84,000. According to Statute of 1850 to account to his co-tenants at its market value at the time of taking. I trust we will carry the proposed amendment by a vote of 73 to 23. Mr. Brock will not vote with us for obvious reasons ... my opinion you will have more trouble with the Brocks than we ever had with Dawson, who with all his weakness was not necessary". Robesonia's ore removal was harder to quantify since they were not part of the Ore Bank Company and did not have to account for their tons, given that they operated solely under the rights to mine enough ore to keep one furnace in blast. The ore removed by Robesonia, further, was against the original 5/6 owned by Robert Coleman and not the 1/6 owned by the Grubb descendants.

Enduring disputes and suspicions, tough economic times, and changes in ownership, the Ore Bank partners found a way to cooperate and operate the mines. On September 27, 1875, the Board of The Cornwall Ore Banks met at the Eagle Hotel in Lebanon at 3:00 pm. Present were George Dawson Coleman, President, R. C. McMurtrie, Attorney for Robert Coleman, Samuel Small, Attorney for Robert H. and Anne C. Coleman, A. Wilhelm, Attorney for Mrs. Anne Alden, Mrs. William Freeman and Sarah H. Coleman, Clement Grubb and Charles B. Grubb [Clement's son], James Reynolds, R Percy Alden and J. Taylor Boyd, the Superintendent of the Mines. It was announced that profits on Ore were $4,457,627.06, representing an average yearly dividend of $417,827.

Chapter 8. Mt. Lebanon

At 1:00 pm on May 14, 1878, nineteen-year-old Debbie Coleman, daughter of George Dawson and Debbie Brown Coleman, married Horace Brock at Christ Chapel, Lebanon[1]. She was the first child of George Dawson and Debbie to marry. The bride's dress from Paris included floral attachments, a veil that descended below her waist, and a layered train. Guests were transported to Lebanon in five private train cars. A reception followed at the family home at 2:00 pm. The employees of the estate and the furnace, with their wives, stood in line to offer their congratulations. Shortly after 5:00 p.m., the newly married couple was on their way to Philadelphia in a private railcar. It was described as "the most brilliant wedding that has ever occurred within the borders of staid old Lebanon County". As a wedding present, Debbie's parents provided the couple with a home nestled in the eastern end of the North Lebanon estate, which the family called Mt. Lebanon. To shield the home from the glare and noise from the furnaces, a large stone retaining wall was built at the southern edge of the estate.

Debbie was the oldest of the children, which included her siblings Sarah, Frances, known as "Fanny", Harriet, Bertram Dawson, Robert Rion, and Anna, born last in 1875. There were four other children born who did not survive past age one. James, born in 1860, died tragically in a riding accident in 1874 at Elizabeth Furnace. His death was very hard on the family. They hired Luther Simon to design a chapel to be built in Brickerville to honor James' memory. The chapel was modeled after a Gothic cathedral and was built with local sandstone. It included beautiful stained glass and a vaulted ceiling with gold leaf. An existing church meeting room from 1750 was incorporated into the chapel. The chapel was built in front of a schoolhouse, which had been built by George Dawson's mother,

Harriet, thirty years earlier. About 300 people attended the dedication in 1877. George Dawson laid the cornerstone at 3:00 pm, followed by a picnic. The invocation was given by Rev. J. M. Galbraith, followed by the hymn "Come Thou Almighty King". A leaden box was placed in the cornerstone. It was 8 inches by 12 inches and contained gold coins from 1874, other currency, newspapers (New York Times, Boston Evening Journal, Philadelphia Inquirer, and Lebanon Daily News), photos of James, and a history of Elizabeth Furnace. Debbie had also written a deeply felt poem written for her lost son. The Elizabeth Mansion was opened, "The rooms are large and airy, and one of them, the parlor, has the wallpaper, carpets and furniture, which the father of the present owner [James Coleman] placed there at the time of his marriage sixty years ago. The Charcoal Furnace, which formerly stood there, has been removed about twenty years, and the property is now better known by the reputation given by Elizabeth cheeses".

The children grew up in the Mt. Lebanon mansion, completed in 1853, which came to be known as the Homestead. The south side of the home featured elaborate floral gardens, sloping down toward the edge of the property. The Homestead contained 39 rooms spread throughout four floors. The main entrance opened to a fine vestibule with tiled flooring. This led to a front hall opening to a grand staircase. At the first landing, there was an elaborate, large stained-glass window. In the west wing, just off the hall, there was a parlor and music room (a large billiard room was added in 1888), and in the east wing, a library and dining room. There were porches and a terrace along the outside of the home. The children maintained their own garden and enjoyed playing in an oversized playhouse. They would also spend time at the Elizabeth Farm, which George Dawson had assumed full ownership of when he purchased his brother's share.

A gatehouse stood at the north-east corner of the property. East of the mansion stood stables and a very large carriage house with a central octagonal base and four rectangular wings extending from the base. Around the carriage house stood a greenhouse and a grapery. There was an icehouse at the rear of the mansion.

The family was very sociable, often hosting extended family and friends. Of the many guests to the Homestead, perhaps the most famous was Ulysses S. Grant and his family[2]. George Dawson and Debbie were guests at the White House. The children of both families shared visits and gifts with each other. As the Coleman children grew up to adulthood, they held extended family gatherings, putting on plays and holding mock-fairs[3].

George Dawson and Debbie Coleman were very active in the community. They generously supported the Pennsylvania Sanitary Commission during the Civil War and outfitted the Pennsylvania 93rd Regiment. The regiment was first organized on September 12, 1861. Uniforms were provided in October, and the volunteers assembled at "Camp Coleman" in Lebanon until they deployed in November. Coleman, the "Father of the Regiment", also provided each member of the "Coleman Rifles", a separate unit within the regiment, with a fire gun blanket. Coleman contributed over $10,000 for the outfitting and support of the regiment, which would translate to over $250,000 in 2014 dollars. The 93rd fought at Williamsburg, Malvern Hill, Fair Oak, Chancellorsville, and Gettysburg, and in reserve at Fredericksburg. Coleman presented the 93rd with a flag "without an inscription, leaving it to the regiment to say by its actions what that inscription should be" and pledged he "would be faithful unto death to the widow and the fatherless". Coleman, his wife Debbie, Debbie's sister Fanny Brown, and Samuel Glover travelled ahead of the regiment to Washington,

D. C., and greeted them upon their arrival. Coleman also visited the regiment in February, June, and September of 1862, to "look after wounded soldiers, ascertain their wants, minister to their comforts, and if thought desirable, have them brought to their homes".

The regiment presented the battle-worn first flag back to Coleman, and on Christmas Day, 1863, Coleman presented the regiment with a second flag. It was blue with a gold eagle and a scroll listing the battles. The 93rd was formally mustered out on June 27, 1865. Bate's History of Pennsylvania Volunteers lists the total number of volunteers as 98 officers, 244 non-commissioned officers, and 1,649 men, with 274 lost. A reunion was held on October 28, 1874, at 10:00 am at the Homestead, paid for by Coleman. The two flags were photographed at 2:30 pm, and Coleman was made an honorary member of the 93rd, an honor later also bestowed on Debbie Coleman in 1884. She paid for the installation of a memorial stone at Gettysburg, where the regiment formed its line at Little Round Top. The monument incorporated a boulder, five feet by three feet, from the apex of the South Mountain at Elizabeth Farms. It was dedicated and presented by George Dawson Coleman's daughter, Fanny, on October 30, 1884.

The family maintained an especially close bond with the Elizabeth Coleman Hall line. In fact, Horace Brock was a distant cousin of Debbie Coleman. Robert Coleman Hall, son of Elizabeth and Charles Hall, married Sarah Ann Watts of Carlisle, and their daughter, Julia, married John Penn Brock. Horace was one of several children born to Julia and John Penn Brock, the son of a successful dry goods merchant in Philadelphia and a landowner. One of the properties included coal fields in the Ashland area, which eventually came under the control of the Philadelphia and Reading Coal and

Iron Company. Horace worked as a civil engineer for the Philadelphia and Reading Railroad.

Descendants of Elizabeth Coleman and Charles Hall, removed from Lebanon County, had not inherited any ownership in the Cornwall Ore Banks or any of the iron-making properties under the original Robert Coleman's empire. They were, though, involved in the development of Greenwood Furnace, Freedom Forge, and the iron industry in Sharon. Their daughter, Louisa, married Francis William Rawle, from a prominent Philadelphia family, and their daughter, Harriet, married William Norris. Both sons-in-law were partners in Norris, Rawle and Co., who put Greenwood Furnace into blast in 1834, having purchased the land in 1832. They also brought in James Hall into the business. As early as 1830, William Norris and his brother John leased Freedom Forge from William Brown and Co. Norris, Rawle and Co. purchased Freedom Forge in 1833. Norris and his brother-in-law, Samuel Patton, left the business in 1835, but Hall and Rawle continued with the business until the fall of 1847, when the Sheriff seized Freedom and Greenwood - the debt on Greenwood was $26,000. James was only 21 when he started in the business and lived at Greenwood from 1834 to 1848. Francis William Rawle was resident at Freedom when many of his children were born.

Charles and Norman Hall, grandsons of Elizabeth and Charles Hall and sons of Robert Coleman Hall and Sarah Ann Watts, became involved in the iron industry in Sharon, Pennsylvania. Norman was two years younger than his brother. He graduated from Dickinson College in 1847 and began working in a dry goods commission in Philadelphia until 1851. From there, he took a position as a clerk at an iron furnace in Marietta, Ohio, for six years, and by 1862 was managing the "Old Sharon" blast furnace for Boyce, Rawle and Co. In addition to serving in Congress as a Democrat in 1886, he was

Vice President of the Sharon Railway and a Director of the Christian H. Buhl Hospital for 10 years. He and his brother Charles built the Hall Furnace, which was acquired by Republic Iron and Steel.

At the time of Debbie and Horace's wedding, George Dawson planned to bring Horace into the management of the North Lebanon furnaces. When he informed his manager, Charles B. Forney, that he would be removed, Forney, rightly so, was quite upset. He started at Elizabeth before George Dawson became the owner. He basically built the furnaces and operated them for over twenty-five years. Apparently, George Dawson took issue with Forney's reaction. On May 2nd, Forney wrote an apology, "My dear Friend—I am sorry for saying what I did about the matter of notice. Your arrangement of giving your son-in-law charge of your property is but natural and my time for stepping out, is about the period I had fixed a couple years ago. I thank you and Mrs. Coleman heartily for the interest you have taken in my boy and trust that he does us all credit. He was the warm and devoted friend of your angel boy, and is filled with pleasant memories of him that will go with him to the grave. All I ask now is to part in peace and to retain you as my friend". Forney received an annual salary more than $2,500. His work had been appreciated as noted by Coleman in 1869, "Please accept the accompanying copy of the 'Works of Hogarth' as a token of my appreciation of your service for so many years, particularly for the interest and zeal you have exhibited in carrying out my plans in the alteration of the No. 1 Furnace. The success of which I attributed mainly to your constant attention. Believe me to be now as Ever Your Friend".

George Dawson died in the afternoon of September 9th, 1878, at 1:50, just a month after his brother, Robert, died in Paris. Robert was not well known in Lebanon, but George Dawson was much loved. The community and his workers grieved deeply as noted in the Lebanon paper, "This simple announcement marks the close of an eventful career and will cause many more than one heart, touched by the memory of other days, to throb on tender sympathy with the bereaved family, for his kindly nature, grand philanthropy, generous impulses, and a spirit of charity more deeply rooted than is common in the hearts of men so beautifully blessed with the good things of life". The funeral in Lebanon at the Homestead was reported in the Lebanon Daily News, "... in the midst of drenching rain those invited gathered in the mansion (1 o'clock) ... corpse reposed in a handsome rosewood casket with ten silver handles, with glass lid, and upon it were placed elegant flowers, and during the services in the mansion was placed in the centre of the hall. ... the church was unable to seat those who were in attendance.... the train moved off amidst a painful silence, the employees and families standing in the rain ... All along the Lebanon Valley Stations people had gathered ... but the most pitiful to witness were the countenances of his two young sons. They seemed utterly unable to comprehend what was transpiring".

George Dawson Coleman was interred at Laurel Hill Cemetery. The family left at 11 o'clock on the day of the burial over the Reading Railroad and reached Falls Bridge Station in Philadelphia at 1:30. Pallbearers included U. S. Senator J. Donald Cameron, William Rawle, John P. Brock, Judge James Ludlaw, Morton P. Henry, Charles Norris, B. Franklin Gowen, and George Keim. When they arrived at Laurel Hill, Judge Biddle, George W. Childs, J. B. Lippincott, W. Heyward Drayton, and others were waiting at the family vault, located in the cemetery at Coleman Circle.

The scope of Horace's responsibilities increased dramatically with his father-in-law's death. George Dawson's sons, Bertram Dawson and Edward, were only thirteen and eleven, respectively. Debbie

Coleman could not handle any business activity, as she was basically an invalid. Arthur Brock, who would marry Sarah Coleman in May 1879, joined his brother, Horace, at the North Lebanon furnaces. Arthur was previously involved in the Cold Springs, New York, ironworks with his uncle, John Brock.

In 1879, Debbie Coleman signed a ten-year lease with the Brocks to manage the North Lebanon furnaces. She wrote to the Cornwall Ore Bank Company, requesting that the Brocks be granted proprietor prices. The family in Cornwall was confused about how to respond. Wilhelm wrote to Robert H. Coleman, "I don't like it besides it certainly indicates a little greed on the part of the latter [Brocks] and strikes me as most unfair toward Dawson's minor children but that is a matter for themselves with which we have nothing to do", and later the next month, "it could almost seem as if the Brocks were plotting against her [Debbie Coleman]", but he does note that friend of the family and legal advisor, Mr. Biddle, states, "it would be madness to deny her that right [to provide proprietor prices to the Brocks]". There was already a precedent in place. The Grubbs leased Chickies and Sheridan Furnaces and were receiving proprietor prices for the ore they used at those furnaces. Despite Wilhelm's comments, he recommended to the R. W. Coleman Heirs that they allow it. Margaret Freeman initially opposed it, but the Cornwall Ore Bank board eventually voted to approve the request. Horace was recognized as the representative of George Dawson's estate. The North Lebanon furnaces were producing upwards of 700 tons of iron weekly and, in late 1878, were committed to ship 10,000 tons to Pennsylvania Steel.

George Dawson Coleman's brother, Robert, had sold his interest in the North Lebanon Furnaces in the early 1850s but retained his shares in the Ore Bank. He married a Frenchwoman, Rosalie Parrant, and lived in Paris for the remainder of his life. Robert and Rosalie had two children, Robert, Jr., and George Dawson. Robert, Jr. had taken his own life in Paris early in 1878, having suffered physically with lung lesions for years. The elder Robert was traumatized by his son's death and fell into a deep depression, which he expressed to his brother,

Dear Dawson,

Your letter of 15th March reaches me this morning on Easter Sunday, a day of Resurrection, if the omen could be accepted: We have all good need of a new life, for the old one is worn & torn. And I for one am well tired of it, I do not know if I will live to see through our wearisome law suits & leave my children no such legacy as that we have staggered under for so long. As I have so little hopes in my luck, it will be just like it to see a gleam of light followed by utter darkness.

Being an enemy of the propagation of our wretched species, I hardly feel authorized to congratulate you on the birth of your little girl. She may be a comfort to you, in her young days; may she be so; as also later, if you are granted life to see her become a woman. I unfortunately see things on their dark side & would be a bad fairy to invite to a christening. Of our sisters we have had little to be thankful for, but they are after all perhaps but little worse than men. Certainly nothing to thank God for, to have the one or the other to foster & love; to be surely tormented by them in after life, I want to die before mine have time to bite me & thanks to my years I will not have long to wait for my last groan, for a pitiful business is it, at

best this famous experiment of human existence. ... With
love to the children and much to yourself my dear fellow,
as we may never meet again.

They never did meet again. The family in America questioned, when
the elder Robert died later that year, if he had not also committed
suicide, but this was flatly denied by Rosalie.

The only person from America who offered condolences to Rosalie
was Edward Peace. Anna had died in 1876 after over two decades of
rejection and estrangement from her family. Rosalie replied, "Dear
Sir & Friend, I learn at this moment that you have greatly wished
to share in my sorrow by writing me a kind letter. I have been so
unhappy that they have hidden from me all the letters of sympathy
which would recall this tragic drama ... You are a man with a heart,
and for that I thank you. Not much consolation has come to me
from America. Therefore, I know how to appreciate those who
express to me sympathy and see only in me a wretched, suffering
woman and who wish to comfort her with kind words".

Robert and Rosalie's marriage had not been popular with the family
in America. When the marriage was first announced, a friend of
the family commented, "The announcement of Coleman's marriage
quite astonished me. I regret the fact of his having chosen a Catholic,
of course poor fellow he will follow his wife's lead and become one
also. It is a step backwards". Harriet Coleman refused to acknowledge
the union in her will, "As my son Robert is unmarried and resides
abroad, I will not annoy him with lumber ...". Instead of physical
property, she left Robert a Rembrandt painting titled Peasant Girl,
which, "was a Christmas present from himself and his brother in
my bright and happy days". After Robert died, Rosalie had to go
through the French and American courts to prove the marriage was
legitimate. George Biddle, one of the executors of Robert's will,

noted the will was not translated correctly and questioned whether it was probated properly. Some of the family went so far as to declare the marriage contract a forgery.

R. C. McMurtrie, who had long been Robert's representative to the Cornwall Ore Bank Company, tried to resolve matters with Biddle, who, along with Rosalie, was designated to hold Robert's voting rights. Biddle recommended to the Ore Bank board that they not recognize Rosalie Parrant Coleman's right to sit on the board. McMurtrie appealed to the board, "I would like to be able to give immediate information to the Widow that her income is likely to be withheld until her right can be established in a court of justice" and individually to Biddle, pointed to a post-nuptial agreement between Robert and Rosalie from August 3, 1858 indicating Rosalie should be entitled to the right to sit on the board. Robert's will named Biddle, representing the Pennsylvania Company for Insurance on Lives and Granting Annuities, in whom the trust for the Ore Banks was placed, and his wife, Rosalie, as trustees for the will. Once the marriage was declared legal by the courts in Philadelphia, the recognition of Robert's 15 shares was split between the Pennsylvania Company for the Insurance of Lives and Granting Annuities, which received 10 votes, and Rosalie Parrant Coleman, who received 5 votes.

At the time Robert Coleman died, he had one surviving son, George Dawson, named after Robert's brother. George was a minor and would not reach his majority until 1883. The will placed the Ore Bank shares in trust for George and specified that in the event Robert's children died without issue, the shares would then be distributed to George Dawson's heirs. There was some confusion on the part of the family as to whether the shares would revert to the elder George Dawson's eldest son or to his nearest next-of-kin. When the younger George died in Paris on October 16, 1891, both

Bertram Dawson Coleman, the elder of George Dawson's sons, and Bertram's aunt, Harriet Drayton, filed lawsuits claiming rights to the trust. This was in addition to a lawsuit entered by Louise Ybanez for the same trust.

The younger George Dawson was described as a "high liver, frequented races, owned a stud of horses and a yacht, dressed extravagantly and gave himself up to pleasure and dissipation". He had married Louise Ybanez on February 9, 1889, after an acquaintance of only three months, but at the time of his death had separated from Ybanez after only four months of marriage. When he died, the divorce was not final. He had returned to his mother, confessing to her that he did not possess the discipline to manage his financial affairs, and pleaded with his mother to help him. He agreed to leave his mother his inheritance, and she agreed to supply him with an annual income of $5,000.

Numerous parties seemed to think that what had been George Dawson's inheritance was up for grabs. Ybanez's estranged wife at the time of his death claimed she should be entitled to the inheritance and sued for it but lost. The Philadelphia Times estimated Robert Coleman's estate valued at between $3,000,000 and $5,000,000 - income from the Ore Banks on December 3, 1891, was $5,139.97, January 29, 1892, at $5,752.37, and March 1st at $6,923.05. The income averaged $70,000 per year, with its best year at $103,000, but by 1893, it was lower due to the national depression. Harriet Drayton and Bertram Dawson Coleman both claimed in separate suits that George Dawson was unduly influenced by his mother, Rosalie, when he signed over his inheritance to her. Bertram Dawson claimed the Ore Bank shares should have gone to him based on his interpretation of his uncle's will. Harriet Drayton claimed the shares should have gone to her since she was the closest next-of-kin to the elder George Dawson Coleman, all her siblings having passed away. Both cases were presented to the Orphans Court of Philadelphia, and both cases were dismissed.

Bertram Dawson was so confident in his efforts that in 1892 he wrote a letter to the Cornwall Ore Bank on Coleman and Brock letterhead declaring, "I desire to notify the Company that I am the owner of the interest in the Cornwall Ore Banks lately owned by the Estate of Robert Coleman, deceased ...". This was premature, since there was no verdict in his suit at that time. It must have been an embarrassment when he lost the suit.

Rosalie became ill later in her life. She adopted Dr. Guido J. Tatiem Hinkel, who assisted her medically. Dr. Hinkel was a grown man, but after so much suffering, Rosalie became attached to Hinkel as if to a son and wrote him into her will. When Hinkel joined the German army during World War I, she disowned him. Hinkel sued Rosalie for $1,000,000, contesting the change, but lost the suit. Rosalie reflected on the pain she felt, "How an aged french woman, hungry for affection to assuage the deaths of her husband and her son, adopted a man, only to disinherit the foster son when he joined the German army...". She had endured the loss of a son and a husband in the same year, been forced through the humiliation of proving the legality of her marriage, watched her only other son suffer and die, and had to fight off multiple lawsuits from relatives. She survived it all. When she died on April 11, 1915, she was in full possession of her husband's shares in the Ore Banks.

Chapter 9. Happy Nine

By the late 1870s, the fourth generation of Coleman descendants in Cornwall were establishing their own identities. Most of them are captured in a photo dated July 29, 1879. It was taken in Lancaster, after having driven from Cornwall in a "Four-in-Hand". Pictured from left to right in the top row, Sue Ellen Coleman's brother John Rae Habersham, Miss Edwards (a friend of the family), Robert H. Coleman, and William C. Freeman. The middle row included Anne C. Freeman, Sophie Montgomery (a friend), Lillie Clarke Coleman (wife of Robert H. Coleman), Edith E. Johnstone (who was partially raised by Sue Ellen Coleman), Anne C. Coleman, and in the bottom row, Edward C. Freeman, Margaret C. Freeman, and Arthur Elliot (a family visitor). William C. Freeman was the oldest of the cousins. He was 32 at the time of the photo and was already actively involved in the iron business, especially with the North Cornwall furnace. His brother Edward was 23, and his sisters Margaret, Isabel, and Anne were all in their twenties. Anne Alden's children, Sarah and Robert Percy, not present when the photo was taken, were married.

In 1865, Sarah married Dr. Richard Derby[1] from New York. She had natural beauty and elegance, which was captured in a portrait painted in 1888 by John Singer Sargent. Anne Coleman, writing to her brother, Robert H. Coleman, reported Sarah's excitement upon her engagement, noting Sarah was writing "all over the world" about it and then added, "How strange it seems that one of our happy nine should break the chain, and start off for herself, a new home for us to visit, a new cousin added to the family, a first wedding to make a fuss over, and to crown all a Dr. with blue eyes a handsome face and the new name of 'Dick' ... Glad the eldest of the girls weds first". Sarah herself wrote to Robert, "My dear Robert, Will you be very much surprised to hear of my engagement to Dr. Derby! It is even so, but speak not on the subject, as it is only known to the family as yet. I hope before long you will see and know Dr. Derby and write to me at once my dear cousin. I want you all to be pleased and to tell me so".

The extended family was very close and enjoyed each other's company – they held frequent family croquet tournaments, took walks together, and travelled together as well. In 1877, Anne Coleman wrote to her brother from Cornwall, "My dearest-Boy, I hear you are going to York and will probably be here tomorrow. Dr. Derby and Sarah are never seen except at meal time when they make themselves agreeable to the rest of the family. They take a long drive every afternoon". Also, in 1877, Anne wrote Robert from Magnolia, Florida, "I know Mother wrote to you yesterday and told you how we got to this lovely place and how much we are enjoying the balmy breezes on the banks of the St Johns River. Percy is delighted to be in the country and there is one walk through the woods to a place called Green Cove Springs. ... Dr. Derby, Uncle John, Percy, Sarah, and I walked over to Green Cove to tea, ... stayed for a sweet concert by an Opera troop. We drove back in a big six seated wagon. We sang all the way home and poor Sarah's hat blew off into the water where it floated for an hour or two, when a boy was sent out in a boat though dark to fish it out".

Robert H. Coleman and his sister, Anne, wrote each other weekly while he was at school, but there were numerous letters shared between the Alden, Coleman and Freeman cousins. Edward Freeman wrote to Robert from St. Mark's school in Southborough, Massachusetts that he often wished Robert were there. Annie Freeman wrote Robert, "I think Anne's photographs are lovely and I wish we had photographed every member of the Coleman-Freeman-Alden family" and signed it "Lovingly your cousin, Annie Coleman Freeman". Robert and Percy Alden shared a strong bond of friendship and love despite their age difference.

In 1879, Anne Alden built a magnificent home in Lloyd Harbor, Long Island, designed by Charles Follen McKim, of McKim, Mead and White. The home, named Fort Hill, sat on the site of an old fort built by the British, overlooking the bay from its position atop a cliff. She would move out of this home to a nearby, much smaller, more primitive home previously owned by the Lloyd family. Sarah and Dr. Derby moved into Fort Hill. Anne Coleman, writing to her brother, was quite impressed with the view from the location, "We were at the site of Dr. Derby's and Sarah's future home. The view is lovely and there seem to be fewer pests there than here. There is a tract of land here, sloping to the water's edge and thickly wooded, for sale and our Cousins are very anxious for you to buy it. It is that point as you land, and consists of 30 acres. Dr. Derby's plan is for you to buy it for $5,000 and have your steam yacht in the harbor nearby, to be summoned by a cannon shot, very noisy and romantic way of getting to sail".

Percy married Mary Ida Warren on June 2, 1878, in Paris. In 1879, Anne Alden purchased property from R. W. Coleman Heirs, which later became the site on which the Alden Villa, Stanford White's first complete residential commission, would sit. Percy good humoredly wrote to his cousin, Robert H. Coleman, regarding the site, "If you interfere with my chosen site I will give you fits when we meet" – since Robert was at the time actively buying land for his first home. Percy and Mary Ida spent the summers in Cornwall. They also had a townhouse in Manhattan and spent a good deal of time in Europe, particularly France.

The family iron business and estates were run by R. W. Coleman Heirs with A. Wilhelm acting as principal advisor to the heirs, especially regarding the furnaces, except the North Cornwall furnace, which was under the supervision of Henry Grittinger. Margaret Freeman and her sisters, Ann and Sarah, often referred to as the "ladies", held the same number of shares in the Ore Bank, the Cornwall Anthracite, and the Cornwall Furnace. The majority shares in the Ore Bank were held by Robert H. Coleman and his sister Anne. Wilhelm had noted to the sisters, "While Robert and Anne's interest is larger than yours in the Ore Hills, your interest in Donaghmore and Bird Coleman are larger than theirs ... hope the results from the furnaces will soon equalize the lot".

Robert H. Coleman had graduated from Trinity College, Hartford, Connecticut, in 1877. His cousin, William C. Freeman, sat down in his office at the North Cornwall office and sent him a heartfelt congratulations, "My Dear Robert: I was glad to hear from Aunt Ellen's letter that you had safely passed all your examinations, and are now a graduate of full standing. As the oldest living College graduate in the family; I consider it my duty to extend my sincere congratulations to the youngest. Hoping to see you soon, believe me your affectionate Cousin, Wm Coleman Freeman". The iron business was stagnant when Robert graduated, still recovering from the Panic of 1873. Although Robert reached his majority, it was decided it would be best to postpone his entry into the business. Rather than stay in Cornwall, he spent a year back at Trinity supervising the construction of a new fraternity house he was funding. It also allowed him time to be around Lillie Clarke, whom he was madly in love with.[2]

There may have been legitimate concerns regarding Robert H. Coleman's capacity to run the business. He was not a good student, receiving numerous warnings and demerits for poor performance and behavior during his preparatory school years. In 1870, his mother, Sue Ellen Coleman, wrote to him from Savannah. "I was grieved to hear today from your letter that you had had a whipping. I think my dear boy that it is a great disgrace, and I hope you will never, never, never get another. We were so proud to say you had never been whipped. I hope you will never again laugh at Grace, for I do not like you to get double checked reports, or be put in Coventry". Later in the year, she again admonishes him, "I did feel very badly to hear of a double check report. You must take care of your tongue, or you will often get into trouble". Robert seemed unwilling to heed his mother's advice. Only a month later he was caught throwing "paper balls" during a lesson.

Still in 1872, a year away from attending Trinity College in Connecticut, Sue Ellen was worried he would not pass his exams. He did manage to pass and gain entrance to Trinity, but his poor performance continued through his college years. He had to make special arrangements to retake his final exams to graduate. Concerns were also expressed by his mother that he was being reckless with his spending, urging him to be more thoughtful in his management of money during his college years.

Sue Ellen Coleman wrote to Robert in 1876,

> Some words of 'admonition' to a young man who has only one parent ... Now I am sure you ought to have all things that will (?) to your comfort and to making your room look pretty, but you must curb your wishes in (?) moderation and be sure not to promise too much away, for your expenditure will be large, as you have both your friends and your board expenses through Senior year. The money is not yet yours, and I must get it for you. In fact, I (?) borrowing it for you. So as I said before curb your desires, for it will make it much easier for you when you have your fortune. If you have everything you can want now you will want everything hereafter and to get everything you want would make even one million a year fly, and you know you have only the interest on that to

spend at best. Then do my dear son keep to being good, and true and honorable and high toned - study - study-study. If the others do not study, now is your chance to step ahead of them and delight my heart. You have great encouragement from Percy to try to (?). He knows what a good education is. I am so glad he appreciates your letters.... Now the lecture is ended.

Sue Ellen's cottage was nearing the end of improvements while Robert was finishing his graduating examinations. Anne wrote him of the progress, "Mr. McArthur is here making plans for the addition. I know it will be lovely, quite large enough but not too large. I have been packing all day the things to go to Colebrook.... I must have all the book cases empty and the books packed also. The Methodist church is to be torn down and the new one will be started shortly now ...". Robert's father had lived at the Colebrook mansion early in his career, and the family retained the mansion as a retreat after the charcoal furnace had been demolished. Robert commissioned Washington Bleddyn Powell to make improvements to the mansion, including a single lane bowling alley.

Business conditions improved in 1879, and Robert started taking a more active role in the business. He got married in January and hired Bleddyn Powell to build a stable and design a new home for himself and his bride. Powell had been First Assistant to John McArthur, Jr., who had been hired to build a stable for the R. W. Heirs at the Cornwall Manor, as well as significant improvements to Sue Ellen's "Cottage". McArthur had also been the lead architect for the construction of the Cornwall Methodist Church, for which Powell drew the plans. The Freeman family and Robert H. and Anne Coleman were the principal contributors to the construction costs. Robert hired Powell, who gave his notice to McArthur starting January 1st, at a salary of $3,000 a year. Robert's stable was a modified copy of the one built for the heirs. When in Cornwall, Cornwall Manor was the center of family gatherings, and while work was continuing on the Cottage, Sue Ellen and Anne stayed at the Colebrook house.

In August 1878, after returning from a trip, Sue Ellen and Anne took a drive over to the Cottage. Sue Ellen was so distraught by how behind the work was that she cried. Captain Hean was supervising much of the work and walked them through the home. Anne reported to Robert, "We were charmed with the Library also the Dining Room and all your portion of the house that is finished except that the stairway is not yet done. I for one was rather surprised to find so much done, and as for the house, I think it is beautiful inside and out, Mother is over there unpacking. I don't know what she intends doing with all the things for I do not see room for them as the closets are not finished. Johnny has got the old croquet ground sodded, also the front lawn and has begun sodding in the shrubbery. I think as soon as your hall is up and the rubbish out of the way, the place will look quite respectable". There were 145 gas burners on the first floor alone, 50 on the second, where the bedrooms were located, and 26 on the third floor. The first floor housed a parlor, a music room, an office, a library, a dining room, a gun room, a buttery, a ladies' book room, storerooms, servants' hall, laundry, kitchen and kitchen lobby. The second floor housed Mrs. Coleman's room, dressing room, Anne's room, bath room, old hall, "Butternut room", "Black Walnut chamber", and "Miss Johnstone's room" (Edith Johnstone was partially raised by Sue Ellen Coleman) and the third floor housed the water tank, hall, Robert's chamber, bath room, college room, guest chamber, waiter's room, lumber room, servants' rooms and other attic chambers.

Benjamin Franklin Hean became Robert H. Coleman's private secretary (and in 1890 was appointed manager of the new

Colebrook furnaces). He volunteered for Company F of the 93rd Pennsylvania Infantry on October 12, 1861, was promoted to Sergeant on October 28, 1861, and 1st Lieutenant on August 4, 1862. He was wounded at Salem Church on May 3, 1863, but returned to the regiment and received a promotion to captain on January 1, 1864. According to Sergeant Franklin T. Miller, a soldier in Hean's company, Hean had a tattoo of the American flag and "B. F. Hean" underneath, "in order to provide means of identification in case of being wounded".

Much later in Hean's career, in 1892, he was elected as Lebanon's Prothonotary, which he served for one full term. In 1895, he informed those around him that he needed to take a trip to Pittsburgh and would be gone several days. Shortly after his departure, it was discovered that Hean had embezzled over $10,000. He never returned to Lebanon. On New Year's Day, 1896, his body was discovered on a beach in St. Kilda, a suburb of Melbourne, Australia, with a revolver in his hand. He had shot himself in the head. Authorities identified the body by his tattoo.

The Lebanon Daily News reported, "In the way of fine residences Cornwall is making some handsome improvements. Mr. Grittinger is occupying a handsome stone mansion recently erected at the North Cornwall furnace. Mr. William C. Freeman has had built for himself a handsome residence on the high elevation west of the same furnace. Mr. Robert H. Coleman is having built on the elevation west of his mother's residence, one of the largest and most complete houses in the state. And it is stated that Mr. Percy Alden had determined to erect a residence on the hill south of the Methodist Church. All these handsome residences in addition to those existing there before will give an ornate appearance to the locality". It is believed Freeman's home was designed by Thomas Ustick Walter[3], who had executed renovation plans for Margaret Freeman's and Sarah H. Coleman's home in Washington, D. C. Robert H. Coleman's first mansion was designed by Washington Bleddyn Powell, and Alden's "villa" was designed by Stanford White. Edward C. Freeman built a home for himself, south of his brother's property, along the Furnace Creek. Each mansion had its own service staff. Edward employed three female servants, all from Sweden.

William C. Freeman built his home in preparation for his marriage to Elizabeth Brown on May 30, 1878. The family was happy for him, given his previous failed betrothal to Miss Mary Heath, granddaughter of the late Hon. John Y. Mason of Virginia. Her father had been Minister to France under Presidents Pierce and Buchanan from 1854 to 1859, Secretary of the Navy from 1846 to 1849 under Polk and Tyler, and Attorney General under Polk. Miss Heath was 18 years old at the time of the broken engagement. Freeman moved from the Cornwall Mansion to his new home, which was close to the North Cornwall Furnace.

Robert was elected President of the Ore Banks Company and started plans for a new furnace in West Lebanon, for which he had begun purchasing land west of Lebanon city. He engaged Charles B. Forney and Hugh Maxwell, who had been at the North Lebanon furnaces, to start planning for the new furnace. As early as December 1878, Hugh Maxwell assisted with the purchase of land. The Lebanon Courier reported the Gingrich farm of 103 acres was purchased at $200 per acre, "The farm is situated a small distance west of the boro limits and lies between the Berks and Dauphin turnpike and the Lebanon Valley Railroad, and is a desirable site for the location of the furnace. Some of the finest limestone is found on the land". In September 1879, it was further reported, "The Cornwall Estate has just made an important real estate investment on the western part of Lebanon at the junction of the Lebanon Valley, Pinegrove and the Cornwall Railroads. It embraces a tract of 58 acres of land owned by Messrs. Funck and Light, and 102 adjoining acres belonging to the estate of Geo. Gingrich deceased. It is probably the best site for manufacturing in this locality - its railroad facilities being unequalled. There are rumors that extensive works - some saying furnaces and others rolling mills will be erected thereon at an early day". A month later, ground was broken. The property would consist of two furnaces. Robert named the new furnaces Colebrook in honor of the charcoal furnace which had been built by his great-grandfather. In 1878, the Bird Coleman Furnaces were producing 250 tons of iron per week, and the new furnaces were being designed to exceed that. Work would continue into 1880 and would require over 150 men to build.

Distributions from the Cornwall Anthracite and the Ore Banks were strong during the late 1870s, never falling below $40,000 per distribution. Robert's share would be over $10,000, the same as his sister received. He needed every cent of the distributions. The cost of the land for his new furnaces and his new home exceeded $60,000. There may have been doubts about his ability to manage when Robert first entered the family business, but by the time he was married, he knew what he wanted to accomplish and set himself on a path to do so. A friend from his college days, Edmund A. Friedman, Insurance Commissioner of Connecticut, remarked, "... am glad you are so much interested in your business and other plans".

Anne reached 21 in October of 1879. On November 11[th,] a deed of trust was established between Anne and Robert, which allowed Robert to vote Anne's shares. The value of Anne's share was substantial. Distributions made to Robert H. Coleman as trustee in 1881 totaled $94,737.23, comprising eight distributions, four from Cornwall Anthracite and four from Cornwall Ore Bank. With control of Anne's shares, Robert strengthened his power in R. W. Coleman Hiers. The family may have thought the exclusion of

Robert and Anne from the Bird Coleman Furnaces equalized the holdings, but they failed to appreciate the forces they awakened in Robert's mind.

Robert and Lillie set sail for an overdue European honeymoon in January. Lillie had been ill, and in the Fall, they had spent time with his maternal relatives in Georgia. Lillie started to recover enough that they felt comfortable with embarking on the journey. They arrived safely in France and slowly moved on toward Italy, making purchases for their new home along the way. They missed William Freeman's wedding to Elizabeth P. Brown.[6] R. Percy Alden wrote to Robert regarding the wedding, "arrived with [?] the Freeman wedding party in Canada last Monday night returning on Friday. We had a good deal of fun, but it was a pretty hard journey on the girls. The Canadians were very hospitable at Ottawa ... Willie's marriage was very quiet and sensible no fuss no nonsense; only 16 people present. We met them the next day at Montreal and they looked like an old married couple".

Robert H. Coleman also, unfortunately, missed his sister's wedding as well. Anne was highly energetic and passionate. She looked at life with an artist's eye. As a young woman establishing her nature in the family and the world, she wrote to her brother in 1874 from Cornwall, "This is the last letter I will write at my little desk this Summer, and I feel dismal, doleful and dreary at having to leave. The country never looked so pretty as it does this evening with the setting sun makes the bright red and yellow leaves glow beautifully and the mountains look like huge bouquets. We have been having an early Indian Summer and a most delightful one and it just seems to be clearing off now". Anne loved activity. When she was young, she took dance lessons and later became an avid roller skater. It was natural that she fell in love with Archibald Rogers, an engineer her brother had met. Rogers was a true outdoorsman, very different than her brother and her cousins. Her mother was not thrilled with the choice, but she had also not been enthused with Lillie at first, thinking Lillie's background was not sufficient to support her son in his future. Anne had lobbied her mother on Robert's behalf when he introduced his intentions toward Lillie, and in May, he needed to return the favor. His mother wrote to him, "We both think it best to wait until you come to talk it all over, but you are the only one we can speak to about it until it is all settled and they are engaged". At the same time, his sister pleaded with him, " ... Oh, I wish it was time for you to come home, you don't know how I want you. I know Mother told you something in her last letter but my Robert, everything looks so dark I want you to come home and cheer me up a little, I have not known all winter what was the matter, but I see it all now. The mischief was done long ago. Poor Mother is so unhappy and she has been so sweet all through ... Oh, Robert, I helped you all I could, your interests help us now, My Dearest Bobba". It is unclear if there is more behind the darkness and mischief Anne reports, but in the end, she did marry Archibald on May 11, 1880. Rogers had taken on the management of a railroad in Wisconsin and taken a house there. In April, Anne appeared excited, "Archie is here with us now. He has his (our house) in Milwaukee on the lake with a beautiful view. The house is being prepared and furnished ... Mother has reached that stage when she wishes I was married. ... Edith got a letter from Lillie the other day which pleased her immensely ... Willie [William C. Freeman] is to be married on Wednesday. The excitement in the Freeman family". For whatever reason, Anne's wedding took place while Robert was in Europe. Sadly, the day before the wedding, Lillie died in Paris after having taken ill in Italy. Robert was crushed. The love of his life was gone.[4]

On May 29, 1880 the Reading Times reported, "Yesterday, Mr. Robert H. Coleman ordered work to cease on his new mansion at

Cornwall and all that has already been done on it will be razed to the ground, so that every trace of what was intended to be one of the finest mansions in the state will be obliterated as nearly as possible - the grounds around it will be plowed over and his desire is to have it done within two weeks". Work had been ordered suspended while Robert was travelling, mostly due to cost overruns. At the time the mansion was ordered to be torn down, the walls of the rear part of the structure reached the second story, but no bricks had been laid on the front walls.[5] While the mansion was torn down, the stables were spared.

One month after Lillie's death on June 9, 1880, the architect, W. Bleddyn Powell, submitted a final invoice to Robert H. Coleman for the work he had done for, "planning and superintending the erection and completion of New stable, ...alterations, additions and decorations to Cottage, ...alterations and additions to Conservatory, ...alterations and rebuilding of Bowling Alley at Colebrook... ventilation of closets etc. in basement, drainage from roof, and decoration of Music Hall". He included a detailed account of the work. Powell added, "it [the new mansion] would have placed me in the foremost ranks of the profession. You can readily see therefore that as a means for advancement to notoriety (reputation being my capital) the structure would have been invaluable. Its annihilation renders me no service. With its destruction let the question of remuneration other than as above and as follows, cease. Regretting the circumstances of our dissolution...". Coleman disputed the invoice and turned it over to his secretary, Captain B. F. Hean.

The dispute was eventually settled. At the end of December, Grant Weidman wrote to A. Wilhelm, "After our interview yesterday I saw Mr. Powell, and explained the matter to him, and he has agreed to accept the sum of three thousand dollars [the yearly salary agreed to at the beginning of Powell's engagement] in full of all claims and demand from Mr. Coleman. He further consents to the proposition that the drawings are to remain with Mr. C., with the understanding that they are not to be made use of, in accordance with our conversation yesterday. Please send me the form of receipt you wish and I will return it to you executed by Mr. Powell. I am glad to have this matter closed in this way, and believe it to be best ended as it is". Included in the final drawings was Powell's design for the new office building at the Colebrook furnaces.

Chapter 10. Partition

It is unclear when Robert H. Coleman first thought of forcing a partition of R. W. Heirs and operating independently of the rest of his family. In March 1880, Wilhelm wrote to him and suggested he "keep in harmony with your cousins". There had been a slight rise in demand for iron in 1879, although prices had not moved much. Wilhelm thought it made more sense to add an additional furnace to Bird Coleman rather than invest in modifications to the Cornwall Anthracite. The Panic of 1873 brought about several years of hard times, but R. W. Coleman Heirs invested $150,000 in improvements to the Bird Coleman Furnaces, including the addition of railroad tracks, engines, pipes, a new pumphouse, and a new stack house. Wilhelm noted, "Now that the steelworks [Pennsylvania Steel] has and will furnish a market for the iron it seems a pity to have $150,000 of capital idle ... since the collapse [of the Coal Combination] we have been able to compete with our western friends and have during the past few months resumed shipments of Cornwall iron to Pittsburgh ... which was closed to us for years". The second furnace at Bird Coleman was added in 1880. Robert H. Coleman did not have an ownership stake in Bird Coleman, but the R. W. Coleman Heirs carried the cost of repairs and improvement of $22,080.29 for 1880. This had been an issue for Robert - the Anthracite provided funds for Bird Coleman's development, but he had no stake in the ownership of Bird Coleman. Robert's feelings were confirmed by Wilhelm, "I was told yesterday again that he thinks he was not treated fairly by our not giving him and his sister the same interest in Bird Coleman as in Cornwall Anthracite, or to use his new phrase, the proportion of interest, that he and his sister furnished the capital to build them". The "capital" was treated as a loan at 6% and paid upwards of $50,000. Both Wilhelm and Small had agreed to not include Robert H. Coleman and his sister with an interest in Bird Coleman Furnaces to "balance" and protect the investment by the "ladies".

By April 1880, conditions still looked a little "gloomy", but Robert had begun construction on the new Colebrook Furnaces. This was a very large undertaking. Wilhelm expressed concerns about the multiple projects Robert initiated, "Robert is young and inexperienced in business and unless he is careful to take proper advice will make serious mistakes". As the year progressed into 1881, Robert became more committed to forcing a partitioning of assets. At the beginning of 1881, the Colebrook Valley Railroad was established. Robert held the bulk of the shares with 2,375 out of 4,000. Sarah H. Coleman, Margaret Freeman, and Anne Alden each held 530. A. Wilhelm had six, Charles B. Forney had five, Edward Freeman had four, and D. S. Hammond had five. By April of 1881, though, Wilhelm communicated to the family, Robert "is looking at things with a view to a dissolution" and then in an additional communication, "Robert left for New York Tuesday ... I doubt not his mission to New York is to consult with Mr. Rogers relative to their future managements for business on partitions which he seems determined upon ... I do not see how you can any longer go on in business as co-partners without jeopardizing your interests in the estate". In July, Robert made it clear to his Aunt Sarah, "I regret deeply to say that there seems absolutely no prospect for such an agreement. Thus, I am forced much against my will to advise under the circumstances that our estate be divided ... hoping we will have a pleasant settlement". (The phrase "much against my will" seems surprising in the context of all the other statements made during this time. Perhaps, the family had underestimated the feelings Robert held regarding being denied a stake in Bird Coleman.)

Robert's sister, Anne, reluctantly agreed to the split. She confided in a letter, "While I have always deprecated a division of the interest in the Cornwall Estate ... painful to me to think of ... but ... better to make the division of interest now than later".

Perhaps Wilhelm's early concerns regarding Robert's business sense were warranted. Robert desired to buy his sister's share of woodland they held in common. His attorneys felt it was a violation of the trust he held on behalf of his sister and instructed Robert that if he took this course of action, it could compromise the entire partitioning. Despite this advice, Robert argued the matter with his attorneys. The fundamental point of law regarding the trust he held for his sister was that he could not benefit individually from any sale of her share of the common holdings and certainly could not buy her share. Fortunately, Robert eventually yielded to his attorney's counsel.

Since the family's efforts to dissuade Robert were unsuccessful, it became clear that the dissolution of R. W. Coleman Heirs was inevitable (there is no record found regarding Sue Ellen Coleman's opinion of the partition). The last transaction shared among the family was a small settlement from a lawsuit against the Robesonia Iron Company. The family was awarded $7,874.51, less all attorney fees of $625, for a net $7,254.51 to be distributed to Robert H. Coleman for $2,267.04, the same amount to Robert H. Coleman Trustee (Anne Rogers), and $906.81 each to Anne Alden, Margaret Freeman, and Sarah H. Coleman. William C. Freeman took the lead on the family's behalf in negotiating with Robert. It was an especially hard year for Freeman. His wife had given birth to a son, William, and died in the afternoon of February 3rd from complications following childbirth. On October 25, 1881, he wrote, "Dear Robert, I think it a pity the coolness existing between this family and yourself should not be made up; if mutual explanations can accomplish this result. If you are of the same mind and would like to have a good plain talk on this subject Edward and myself will meet you, if you will appoint a time and place where we can discuss this privately. Yours Affec. Wm Coleman Freeman".

Robert was unwilling to compromise on property divisions, which made for straighter lines of demarcation and other details. By November, Freeman was losing his patience, "... As the family have been so willing to accommodate you; I think it is only fair you should make some compromise in this matter". The frustration was echoed even deeper by William's brother Edward, "We have no intention of calling either at your house or office while the present state of affairs exist and are much surprised that your own Common Sense does not tell you after the manner you have treated us throughout this would be utterly impossible. Anytime, you name Willie and myself will meet you at North Cornwall office". It seems during this period, Wilhelm was having difficulty watching the Coleman estate he had devoted his life to being split, as Freeman expressed, "... I find it makes trouble on the Estate. Mr Wilhelm being so firmly wedded to the old system. I think no changes can be made without making trouble while he remains in the management at Cornwall".

By December 1881, the new Colebrook Furnace was producing between 45 and 50 tons per day, which was considered an unprecedented yield for Cornwall ores. The furnace used Whitwell box blast stoves exclusively. On the last day of the year, the partition was final.

> Notice is hereby given the co-partnership of the undersigned heretofore existing under the firm name of R. W. Coleman Heirs Company has been dissolved this day by mutual consent. Signed Anne C. Alden, Margaret C. Freeman, Sarah H. Coleman, Robert H. Coleman, Robert H. Coleman Trustee, ten parcels in sub-division:

(1) Anthracite Furnace, (2) Dairy Farm (with property on the other side of turnpike opposite Robert H. Coleman mansion between Cornwall Railroad and its branch to furnace, (3) Robert H Coleman property (less a triangle to go to 2), (4) property adjoining Mrs. Alden's land (with land added from 5), (5), (6) including Bird Coleman Furnace and Charcoal Furnace, (7) including Speedwell Forge upwards 1,000 acres of woodland, (8) including land between Miss Coleman and the road separating hers from Robert H. Coleman, (9) Donaghmore Furnace - to be bid on and (10) divided or sold, Robert H. Coleman and his sister (held in trust) to possess 1, 3 and 5.

Robert received the Cornwall Anthracite furnace, land in nearby Cold Spring and West Lebanon, and some cattle and livestock. The family received Donaghmore, the Cornwall furnace, woodland, other lands, Speedwell, and some cattle and livestock. Margaret Freeman, Anne Alden, and Sarah H. Coleman each paid Robert and his sister $67,647.64.

Donaghmore was indebted to Cornwall Anthracite for $47,836.12, and Bird Coleman for $227,074.07 - the credit balances of the proprietors were kept in proportion to their interests in Cornwall Anthracite. If the rest of the family had paid the debt of Donaghmore and Bird Coleman to Cornwall Anthracite, then the amount paid would have belonged to the Common Fund of Cornwall Anthracite and would have been distributed proportionately. To defray expenses, the family decided to auction Donaghmore but were unable to realize a reasonable bid.

Robert purchased the majority shares of the Lebanon Iron Company, the successor to the Aurora Iron Company, which was formed in 1865 by Aaron Wilhelm, D. S. Hammond, A. R.

Boughter, William Shirk, and P. L. Weimer. It was a natural fit for Coleman. The Colebrook Furnaces would supply the pig iron, and the Lebanon Iron Company further diversified the product line that Coleman could produce. The original owners erected a plant east of Fourth Street in Lebanon to manufacture butt-welded wrought iron pipe for gas, steam, and water. The name was changed to the Lebanon Tube and Iron Works, but it was never overly successful. With Coleman's entry into the company in 1882, it was reorganized as the Lebanon Iron Company and operated primarily as a bar iron rolling mill. Coleman was elected President, with Abraham Hess, Coleman's Assistant, elected as Secretary and Treasurer. A new plant was built at a cost of nearly $200,000, and Thomas Evans was established as the General Superintendent. Wilhelm and Hammond remained as directors. The new plant had a capacity of 12,000 tons per year of puddle bar-iron and employed two hundred men. By the end of 1883, they were running at full capacity and announced the addition of three additional puddling furnaces. The use of puddling furnaces at rolling mills was common by the late 1880s. Separating the iron from the fuel allowed the iron to be manipulated without removing it from the heat, and the use of grooved rolls further increased efficiency.

Late in 1882, Artemus Wilhelm, no longer advising Robert H. Coleman but still active in the interest of the rest of the Cornwall Coleman family, became concerned that Robert was showing signs of financial weakness and suggested to Sarah H. Coleman and Anne Alden that they sell their shares in Robert's Dime Bank.[1] It concerned Wilhelm that Robert was borrowing from the bank without security, and in November, the bank ran out of capital. Robert agreed to buy the shares at $35 per share. On December 29, 1882, Wilhelm met with Robert at the Dime Bank. A total of 504 shares were transferred, 145 of Sarah H. Coleman's, 48 of Anne

Alden's, and 311 of Wilhelm's. Wilhelm received $17,640, Sarah $4,507, and Anne $1,680.

Wilhelm's aggressive opposition to Robert H. Coleman was problematic. William C. Freeman thought it best to reduce the strain in the family's relationship with Robert by parting ways with Wilhelm. He was basically forced into retirement from his long dedication and career with Coleman interests. His final action was withdrawing from the Cornwall Ore Bank, "Under existing circumstances I deem it my duty to retire from the Secretary ship of the Cornwall Ore Bank ... I do it with much concern ... Judge Watts, Mr. Small, Mr. McMurtrie and myself are the only survivors who took part and were identified with the organization of the Cornwall Ore Bank ...". Wilhelm was saddened to leave the employment of the Colemans. He did, though, have other business activities. He was active as a director with other Central Pennsylvania ironmaking and industrial concerns, including the reorganization of the Reading Railroad. He had a home in York, Pennsylvania, and a country estate and farm in Paxtang, just outside of Harrisburg, where he died in 1887, after an illness of ten days. The Harrisburg Telegraph noted, he "was a 'self-made man', a thorough, practical, energetic, capable businessman. Always busy, he was tireless in the acquisition of knowledge of every detail necessary to the successful management of the large affairs entrusted him ... no man had a more extensive knowledge of men and his extensive acquaintance all over the United States drew to his York and Harrisburg residences men prominent in all circles of life. His delight was to dwell on the events of his early life, his struggles and success, in itself a regular romance, and of great interest".

Following the partition, Robert began a push for control of the Cornwall Railroad. Since he could not gain control, he decided to build his own independent road. Wilhelm expressed his frustration to William Freeman, "to me it is sad to think of a young man claiming the name of Coleman to say to his aunts 'Now unless you surrender to me the entire control of your property in which you have a large controlling interest either by lease or otherwise, I will build another road to destroy it'". Coleman had already chartered a new road, the Colebrook Valley Railroad, to run from Elizabethtown to the Ore Banks. Since efforts to gain control of or lease the existing Cornwall Railroad failed, Robert H. Coleman began construction of a new road, the Cornwall and Lebanon Railroad, which would run parallel to and on the easterly side of the Cornwall Railroad from Lebanon to Cornwall. The new road would cross over the tracks of the existing Cornwall Railroad in Cornwall before connecting to the Colebrook Valley Railroad and continuing to Mt. Gretna and beyond.

The Cornwall only carried freight, but when the Cornwall and Lebanon planned to open its line to passengers, the Cornwall did the same. Both roads opened to passengers on October 1, 1883. Wilhelm was concerned about the competition, "The situation in regard to Robert and the railroad matters seem in about as unsatisfactory shape as possible. I have not seen Robert for several weeks, but from information received of Messrs. Freemans he is more unreasonable now than ever and nothing can be done to let him (?) the competing railroad which will not only destroy the Cornwall Railroad but fear the control of the competing railroad as well as the Colebrook Valley ... it is hoped however that reason and common sense may yet prevail, but I am sorry to say that Robert does not seem to possess much of either".

Early in 1883, Wilhelm was voted off as a director of the Colebrook Valley Railroad (in 1886, the Colebrook road was merged with the Cornwall and Lebanon). His response was emphatic, "I regret to say that I see nothing but trouble ahead, all growing out of vain ambition of the young man ... and will not make him (as he told me ...) the 'greatest man in Lebanon County'". He added, "I do think that Robert's conduct as present toward the Board of Directors is as well as has been contemptible without precedent and believe the Czar of Russia would actually blush at the thought of doing what Robert does and assumes to do as if he were 'Monarch of all he surveys and there were none his rights to dispute'". Five of the nine directors were under Robert's control. It was Wilhelm's opinion that Robert acted vindictively with anyone who voiced a difference of opinion.

Connecting the Cornwall and Lebanon to the Ore Banks was problematic, and in trying to resolve the issue, Coleman was looking at the possible need to encroach on the property of his aunt, Sarah H. Coleman. He wrote, "before touching your land I must make (?) effort to avoid running through your property ... You remember at one time the Cornwall Railroad had agreed to give us the right of way which you know would have enabled us to reach the hills without inconveniencing anyone". R. Percy Alden pleaded with Robert to re-consider going through the "grounds that have been for a hundred years the delight of the 'Coleman Family'".

The Coleman family took great pride in the Cornwall estate, which had been in the family's possession since 1798. The mansion home, originally built by Curtis Grubb and later added onto by Coleman descendants, sat at the top of a slight rise to the north of the Cornwall Charcoal Furnace. From the veranda, the view included extensive gardens with rows of flowers and hedges, vegetable gardens, a circular fishpond, and meadows extended beyond the gardens. Numerous outbuildings were contained within the borders of the estate, including an elaborate stable (now Bradley Hall) and a greenhouse, added in the early 1880s.

The hard feelings between William Freeman and Robert were further exasperated since the Cornwall and Lebanon was carrying three-quarters of the freight, reducing the previous freight and profits for the Cornwall Railroad. When the Cornwall and Lebanon started to build a connection to the Ore Banks through the meadow leading to the pit, Freeman ordered his workers to tear up the new track, which in part ran through land Freeman owned. October 29, 1883, edition of the Harrisburg Daily Independent reported the incident,

> About 5.30 o'clock on Saturday evening about fifty workingmen of the old Cornwall railroad went out on the workingmen's train from Lebanon to Cornwall, and all the Hungarians (one hundred in number) were taken from the ore hills, and all of Contractor Reilley's men from the Mt. Hope railroad were brought down, the whole force being about two hundred and fifty men. This was unexpected to Mr. Coleman's workmen, as there were only about fifteen of them besides Mr. March's force of twenty men. The Cornwall and Lebanon railroad men, with March's men, were working upon it during the day at the ore hills. While they were working on the road, laying the track, etc., Mr. Freeman came to where the men were working, and gave orders to all his men to be out on Saturday evening. While Jimmy March's men and the repairmen were eating their supper, Mr. Freeman put his men to work at tearing up the railroad track, etc., which the Cornwall and Lebanon railroad men had just put down. The men obeyed orders, and tore up the track, with six mules hitched to the rails. civil engineer as a peacemaker. A Mr. Kendall, of the engineer corps for the new road, told his men that being too short handed, and

not wishing to create any further disturbance, they should gather the tools and put them safely away and not molest the old road men, but go home and he would see that the law would decide as to who is right or wrong. While Engineer Kendall was giving his orders to the men of the new road, a Hungarian raised a pick and wanted to strike Mr. Kendall with it. During the melee quite an excitement was created, and it was feared that serious results would occur. The news spread like wild-fire in Lebanon, and lots of men were ready at a moment's notice to respond in behalf of Mr. Coleman. The sympathy of the entire community is with him, and condemnations of Mr. Freeman were severe. The police were on the alert, and they at one time, the way the reports came in, thought they would be called out. Work will be resumed on Mr. Coleman's branch from Cornwall to the ore hills on Monday, but no doubt the workmen will meet with opposition. It was feared at one time that the Sheriff, with a posse would have to go to the scene.[2]

William C. Freeman took matters into his own hands when he ordered his workers to tear up the Cornwall and Lebanon tracks. This resulted initially in a fight between workers on the respective railroads but gave way to a battle in court. It was decided that Coleman did not have the right to cross over Freeman's land. Eventually, the Cornwall and Lebanon did construct a spur to the ore banks.

In December 1886, an agreement was reached between the competing roads, which gave the Cornwall priority in resolving traffic over the crossing point in Cornwall Center. The Cornwall and Lebanon also agreed to stop at least two hundred feet from the point of crossing and wait for a signal from a watchman until proceeding. The Cornwall and Lebanon would often stop eight to nine hundred feet from the intersection, which was too far a distance for the watchman to see, and there were cases of the Cornwall and Lebanon not stopping at all. The Cornwall Railroad filed suit against the Cornwall and Lebanon, citing these objections with additional claims of loss due to delays on the part of the Cornwall and Lebanon. During the appeal, it was determined that stopping eight to nine hundred feet was too far beyond what would be a reasonable interpretation of "at least two hundred feet". Work began in 1890 on the inevitable solution - Robert H. Coleman built an iron trestle bridge, supplied by Croford and Saylor of Pottstown, to carry his road over the existing Cornwall Railroad tracks.

Robert H. Coleman insisted passengers travelling from Lebanon to Mount Gretna had to start their travel in Lebanon with his road – passengers could not travel to Cornwall on the Cornwall line and transfer to the Cornwall and Lebanon at Cornwall (the Cornwall did not have their own station in Lebanon, but through special arrangement used the Philadelphia and Reading Lebanon station). Both Coleman and William Freeman competed fiercely for the passenger fare between Lebanon and Cornwall.

This became an issue in August 1887 when soldiers on their way to the new encampment in Mount Gretna, having travelled to Cornwall on the Cornwall Railroad, were refused passage to Mount Gretna on the Cornwall and Lebanon. Coleman had spent $55,000 of his own money to prepare the campsite and another $180,000 on new steel rails. Freeman had erected a high fence between the two roads to prevent passengers from switching trains. Freeman was urged to consent to allow the transfer and was promised a cent a mile for each of the soldiers (National Guardsmen) for each of the six miles between Lebanon and Cornwall.

Through a clerical error, soldiers travelling west on the Philadelphia and Reading were to have disembarked at Lebanon and then boarded the Cornwall and Lebanon to Mt. Gretna, but instead ended up at the Cornwall station. Six carloads of soldiers and Battery were denied transport to Mt. Gretna. The soldiers were quite restless and even unsuccessfully attempted to take control of one of the locomotives. Discussions between the two roads were slow. In the end, the infantry marched the four miles from Cornwall to Mt. Gretna (along the way they broke into a tool shed in Cold Springs and "stole" a truck, which about 25 of the men boarded), and the Battery was returned to Lebanon, where it was transferred to the Cornwall and Lebanon.

In addition to the Cornwall Railroad and the Cornwall and Lebanon main tracks in Lebanon, there were spur lines that wove their way into the Colebrook and North Lebanon plants. The mass of tracks in Cornwall was perhaps even more confusing. In addition to the parallel lines of the two competing roads, tracks were running to and from the Ore Banks and extensions into the local furnaces. Both major roads had connections with the Ore Banks. The Ore Banks added their own tracks to move material around inside the pit. In 1865, they began construction of a spiral railroad that wound its way through the Big Hill. Track was added and removed throughout its time in operation.

With the dissolution of R. W. Coleman Heirs, the family formed The Cornwall Iron Company, Ltd. in October 1886. Anne Alden, Margaret Freeman, and Sarah H. Coleman each subscribed for 1,999 shares, each share valued at par of $100. William Freeman, Edward Freeman, and Percy Alden each subscribed for 1 share. The character of the business would be "in the manufacturing and sale of iron and steel, and generally the transaction of all matters pertaining to the said business". William C. Freeman was established as Chairman, and Percy Alden as Secretary. In addition to the furnaces, the company managed land owned by the Cornwall and Mt. Hope Railroad and the Cornwall Railroad, as well as the Cornwall Furnace lands. After the dissolution of R. W. Coleman Heirs, the sisters, Anne, Margaret, and Sarah, put the old Cornwall furnace permanently out of blast on February 11, 1883 (numerous sources, in print and online, falsely attribute the shutdown of the Cornwall Iron Furnace to Robert H. Coleman). They also conveyed the deeds for Bird Coleman Furnaces and Donaghmore Furnace to the Cornwall Iron Company. Provisions were included for partners wishing to pull out of the company. If any partner wished to sell their shares, they had to first be made available to the other members for 30 days. Two managers would constitute a quorum. The managers were William Freeman, Edward Freeman, and Percy Alden. At the very first meeting of the Cornwall Iron Company, William Freeman and Percy Alden attended and brought forward a motion to insure the company's boilers and locomotives, discussed the Ore Roasters at Bird Coleman Furnaces, and the erection of a house for the Manager of Bird Coleman.

Chapter 11. Competition

In the 1880s, the Colebrook Furnaces, the Cornwall Iron Company, and the North Lebanon Furnaces competed with each other. Some steel companies, such as Pennsylvania Steel, purchased iron from all three, as well as ore from the Ore Banks. The three entities were very aware of the status of each other's furnaces and often made decisions on their production based on their knowledge of what the others' furnaces were producing and whether they were in blast or out. The Colebrook Furnaces were owned by Robert H. Coleman, The Cornwall Iron Company by Anne Alden, Margaret Freeman, and Sarah H. Coleman (except for the three shares owned by William C. Freeman, Edward C. Freeman, and Percy Alden), and the North Lebanon Furnaces by George Dawson Coleman's widow, Debbie Coleman.

The owners of the three companies still had to work together through the Cornwall Ore Bank and other occasional activities. The Cornwall and Lebanon area was well known in the iron industry and attracted the attention of outside groups.There were engineers and other professionals who travelled to the ore banks just to see and, in some cases, study the mines, but the mines attracted sight-seers as well. The rapid technological advances were big news in the country. One observation, perhaps a bit over the top, reported, "The entire 'Cornwall Estate', its mountains of valuable ore, its immense iron-producing manufactories, its magnificent farms, improved livestock, and herds of the purest blood, are unequal in the universe, and are far more worthy of a visit than famed Niagara or Mammoth Cave".

The Eastern Pig Iron Association included a visit to the area as part of their annual meeting in 1884. The association members left

Philadelphia on Wednesday, June 18, at 9:50 am, arriving in Lebanon at 12:35 pm. They visited the Colebrook Furnaces and then rode to the Ore Banks on the Cornwall and Lebanon, having lunch on the train. They then proceeded to Steelton to view that borough's massive steel plant. In 1890, the Iron and Steel Institute of England and the Society of German Metallurgists and Civil Mining and Mechanical Engineers visited Lebanon, arriving in twenty-three Pullman cars. A local committee, which included Horace Brock, Robert H. Coleman, William C. Freeman, P. L. Weimer, and John Binkenbine, was organized to host the visitors. In addition to the North Lebanon furnaces, the Colebrook furnace, the Cornwall Ore Banks, and other furnaces in the area, the group also visited the Weimer Machine Works.

In 1887, the Harrisburg Telegraph reprinted an article that first appeared in the Philadelphia Press. The article provides a brief history of the Ore Bank and iron works in the Lebanon and Cornwall area.

> ...which covers over 22,000 acres ... and which contains, as its heart, at once the cause of its existence and the source of its life, the most remarkable deposit of iron ore in the United States. The Cornwall ore bed has been called the most remarkable in the country, but the adjective is too vague for exact use. Certainly, the deposit is a wonder, and the direct effects of its existence upon human life in this region are phenomenal. In the kind of ore, the size of its bed and quality, the deposit is unique in Pennsylvania. To say that at Cornwall there are three great hills of ore, one 312 feet high above the water level: another 98, and another 78; that a drill has been sunk into the ore for 300 feet below water level without reaching the bottom of the deposit; that the bed has been mined since 1740, and that

7,000,000 tons have been dug from its sides, equivalent to 3,500,000 tons of pig iron to state such tremendous facts and figures may be impressive enough. But such cold statistics, while they appeal to the imagination, fail utterly to convey any adequate idea of the astonishing spectacle presented by this triple mountain of iron. Nor can any description suffice. It is a wonder which must be seen to be realized, and repeated visits could never accustom the beholder to the phenomenon.

The article attempted to calculate the value of ore mines and the iron works. Using an estimate of 500 tons of iron produced per week, the yearly production of iron was figured at 286,000 tons. Since Cornwall iron was selling between $15 a ton and $19 a ton, the article used an average selling price per ton of $17, arriving at annual sales of $4,862,000. The cost of production estimated by an "expert" was determined to be $10 per ton, leaving a profit of $7 a ton, for a yearly profit of over $2,000,000, spread out between all the different family operations.

As early as 1882, the Colebrook furnaces began using one-third of coke in their fuel mixture. Charles B. Forney, who took over as manager of the furnaces in 1888 (his father, also Charles B. Forney, had overseen the construction of the furnaces and served as the first manager), had performed experiments and discovered that a fuel mixture of 7/8 coke and 1/8 bituminous coal worked best. Eventually, all the furnaces in Lebanon and Cornwall added their own coke ovens. The coke was derived from specific types of bituminous coal, which was heated in ovens generally about 13 feet by 8 feet.

Using well-roasted ore and Whitwell stoves to heat the air, the furnaces were producing a very high yield of iron, but early on, the No. 1 furnace did poorly. No. 2 worked "splendidly," according to Abraham Hess, formerly a clerk for R. W. Heirs at Cornwall and now working at the Colebrook Furnaces. He reported that at the start of April 1883, they did 1,098 tons the week before, against expectations upwards of 1,020 to 1,050 tons per week. He projected, "At present I do not think it safe to estimate the cost of making iron less than $15 per ton. In regard to iron for Bethlehem on your individual account, if we do not make more 1 & 2 than we have been doing we will not have it to spare". Robert H. Coleman rebuilt the Cornwall Anthracite furnaces with the No. 2 furnace at 80 feet by 14 feet (furnace measurements indicated the height of the furnace by the diameter). By the late 1880s, he had a combined five furnaces between the Colebrook and Cornwall furnaces.

Colebrook sold iron to steel producers such as Lackawanna Iron and Steel and Pennsylvania Steel. In 1884, they agreed to sell 5,000 tons of No. 1, 2, and 3 Colebrook pig iron at the rate of 150 to 200 tons per week. Robert H. Coleman used his own railroad to deliver iron to Pennsylvania Steel. Luther Bent wrote to Coleman in 1885, "It is also understood that if we screen the iron, we will give the preference to Colebrook Valley and Cornwall and Lebanon Railroad of all freight coming from your furnace and ore from the Cornwall mines during same period". During much of the 1880s, the furnaces generally operated smoothly but began to show wear by the end of the decade. One of the furnaces went out of blast in 1888, while the other was running poorly. By 1889, though, both furnaces were again running smoothly. Unfortunately, on November 16, 1889, there was a tragic accident at Colebrook. The Daily News printed a horribly graphic account,

Enoch Eisenhower, Harvey Bohr, Henry Ferteg, Wm. Snyder, Ben Neville, E. Isaac Siegrist, Harvey Beck, John Bohr and many others were employed on the night turn. Suddenly, and with a tremendous report, the pavement on which the men stood arose, and instantly a flood of red-hot iron bulged up as if from the bowels of the earth and completely deluged the unfortunate men, almost instantly incinerating them before they had time to move five paces. Their destruction was complete and awful. Instantly the interior of the furnace was ablaze and the victims were lost to view in the sea of molten metal, and veiled by clouds of steam and smoke. In a few hours the place was flooded, and the contact of water with red-hot slag caused a number of violent explosions, but the remains of the men were not blown to pieces, because they were deeply embedded in the molten iron. Eisenhower and Beck leaped for their lives, but they fell back. Eisenhower waded out of the molten iron, but he inhaled the fumes and perished after being taken home. William Snyder's body was first found. He was on his hands and knees, hardly a semblance of a human being. Siegrist and Ferteg were clasped in each other's arms and buried in the hot slag. They were burned to a black crisp. They lay as in a bed of red-hot coals. Harvey Beck was found lying on his face deeply embedded in the molten iron. A local paper says Coroner Ristenbatt and a jury took testimony all day. Witnesses swore that the furnace was one of the best and the accident was unavoidable, and that a break of that kind was likely to happen any time. Millionaire Robert H. Coleman, who owns the furnace, pasted the following notice: 'We will care for the widows and children of the seven men who were killed, as they died while at work in our service, and we will look after their families as long as it may be necessary to do so'.

Coleman made a point to acknowledge his workers. Upon completion of Colebrook Furnace No. 2, he hosted a dinner for 300 guests, most of whom were workers from the furnace. He proposed the first toast to the "stalwarts," the 110 laborers who worked 10 hours per day to complete the construction. The dinner was reported in the local news with the title, "Capital and Labor Celebrating Together". He gave an annual banquet at his Music Hall in Cornwall to his 40 or more managers and clerks. There was music from the grand organ and "fine vocalism added much to the pleasure of the occasion". In 1886 there was a performance of a piece which Coleman himself wrote. He also hosted all his employees, over 500, around the holidays for a Christmas party, giving turkeys, gifts to children and cash payments. He added a large bath house over the Quittapahilla Creek for the employees and in 1888 laid the cornerstone for Trinity Chapel, built across from the furnaces. The chapel opened for services on May 27, 1888.

Robert H. Coleman remarried in 1884 to Edith Elliot Johnstone. Born in Beaufort, Georgia, her family was connected to the same intimate network as the Habersham family. In fact, Sue Ellen Coleman was distantly related to Edith's mother, Mary Barnwell Elliot Johnstone, the second wife of Alexander Johnstone. Alexander owned and operated rice plantations in the Georgetown, South Carolina region, but the impact of the Civil War reduced the family's income. While inspecting his summer home, Beaumont, in Flat Rock, South Carolina, in 1864, Alexander surprised three Confederate deserters who were camped out in the home and was brutally murdered. Mary Johnstone had no choice but to abandon the properties. She moved to Baltimore in 1868 with her three youngest daughters, Fanny, Emma, and Edith, and found a position at Edgeworth School for Girls, where she worked for another twelve years until her daughters graduated. Edith was only six years old when her father died. When she graduated Edgeworth, Mary went to live with her daughter, Emma, with whom she remained until Mary died in 1909.

Sue Ellen Coleman sent her daughter, Anne, to Edgeworth as well, and Edith and Anne developed a close bond that would last throughout their lives. Edith would spend long periods living as part of Sue Ellen's household, spending time with the family in Cornwall and New York at Sue Ellen's townhouse at 340 Madison Avenue. Edith even had her own room. When Edith graduated, she served as a social secretary for Sue Ellen.

Having grown up together, Robert H. Coleman and Edith Johnstone built upon their childhood bond following Lillie's death. They were married on October 1, 1884, in Grace Protestant Episcopal Church, Baltimore, by Rev. Chandler Hare, rector of St. Luke's Church, Lebanon. The couple moved into the family home in Cornwall, and not long afterward, Robert engaged Hewitt and Hewitt, architects from Philadelphia, to design a new home adjacent to the existing "Cottage". Hewitt and Hewitt also designed the main terminal and the Cornwall station for the Cornwall and Lebanon Railroad.

While the furnaces in Lebanon and Cornwall sold pig iron to steel companies using Cornwall ore, the Cornwall Ore Bank also sold ore to outside entities. In 1885, an agreement was written between the Cornwall Ore Bank and Pennsylvania Steel for five years, 8,000 tons of "Run of Mine" ore per month at 13% of the price of No. 1 iron on which proprietary price rates were based. Orders filled to the Scranton Steel Company for 1885 were averaging between 4,000 and 6,000 tons per month at $26.50, yielding a price above $100,000 per month. Horace Brock commented on the sale to Pennsylvania Steel, "I am in favor of making the sale provided it does not interfere with the supply to proprietors and that it is understood the price shall be made monthly". There were concerns that Robert H. Coleman was negotiating with Pennsylvania Steel before gaining approval from other Ore Bank members. William Freeman's opinion on the sale of large quantities of ore being sold was deeply reflective, "I have been obliged from time to time for a considerable period to consider what is the true interest of the owner of the ore banks with reference to the distribution of their ore and I have never been able to reach any other conclusion than that if the furnaces which have been erected in the immediate neighborhood of the Ore Banks belonged to entire strangers, it would be the true advantage of the owners of the ore to confine their sales to them as long as their consumption amounts to this very considerable number of tons those furnaces now require ... I believe the true policy of the owners of the ore is to maintain a reasonable demand for it at a good price, rather than to throw it indiscriminately upon the market ... If, therefore, I represented only owners of the Ore Banks, I would feel obliged to oppose the proposition you mention". The ore at this point was testing with a lower percent of iron content, however a portion of the ore was still testing at above fifty percent.

The Ore Banks continued to produce a dividend for the shareholders. As an example, Anne Roger's share for December 1885 was $9,390.03, for February 1886 $11,164.03, March $11,390.55, and April $12,165.14. The dividends for the remainder of the year paid between $7,000 and $8,000, with the exception of July, which paid over $8,000, and December, slightly less than $7,000. (During the year, she also received a 1/8 share in the sale of the Castle Finn property, receiving $1,125.20, and received an interest payment of $1,000 on March 29, 1884, on a note from her brother, who had provided a loan of $40,000 at 5% for 6 months.) By 1892, and for much of the early 1890s, ore realized lower prices.

J. Taylor Boyd published a monthly report to the Ore Bank Board. He covered production numbers, alerted the board to issues, and made suggestions for improvements. For example, in one report in 1888, it was noted that a bed was apportioned at Good Samaritan for $300 a year in case of accidents requiring hospitalization. The same report stated, "Owing to the amount of repair work which is required in keeping our power drills in order and consider it would be a matter of economy for your company to have a small machine shop …". He would also make recommendations for other issues, including the need for housing and research.

The Ore Bank Company took good care of Boyd. His 1866 salary was $2,000. In 1872, the company increased his salary to $2,500 per year, and over the next two decades, continued to increase his annual wage. His housing was provided for, and by 1884, a separate multiple-story stone residence with a large front porch was built for Boyd and his family just south of the office, replacing a previous wood frame home. In 1868, the company built a workshop costing $1,050, and through the years continued adding testing and laboratory facilities to enhance the evaluation of the ore quality. Boyd kept watch on the activities and needs of the mining operations and advised the Ore Banks board of future concerns, as well as reported on current conditions.

The company never had enough housing for the miners. In 1866, Boyd reported to the board regarding tenement homes, "I would suggest brick houses, which I think can be built for 2/3 of the cost of sandstone; our want of tenement houses for our workmen is a great drawback, for, had we houses we get a much better class of men, and control them better, should labor be in demand elsewhere".

A year later, the company had 13 worker homes, including the four double dwelling tenant homes constructed in the past year at a cost of $2,360 for each double house. Boyd commented on the inadequate housing capacity, "taken into consideration the number of men employed, is a very small number". By 1874, there were 21 tenant houses to support an average work force of 80 to 90 men. Boyd estimated they needed at least thirty houses "for the accommodation of our better class of workers" and further recommended, "We think it would be good policy to continue building one block per year until we get to 30 houses". Boyd believed they lost good workers as a result of an inadequate amount of housing. The size of the workforce at the mines grew slowly through the last decades of the 19th century and by 1890 stood at about 300 workers receiving an average daily wage of $1.65, according to the Philadelphia Inquirer on July 7th.

Also, in 1866, Boyd brought to the board's attention the "necessity of having a bell placed on this office to regulate the working of the men. We are now controlled by the bell at the Anthracite Furnaces, which does not suit the hours we work". In 1867, a new bell was placed in the circular tower, which anchored the north-west corner of the office. The office overlooked the mines on the eastern edge of the middle hill and originally contained living quarters for the Superintendent, before separate quarters were established for the Superintendent. Steps were installed that descended from the office to the base of the middle hill.

It was important to the company to retain quality workers, which resulted in the company needing to carry the workers during lean times when ore was in less demand. In 1872, Boyd reported, "Labor is now scarce, and will be after the 1st of April, very much so. It has become a serious question whether we can hold on to our present system, or whether it would not be policy to reduce the hours worked during the summer, to say 11 hours ... the men do not seem to appreciate that we have been paying full wages during the winter while they only worked about 7 or 8 hours per day". The company also did their best to address employee safety and take care of workers who were injured. In his monthly report Boyd addressed one case, "Daniel Wise, who was blown up last Winter by the premature explosion of a blast was badly hurt; the doctors say one eye is destroyed, and there is little hope of him being able to see sufficient with the other to do any kind of work; he has a helpless family of eight children, one being an idiot ... Resolved, that Daniel Wise be allowed half the usual wages till the next meeting of the Board, in consideration of his injuries in the service of the company ... and that his physicians will be paid". There were also cases of the board's financial support of workers' families when workers suffered a fatality.

The Cornwall Iron Company improved its furnaces in the 1880s. By 1890, between Bird Coleman and North Cornwall, they had three stacks in operation. The Bird Coleman Furnaces were rebuilt in 1885 to 75 feet by 18 feet furnaces. North Cornwall operated a single 80 feet by 18 feet furnace. They used Whitwell stoves and Cornwall ore exclusively. They also switched over to coke for a fuel source. Donaghmore steadily declined in performance and was permanently put out of blast and abandoned in 1891. In 1887, total production for three months at Bird Coleman was 14,445 tons, and at Donaghmore only 2,666. The company earned $343,825.26 with operating expenses of $236,597.52 and improvements of $19,610.04. The Receipts Over Expenses were $96,917.70. Receipts over Expenses fell to $38,386.12 in 1888, primarily due to improvements, but were back up to over $90,000 the following year.

Production increased dramatically in 1890 with Receipts Over Expense above $100,000 and Dividends Paid over $90,000.

Andrew Brady, the Manager of Bird Coleman Furnaces, noted that Furnace No. 1 was taken out of blast in 1888 due to "... dull times", but in December, it was put back in blast using coke. There seemed to be some concern over the iron provided to Pennsylvania Steel. He wrote to the brokers, Messrs. J. J. Lea and Company, "if we are to grade iron according to sales fixed by Major Bent and yourself [of Pennsylvania Steel] we should know exactly what your idea of grade is ... we have only 37 tons of white iron on hand ... I have gone over Pennsylvania Steel Company's statements of grading very carefully and must say if this is a sample of a 'liberal spirit' ... they cannot have any more iron after expiration of existing contracts ... I have seen a great deal of the iron made at Bird Coleman both in November and December and am positive grading is better than it has been for a year past ... I think your Mr. Ellis Lea has been misled by comparison (?) in Cornwall Iron ... if he would like to spend a day at Cornwall perhaps we can teach him something about grading iron". Ore was graded according to its composition. No. 1 contained 5.267% Silicon and .034% Sulphur, No. 2 with 5.013% Silicon and .053% Sulphur, and No. 3 4.308% Silicon and .081% Sulphur. Some of the steel companies were pulling out of contracts. Brady reported, "If Bethlehem Iron Company will not let us resume shipments ... keep Bird Coleman No 2 out of blast until Major Bent comes to his senses. Any No 2 we may have can be sent back". Brady was very clear where he stood, "I am positive iron was correctly graded, and no amount of talking or persuasion can make me (?) we have been fairly dealt with. Pennsylvania Steel Company had better pay their bills promptly before taking such high moral ground".

1889 was a busy year for the Mt. Lebanon Coleman and Brock families. At 1:00 pm on the 22nd of May 1889 Harriet Dawson Coleman, daughter of George Dawson and Debbie Coleman, married Harry Sheaf Glover at Christ Church, Lebanon, Pennsylvania with the Rev. S. A. Martin presiding. It was reported as, "one of the most brilliant weddings ... everything that wealth could command being made tributary to the royal entertainment". Six parlor cars brought guests from New York. Harriet's dress of cream-colored satin was made by Worth of Paris. A reception was held at the Homestead from 2:00 to 4:00, and employees were invited to the house, each receiving a box filled with wedding cake as "they marched in regular file [to] the office". The new couple departed on a special car, the "Ariel", at 8:00 pm.

One month later, in June, Bertram Dawson married Anne Churchill Mason at St. Paul's Episcopal Church, Sing Sing, New York. The wedding party of the bride included Annie and Fanny Coleman. Groomsmen were Edward R. Coleman, best man, William Heyward Drayton, and Horace Brock. In attendance were Mr. and Mrs. Percy Alden of New York, Mr. and Mrs. Alexander Biddle, Mr. and Mrs. Isaac Norris, Mr. Henry Rawle, Mr. and Mrs. Coleman Drayton.

In January 1889, an agreement had been reached for five years between Bertram Dawson, his brother Edward, and Arthur and Horace Brock to form Coleman and Brock, an equal partnership established for the business of buying and selling iron. The company would continue along the same lines as the partnership Arthur and Horace had with Debbie Coleman, the actual owner of the Lebanon Furnaces. Coleman and Brock would continue to buy "Cornwall Ore" and would pay Debbie Coleman on the 15th of each month for the previous month.

Later that year, in September, Coleman and Brock purchased three-quarters of The Pennsylvania Bolt and Nut Company. It was founded in 1882 by James Lord and brothers Henry S. and George B. Eckert of Reading, Pennsylvania, who ran the Henry Clay furnace in Reading, which had been started by their father, Isaac, and their uncle, Dr. George N. Eckert. Lord had been Chief Clerk at J. H. Sternbergh's Bolt and Nut works in Reading since 1871, when he left to start the new company. The plant was constructed at the east end of Lebanon along the railroad tracks. Also involved with the business were Aaron Wilhelm[1] and Herman Meigis, Henry S. Eckert's son-in-law.

The Eckerts sold part of their interest to Wilhelm in 1888, and when Wilhelm died in May 1889, his son, Charles, assumed the presidency, and the deceased's brother-in-law, Walter S. Davis, became Vice-President. In September, all shares, except the one-fourth held by Lord, were purchased by Coleman and Brock. Charles Wilhelm, along with his uncle, turned around and formed the National Bolt, Nut and Rivet Works in Riverside, North Reading.

Arthur Brock assumed the office of President with Lord serving as General Manager, Secretary and Treasurer. Other directors were Horace Brock, Bertram Dawson Coleman, Edward Coleman, and John H. Hoffer[2]. A supply of pig iron was provided to the bolt and nut works from the Lebanon Furnaces. The furnaces and the bolt and nut works were run in harmony with each other under the management of Coleman and Brock. They treated their employees as one, as evidenced by the distribution of 1,100 turkeys on Christmas Eve Day 1890 to the combined workforce of the furnaces and the Pennsylvania Bolt and Nut Works.

Chapter 12. Collapse

In a little over a decade, Robert H. Coleman brought into blast two furnaces at Colebrook, built a railroad network which spanned from Lebanon to Elizabethtown, opened the Mount Gretna Park as one of the stops on his railroad, and invested in Florida transportation, especially the Jacksonville, Tampa and Key West Railroad. His mother and other family members had spent time around St. Augustine for years, and Robert was drawn to both the climate and opportunity. In 1883 he invested $365,000 in the Florida Construction Company, manufacturers of railroad supplies. He also purchased shares in the Jacksonville, Tampa and Key West Railway. Closer to home, he built short spur lines off the Cornwall and Lebanon to extend access to his railroad for other businesses. Never realized, he began plans to extend the Cornwall and Lebanon to New Holland and to Lancaster. All of this required, and would require, an enormous amount of money.

As early as 1882, Robert began aggressively borrowing money to fund his many projects. He took out an $82,000 mortgage on his furnaces as well as a loan against the Colebrook Valley Railroad for $150,000. Artemus Wilhelm stated there was, "evidence that Robert is short of cash ... and this is one of the causes of outrage being committed on the minority stock holders of Cornwall and Lebanon Railroad by delaying the construction of their road". In 1885, he was denied a loan from Drexel and Company for his Florida railroad projects. He ended up taking a loan for $100,000 through the Farmers and Mechanics National Bank and an additional $100,000 with the Pennsylvania Company for Insurance on Lives and Granting Annuities. He took on loans from family as well, including a $50,000 loan from his sister and five loans at different times totaling over $200,000 from his brother-in-law, Archibald

Rogers. Kendall Brothers, a civil engineering firm in Reading, negotiated a loan for $100,000 with the Continental National Bank of Boston, offering railroad bonds as collateral. Kendall Brothers pointed out that Coleman received an annual income of $120,000 to $130,000 from the Ore Banks alone. At that time, Coleman had three furnaces, which he built for a combined cost of around $600,000, and he was looking to add a fourth. The bank expressed concerns that "half the furnaces are out of blast … the iron interest is so depressed", but Kendall countered that the "Coleman's [Robert's furnaces] are making money now, when others must stop, and that Mr. Coleman is worth 'several millions'".

On top of all of Robert's activities, he invested in rice fields with his relatives in Georgia. In 1885, Coleman placed Hugh Maxwell, who at that time was managing the Colebrook furnaces, in charge of his interests in Georgia. Coleman's uncle, R. B. Habersham, anxious on a debt he had taken on Robert's behalf, wrote to Maxwell in 1888 from the Upper Rice Mill Company in Savanah. "Advise Mr. Coleman that it is all important that I should know whether he will this year continue the payments of my interest. Otherwise I will be compelled on December 1 to write Mr. Blake of my inability to pay and take steps to sell my share". Robert also sought investors to bring in cash to the operations. One broker wrote, "Since my interview with you I have succeeded in interesting some Philadelphia capitalists in our rice enterprise … it would be advised to have your Mr. Maxwell of Savannah, meet us at New Orleans". Robert's financial maneuverings strained his relationships with family. When Robert sold a property, he questioned his Uncle William Neyle Habersham's request for a portion of the proceeds "I never knew that you had one-dollar interest in the $37,000 which was handed to me for investment".

His investments in Florida, though, were his riskiest. He formed partnerships in Florida with Henry Flagler and others. Flagler, John D. Rockefeller's longtime partner, was drawn to the vastness of the Florida east coast south of St. Augustine. At the time Robert became involved, Flagler was in the process of divesting himself from his railroad partners, thus gaining sole control of his development of the Florida East Coast. Coleman assumed the costs associated with buying shares to facilitate Flagler's exit from the partnership. The financial stress and demands for railroad development were deep and constant. While the Florida railroad did show profits, they were not consistent, and Robert never broke even on his investment. The Indian River Steamboat Company was unprofitable when he bought it and never realized a profit.

The cracks in Coleman's business affairs started to widen in the early 1890s. Certain world events beginning in 1890 resulted in the Great Depression of 1893. In the United States, investors began withdrawing from the gold supply, dropping the reserves below a danger level. Railroads were over-extended. The Philadelphia and Reading was among the first to be put into receivership. The avalanche flowed into lesser roads, of which the Jacksonville, Tampa, and Key West was one impacted. Loans were called in, and bankruptcies emerged. Coleman for years, had borrowed money just to pay the interest due on loans or re-negotiated the loans. In January 1891, he borrowed $500,000 from the Pennsylvania Trust Company to pay interest due on loans, and in February had to take a forced loan of $1,500,000 with the Pennsylvania Company for Insurance on Lives and Granting Annuities. Then in June, he took out a mortgage of $62,500 to pay further interest due on loans. By August 1893 as loans were called in and credit dried up, Coleman had run out of options and went into receivership, requesting his brother-in-law, Archibald Rogers, and Henry T. Kendall, Vice-President for the Pennsylvania Trust Company, be assigned as the Receivers. Rogers declined, but Kendall accepted. In place of Rogers, the Pennsylvania Company for Insurance on Lives and Granting Annuities was appointed as assignee. The Florida railroads were shut down, and in September, the last of his furnaces were blown out. There were general problems with Coleman's debt level and financial behavior, but public consensus blamed the downfall on the Florida investments. The News Journal of Lancaster, Pennsylvania, declared it was "an evil day he invested in Florida lands".

His mother, Sue Ellen Coleman, had died in 1892 and did not have to watch the painful fall of her son. He moved into the Cornwall Anthracite Manager's home while he prepared to depart Cornwall. In December, Robert, Edith, and their five young children left for a Christmas holiday with his sister in Hyde Park, New York. The family would then move to Saranac Lake. Both Robert and Edith suffered from tuberculosis, and Saranac was a leading healing center. Plans were drawn up in 1896 for a home. The site for the home, which was put in Edith's name, was on a ridge overlooking Saranac Lake. After settling the bulk of his affairs, Coleman had about a quarter of a million dollars. His empire evaporated, but he still retained enough to live comfortably.

The iron interests and properties in Cornwall and Lebanon were his greatest assets. The value of Coleman's estate was estimated at $4,441,126.92. $3,439,948.68 was in real estate and $712,177.92 in personal property in Georgia and Florida. A judgment in favor of Archibald Rogers was settled quickly, but there were numerous pending suits brought against Coleman. His Assignees published their assessments by late 1894. They valued the Lebanon bank building at $65,000, the Colebrook Furnaces at $600,000, the Cornwall Anthracite at $149,700, the Cornwall Ore Bank shares at over $2,000,000 based on a single share's value at $135,000, and the Cornwall and Lebanon shares at $338,500. Many of Coleman's non-industrial assets, such as farms, were not liquidated. These assets also included the old Colebrook properties and investment holdings, including 60 shares of Pennsylvania Steel. Arriving at sound valuations was complicated by the fact that some of the properties had liens against them.

Fortunately, Lackawanna Iron and Steel was interested in the iron properties. Joseph Scranton was the primary driving force in the Lackawanna Iron and Coal Company and became very wealthy, but his control of the company became diluted through years of taking on new investors. When he died in 1872, his son, William Walker, became General Manager. William had aggressive plans for expansion and improvement, but the Board of Directors for the company declined to entertain the proposals. He resigned and, with his brother, Walter, formed the Scranton Steel Company in 1881, directly competing with the Lackawanna Iron and Coal Company. The Colebrook furnaces were regular suppliers for Scranton Steel. Colebrook was shipping between 3,000 and 5,000 tons of iron to Scranton throughout the mid-1880s. In only a decade, Scranton became so successful that it merged with their old company, taking the lead in the newly formed Lackawanna Iron and Steel. William was President, and Walter was Vice-President. When Robert H. Coleman went into receivership, it made sense to step in and purchase the Coleman properties. They were familiar with the quality of iron and were regular customers. They purchased the Colebrook Furnaces for $300,000, half the estimated value, and the Cornwall Anthracite Furnaces for $100,000, two-thirds the estimated value.

Walter Scranton visited Lebanon multiple times to inspect the properties and finalize the purchase, after which he represented Lackawanna on the Ore Banks board. Lackawanna Iron and Steel agreed to pay $2,729,640.50 for Coleman's furnaces, shares in the Ore Bank, and the Cornwall and Lebanon Railroad. The fifteen and 5/8 shares of the Ore Banks were valued at $2,109,375. Lackawanna received 6,906 shares of capital stock in the Cornwall and Lebanon valued at $219,265.50.

By December 1894, the assignees had realized $3,181,586.45 to settle claims of $3,029,276.04. There remained unsold real estate in Florida, Savannah, and Pennsylvania valued at $345,498.68. The Pennsylvania properties included Cornwall Hall, valued at $75,000, a one-half interest in Colebrook Farms, which had been in the family for over one-hundred years, and the Conowango Mine. In addition to the properties, there was money due Coleman totaling almost $1,500,000 (mostly from his own companies). He also owned a fair amount of stock certificates.

Eventually, the claims against Coleman were settled. The Dime Bank depositors were paid 70 cents on the dollar, but as late as March 1896, McClure Coke Company of Pittsburgh was still trying to collect $150,000 for coke delivered before Coleman's failure. Much of Coleman's personal property was sold or auctioned off. The University of Pennsylvania acquired at auction in February 1897, Etruscan pottery, bronzes, and a cinerary urn from his collection. The unfinished mansion needed to be kept in good condition while final disposition wound its way through the courts. There was even a night guard stationed at the mansion. In 1901, William C. Freeman bought the mansion, the stables[1] and additional lands from Henry T. Kendall and the Pennsylvania Company for Insurance and Granting Annuities, assignees for the estate of Robert H. Coleman, for $30,000 (Freeman had previously purchased other property which had belonged to his cousin). Freeman finished the slate roof and other minor improvements; however, he never lived there, remaining at his home in North Cornwall. As late as 1917, the Assignees auctioned Coleman's old Colebrook properties.

Robert H. Coleman was only forty when he and Edith moved from Cornwall. After struggling for many years, Edith died in 1903 while at a health resort in New Jersey. Anne Rogers helped send the children to a private boarding school. Further tragedy struck when his son, Ralph Elliot, died from a self-inflicted gunshot in a park in Buffalo, New York, reportedly over a failed love interest. Robert had to identify the body.

Robert did find some pleasure in his later life. He had a tennis court built, and family, relatives, and neighbors enjoyed regular, friendly tournaments. He resurrected his hobby of "bird watching", which he had been interested in as a young man, and published a "List of Adirondack Birds" in 1921. His sons all gravitated toward engineering careers. When World War I broke out, his three surviving sons joined the fight. Coleman kept a large flag flying in his yard during the war.

Robert would spend long visits at his sister's home. There is an intimate photo from 1917 of Archibald Rogers and Robert, along with Archie's son Edmund, son-in-law John Griswold Webb, and grandson John Griswold Webb, Jr., sitting on the back porch at the Rogers' home in Hyde Park, smiling and enjoying themselves. After feeling ill for months, he made his last visit to Anne's home, where he died on March 15, 1930. He was the only Coleman to ever lose their fortune. He was buried at the family plot in Laurel Hill Cemetery overlooking the Schuylkill River in Philadelphia, resting between the graves of Lillie and Edith.

Archibald and Anne Rogers built Crumwold Hall on a high bluff overlooking the Hudson River at a turn called Crum's Elbow. They married in 1880, and in 1883, "Archie" started buying land for the estate. Richard Morris Hunt designed the home in a style similar to another of Hunt's designs, Grey Towers in Milford, Pennsylvania, for the Pinchot family. Construction began in 1886, and by 1889, the family moved into their home. Hunt anchored the home with a large turret on the south-east corner, echoing with smaller turrets at other points. The land purchases were over $120,000, and the construction cost $400,000. Their neighbors to the south were the James Roosevelts, parents of Franklin Delano Roosevelt, and their neighbors to the north were the Frederick K. Vanderbilt family.[2]

Primarily, it was Anne's wealth that provided the funds for the estate. Archie watched over the portfolio and planned and managed the vast estate, including establishing a reforestation program on the property. He was instrumental in having the trusteeship which Anne had given to Robert voided, in addition to overseeing the payment due to Anne from the sale of her shares in the Cornwall Ore Banks.

Archibald Rogers did not grow up wealthy. His boyhood home down the road from Crumwold was modest. He attended Yale and started his career as an engineer after graduating. Before Archie and Anne were married, he worked on the Delaware, Lackawanna and Western Tunnel and started work on the Milwaukee, Lake Shore and Western Railroad as Treasurer and General Manager. After they were married, they lived in Milwaukee until making the move to Hyde Park. Archie did serve the Jacksonville, Tampa and Key West Railroad as President, the Cornwall Lebanon Railroad as President, and formed Pancost and Rogers as sales agents of the Reading Iron Works and Cornwall Ore Banks.

Archie's love of nature led him to serve as a trustee and member of the Executive Committee for the American Museum of Natural History. He hunted, raced iceboats on the Hudson when it was frozen, and studied plants and animals his entire life. He was at Theodore Roosevelt's home in New York in December 1887 when the Boone and Crockett Club was first proposed. At that dinner were James Coleman Drayton, Elliot Roosevelt, George Bird Grinnell, and others. He was Secretary and Treasurer from 1888 to 1901 and Vice-President in 1903. He was a different breed than the young men Anne knew growing up, and he was not Sue Ellen Coleman's idea of a mate for Anne. There was a bit of discomfort in Sue Ellen's heart regarding Archie, which never disappeared. Anne wrote to Robert in 1888, "Archie is I fear 'a thorn in Mother's flesh' ... during Mother's last visit he was very disagreeable I think Mother rather worries to death everytime Archie has a club meeting or anything to take him out in the evening alone ... she doesn't understand him ... Archie has gone to Virginia and may go further south".

Anne and Archie's children were friends with Franklin Delano Roosevelt, and they were even homeschooled together at Crumwold. Franklin and the Rogers children, especially Archibald, Jr., and Edmund, were close friends along with the Derby children. Anne Rogers remained close with Sarah Derby, and the Derby family would often visit Hyde Park. Young Franklin was closest to Archibald, Jr., and Franklin was quite devastated when Archibald died at only nine years old. Eventually, the close bond shifted to Edmund. Franklin, the Rogers boys, and the Derby boys all attended Groton and remained close. Roger Alden Derby and Franklin remained close following Groton.

The Rogers were very sociable and involved in the community. Archibald served as a Vestryman for the Hyde Park Episcopal

Church. The Rogers ran a dairy farm and other operations on the property and employed many residents of the community. Every Christmas, Anne and Mrs. Frederick K. Vanderbilt organized events and charities for the town. Anne loved to entertain. Parties at Crumwold were large and festive events. As many as sixty people would sit down to dinner, requiring over twenty staff members to attend to the guests. She and Archie always threw an elaborate New Year's Eve party with plenty of dancing, and their fireworks displays on July 4th were greatly anticipated, ending with the American flag exploding in the sky.

Chapter 13. Allied Interests

When Lackawanna Iron and Steel purchased Robert H. Coleman's Lebanon and Cornwall holdings, the Lebanon Daily News commented, "Who would have thought years ago that the Coleman interests in the Cornwall Ore Hills and allied interests would fall into other hands". The Grubb descendants still held their 1/6 interest in the Ore Banks, and the Robesonia group held its rights to extract ore to support one furnace, but the remainder of the Ore Banks and the Cornwall and Lebanon furnaces had been owned and operated by Coleman descendants until Lackawanna purchased the interests of Robert H. Coleman in 1894. There were many more changes ahead.

The long-term impact of the 1893 depression was felt throughout the country, and it was no different in the Lebanon area. Iron workers found themselves out of work as all the furnaces in the area either cut back production or shut down. The Dime Bank was bankrupt, and many investors faced losing their entire deposits. The failure of the bank also affected the Ore Banks as was noted in their minutes, "Owing to the closing of the Bank at Lebanon in which the account of your 'mines' has been kept ... since August 5th using 1st National Bank of Lebanon ... the general prostration of all business the last two months and the going out of blast of the greater part of the furnaces to whom we have been shipping ore has very much reduced our output". Local prosperity was tied to the health of the iron business and both continued to struggle through the depression. In 1896, the minutes for the Ore Banks reported, "Since the depression in iron and the blowing out of several of the furnaces which we have been furnishing with ore, we have been cleaning up our workings ... put your 'mines' in good order". Despite the harsh conditions, the Ore Banks still realized a net gain of $231,859.61 for the first six months of 1896.

Financial conditions for the Ore Banks were made worse by the decreasing quality of the Cornwall iron ore. As the mining continued to go deeper underground, the percentage of iron in the ore continued to decline, slipping below 50% iron content. J. Taylor Boyd emphasized the situation to the Ore Bank board and summarized his thoughts at the March 21, 1894, meeting,

> Your committee took up the question of the concentration of the ore by electro-magnetic process and carefully examined ... a car load of the ore was sent to Dr. Thomas Edison at Orange, NJ, and many interesting experiments upon it were made by him in the presence of the members of your committee ... no inherent or physical reason why the Cornwall Ore could not successfully concentrated to at least 60% and that in this concertation or separation the sulphur pyrites ... are eliminated to probably a greater degree than is attained by the best practice now in use in roasting the Cornwall Ore ... sulphur and copper in such a form as to be valuable by-product ...Your committee asked Dr. Edison's assistance in devising some mechanical means for selecting the ore and after experimenting for some time he announced to the Chairman of your committee that he was prepared to guarantee the successful operation of an electrical magnetic separator of his invention to crush and separate 2,000 tons of Cornwall Ore in 10 hours ... raising the average grade of the ore considerable above 50% ... an analysis of the ore after the treatment by Edison showed metallic iron 50% and sulphur .75 of 1% ... On an output of 600,000 [?] tons per annuum ... have been

sending to their furnaces and in the last ten years paid to the Association or it more than $71,000,000 [?] ... Dr. Edison estimated the entire cost of selecting the ore by his machinery including his royalty at not over 17 cents per ton and the cost of his machinery put up and ready for use at $55,000 with a small addition ... Edison is operating a very large concentrating plant at Orange, NJ and is offering to sell and selling his concentrated ore at Reading ... at 6 cents a unit of metallic iron ... about 62% in richness in metallic iron and the ore from which it is obtained contains about 15% iron. Another most dangerous competition is the ore from the New Mesabi mines at Bessemer Ore of about 65% ... being sold at Cleveland today at $2.35 ... There are 52 patents for magnetic separating machines almost any of which is equally well accepted.

Sales were very far down, and furnaces were put out of blast. There was no movement to buy or build a concentrator despite the challenges facing the owners.

By late 1893, the Cornwall Iron Company felt the strain from the hard economic times. On top of this, on March 22nd Sarah H. Coleman died, and both Margaret Freeman and Ann Alden passed the following year. The ownership of the company was inherited by William, Edward, and Isabel Freeman, Margaret Buckingham, Percy Alden, and Sarah Derby. The active management of the company was conducted by William, Edward, and Percy. Of those three, William Freeman was the only one with a practical knowledge of the business. Even though in June 1895 the Bird Coleman Furnaces, idle for two years, were being readied to be put back in blast, the future market for iron was far from clear.

There were three notes due between late 1893 and the fall of 1894 for a total of $125,000. They were due $22,104 by Pennsylvania Steel. Wages were reduced effective November 1, 1893, and all single men had been discharged. Only married men living in the company houses were retained, and they were only working half-time. The company still managed to pay a dividend of $258,000 – salaries for the same period amounted to $54,773.34.

At a special meeting of the Cornwall Iron Company in August 1894, held at William C. Freeman's home, William, his brother Edward, and R. Percy Alden met to "reduce expenses to the lowest possible limit by dropping a number of names from the payroll and continuing the remainder on half time'. The minutes continued, "Chairman authorized to borrow $15,000 and repay himself $4,500 he advanced the company". In October, meeting again at William C. Freeman's home, the directors resolved to "retain 8 or 9 men out of 57 now on payroll". The previous authorization to hire an Associate was revoked. A further resolution, proposed by Alden and seconded by Edward Freeman, authorized the Chairman, William, to ask for the resignation of Andrew Brady[1], who had been with the family for 17 years and was the current manager of Bird Coleman, effective on the last day of the year.

On December 28, 1896, a meeting was held at the company's office, in the old Paymaster's office across from the Charcoal Furnace, at 11:00 am. Edward Freeman entered into the minutes, "I, Edward C Freeman, a manager of the Cornwall Iron Company Ltd., wish to bring formally to the attention of the Board of Managers the fact that at the last meeting of the said board, October 6, 1896, a resolution was passed directing the Chairman to request the resignation of Mr. A. Brady ... the Chairman has failed to carry out the instructions of the Board and request that this my protest be entered". Then, on December 28 the following from William

Freeman was read, "To The Board of Managers, Cornwall Iron Company, Ltd., Dear Sirs: Wishing to relieve my associates in the enlargement of the Directory and new policy they propose to inaugurate I will not attend meetings of the Cornwall Iron Company, Ltd. held this day. At the same time, I desire to give notice, that I will neither approve of or consent to any change in the Articles of Association of the Cornwall Iron Company, Ltd. So much criticism has been manifested and shown by my associates towards me; that I desire to relieve myself from any further wrong and annoyance on that score, and hereby declare to serve any longer as Chairman or manager of the Company. Any policy wrong in principle never becomes right in practice and it must be obvious to all that if the Chairman is to manage and direct the affairs of the company he must have the appointment and control of his subordinates free from the interference of any Board of Managers. Yours Truly, William C Freeman".

At this time, the shares in the Cornwall Iron Company were held by William and Edward Freeman, R. Percy Alden, and Alden's sister Sarah Derby, Margaret Freeman Buckingham, and her husband Benjamin H. Buckingham[1] to whom Margaret had transferred 5 shares. Margaret Coleman Freeman and Benjamin Horr Buckingham were married on December 6, 1894. The Times of Philadelphia reported the ceremony was "simple and private" as the family was in mourning. Buckingham, born and raised in Virginia, was a Lt. Commander in the U.S. Navy and a graduate of the U.S. Naval Academy. During his career, he served as a Naval Attaché in London, Paris, Berlin, and St. Petersburg. He also served as an assistant to Theodore Roosevelt when he was an Assistant to the U.S. Navy. Buckingham died in 1906.

Following the dispute over the firing of the Bird Coleman Manager, only Edward was present at a January 1897 meeting, forcing another meeting to be held on the 16th. At that meeting at R. Percy's Villa, the following letter from William was read into the minutes, "Dear Sirs: ... desire to place upon the minutes of the Cornwall Iron Company, Ltd. ... in reply to the protest of Edward Freeman ... feel constrained to accept the situation you have forced upon it [the company] ... and would be glad at any and all times to receive your advice". William had sent Edward the seal of the company, the checkbook, unpaid requisitions, and unsigned paychecks. William's resignation was accepted at that meeting. He also submitted reports he would normally present in person, showing a profit of $111,317.56, improvements of $18,456.16, Capital Stock of $600,000, an account with the 1st National Bank of Philadelphia of $85,000, and an account with Valley National Bank of Lebanon of $3,000. He further outlined a net loss for the Cornwall Iron Company, Ltd. of $33,483.84.

With William C. Freeman no longer active with the company, no other member had the expertise to oversee the iron operations. In December 1897, the company leased the Bird Coleman Furnaces to Lackawanna Iron and Steel for five years. The stock on hand was appraised and sold. The terms of the lease specified that Lackawanna would pay a $.60 per ton royalty on each ton of pig produced, not to exceed $50,000 per year and not less than $2,083.33 per month. They were obligated to use the Cornwall Railroad, "The party of the second part shall be entitled to what is known as 'Proprietor's Rights' for all ore taken from said ore banks and mine hills and ore at the furnaces ... herby leased". The royalty was later reduced to 50 cents.

Lackawanna put the North Cornwall Furnace into blast in February 1898. It was quite the affair as reported in the Lebanon Daily News, "Another Furnace Lighted Amid Blowing Whistles and Cheers of Bystanders. The North Cornwall Plant Idle for many years. At 11:00 put into blast amidst the blowing of whistles, waving of handkerchiefs and loud cheers from a large number of employees and spectators ... plant recently leased by the Lackawanna Steel and Iron Company of Scranton, General Superintendent F. L. Grammer ... 150 men will be affected ... Third furnace put in blast at Cornwall since January 1 ... Miss Julia Gilroy, the bright young daughter of Mr. H. E. Gilroy, 9th and Cumberland, stepped forward with a beautiful silver mounted cane to the lower end of which was attached a quantity of cotton waste saturated with oil and lighted ... among spectators Mr. & Mrs. Grittinger".

The lease with Lackawanna proved profitable. Lackawanna was prompt with its payments, and the company considered extending the lease. William Freeman, while not active, still held shares outright and as trustee for his mother's estate and was opposed to the lease extension. The rest of the family tried to force his signature through the courts. William Freeman held that a unanimous vote was necessary to allow Lackawanna to use ore from the banks and lease the furnaces. The company believed a majority was all that was necessary. In answer to the petition, William C. Freeman asserted he was the only one of the shareholders competent to manage the business or to oversee disposing of the property. The only solution he suggested was the employment of a manager to run the plant, or to sell the property at a public sale. The suit was dropped, and the company was dissolved.

On top of everything else, during this period, the company also had to deal with encroachments on its property by the Ore Banks. At the January 1900 Cornwall Ore Bank Company board meeting, it was noted that mining operations were extending "beyond the limits of the Clark Survey ... damages by the Cornwall Ore Bank will be paid to the Cornwall Iron Company". The company looked at its situation and concluded that what made the most sense was to divest itself of its properties.

At the start of 1901, Howard C. Shirk and John Hampton Barnes were elected as liquidating attorneys, and an auction was planned at the Donaghmore Station of the Cornwall Railroad. The minimum bid was set at $550,000. Edward Freeman, R. Percy Alden, Sarah C. Derby, Margaret Buckingham, and Isabel Freeman held 4/6 of the shares and proposed to buy the 1/6 share of William Freeman, as well as 1/6 share from Edward Freeman and William Freeman as trustees, for $183,333.33. William Freeman agreed to the terms. Edward Freeman and William Freeman sold the 999 shares they held as trustees to Isabel Freeman and Margaret Buckingham. William Freeman sold his 1,000 shares to Edward Freeman, Margaret Buckingham, and Isabel Freeman. The public sale of the Bird Coleman Furnaces, Cornwall Furnace (cold blast furnace), and Donaghmore Property was set for Saturday, March 9, 1901.

The auction notices explicitly stated that William C. Freeman was no longer a stockholder. Liquidating trustees were B. H. Buckingham, Howard C. Shirk, and John Hampton Barnes. Property consisted of the North Cornwall furnace, including dwellings, Bird Coleman, Cornwall, and Donaghmore. Purport No 1 included the North Cornwall Furnace and frame buildings with a total of 56 acres, Purport No 2 included the Erb farm of 134 acres, Purport No 3 included the stone manager's residence, Purports No 4 and 5 included land toward Bismark (now Quentin), and Purport No 6 included a brick dwelling. The furnace capacity was 150 to 200 tons of pig iron daily. The Bird Coleman Furnaces included brick, stone, and frame buildings, and had an upward capacity of 300 tons per day. The Cornwall furnace included 40 stone and framed dwellings, as well as the Cornwall Steam Grist Mill, and Donaghmore included a stone mansion. All three furnaces were to be sold as a whole, but the properties failed to reach the minimum bid. The company decided to extend the lease to Lackawanna for twenty years.

The Cornwall Iron Company, Ltd. was retired, and The Cornwall Iron Company Incorporated was chartered with shares held by Edward C. Freeman, R. Percy Alden, Isabel C. Freeman, Margaret C. Buckingham, and Sarah C. Derby. The company owned the Bird Coleman Furnaces, the Cornwall Charcoal furnace, and the North Cornwall Furnace. The purpose of the company was for "the manufacture of iron and steel, or both; or any other metal of or of any article of commerce from metal or wood or both. The purchasing, leasing, holding, mortgaging, and selling of real estate and mineral rights; mining, erecting furnaces, forges, mills, foundries, manufactures ... to exist perpetually until dissolved". Annual salaries were set for D. S. Hammond at $2,790, H. C. Shirk at $1,150, A. Brady at $9,460, and eight others combined at $25,175. The company was capitalized at $500,000 with 6,000 shares, Edward C. Freeman with 1,556 shares, Isabel C. Freeman with 1,555 shares, Margaret C. Buckingham with 1,555 shares, R. Percy Alden with 667 shares, and Sarah C. Derby with 667 shares. The Bird Coleman Furnaces were valued at $360,000, and North Cornwall at $179,000. On February 2, 1901, Lackawanna Iron and Steel renewed its lease for 20 years with the Cornwall Iron Company. Lackawanna, through its previous acquisition of Robert H. Coleman's properties, held a controlling interest in the Cornwall and Lebanon Railroad and a 1/6 interest in the Cornwall Ore Banks. They built ore roasters and 700 coke ovens at Colebrook. The iron they produced in Cornwall and Lebanon was used at their plant in Buffalo at Stony Point, New York. On the last day of 1902, an agreement was reached between the Cornwall Iron Company and Lackawanna by which Lackawanna purchased shares in the Cornwall Iron Company and the Cornwall Railroad, paying 66 2/3 cents per share for the company shares and $4 per share for the railroad shares.

H. B. Cox was made Superintendent at Bird Coleman and Patrick Eagon his assistant. The No. 1 furnace, which had been rebuilt in 1895, stood at 81 1/4 feet. It was fueled by coke, used Cornwall ore exclusively, and had a total annual capacity of 125,000 gross tons. North Cornwall, in contrast, had an annual capacity of 45,000 gross tons. Lackawanna's Board of Directors in 1902 included Walter Scranton, William E. Dodge, Warren Delano, Jr., D. C. Blair, J. J. Albright, Cornelius Vanderbilt, Moses Taylor, Edmund Hayes, Arthur Scranton, Henry Wehrum, Stephen Palmer, Austin Blair, B. H. Buckingham, and Arja Williams.

Despite all the changes, iron making continued to go smoothly, but the Lebanon workers for Lackawanna received devastating news in September 1903. Lackawanna Iron and Steel, which had moved its operations from Scranton, Pennsylvania, to just south of Buffalo, New York, was still completing its construction there. On September 22nd the Lebanon Daily News reported, "In view of the startling rumors of a general shut down of the Lackawanna Iron and Steel Co's plant in Lebanon County and City carrying with such active general discharges, Vice President Buckingham was asked for a statement and confirmed the reports to a shut-down in a few days; that it affects about 500 men; that operations will not be resumed here until probably next spring. Asked for a cause, Mr. Buckingham states that the steel mills at Buffalo are not ready; that their completion has been delayed far beyond the time set; that the company now has sufficient pig iron on hand, stacked". The next day, the workers put in their last day, at the end of which they were paid all outstanding wages. There would be no iron made in Cornwall or at Colebrook. The only production in the county was at the Pennsylvania Steel North Lebanon Furnaces.

While the furnaces were down, Benjamin H. Buckingham retired as Vice-President in charge of Lackawanna's Lebanon and Cornwall furnaces and was replaced by J. R. Savage. Rumors circulated in early 1904 of operations resuming at the Lackawanna plants, but were denied by Savage. Work did resume within a few months, but workers had found other jobs during the long blow-out, many having to move out of the area. It was a rough time for the workers, the community, and Lackawanna Iron and Steel. By August, it was reported that Pennsylvania Steel was interested in buying out Lackawanna's Lebanon interest and would then build a large steel-making facility, but the rumors were never realized. Eventually, production returned to previous levels.

William Freeman removed himself from the Cornwall Iron Company but was still involved with the Robesonia Iron Company. When William White, Sr. died, he left his shares to his son William White, Jr. and his daughter, Mrs. Henry P. Borie, and they purchased Ferguson's interest. On April 1, 1885, they formed the Robesonia Iron Company, Ltd. with a 20-year charter. They also brought in minority partners, William and Edward Freeman and Joseph Tatnall Lea, who had a longtime relationship with the Cornwall Iron Company, selling iron and ore. Shares were valued at $100 per share, and the shares were purchased by Henry P. Borie, on behalf of his wife, for $149,900, William White for $149.800, Joseph Tatnall Lea for $100, William C. Freeman for $100, and Edward C. Freeman for $100. Eventually, the Freeman interests grew, and other members of the family were brought into the company. According to the Lancaster Intelligencer, by 1886, they owned 5/8 of Robesonia for which they had paid $700,000. Sarah H. Coleman, in her will, left her shares in Robesonia to her nieces, Isabel and Margaret. These shares, though, were to be managed by her executors, Margaret C. Freeman, William C. Freeman, and Edward C. Freeman. After leaving the Cornwall Iron Company, William C. Freeman grew his holdings in the Robesonia Iron Company to the point that he eventually assumed the role of Chairman.

William C. Freeman passed away on February 7, 1903. He had gone to Princeton to visit his son, who was ill, but ironically, he himself fell ill and died Saturday at 3:30 am from complications of kidney and heart troubles, which he developed from a cold during the trip. His sisters Isabel and Margaret quickly left Washington, DC, to be by his bedside. William, Jr. would eventually replace his father as Chairman of Robesonia, and Robert C. Lea would assume the sales responsibilities.

Shortly after the Civil War, J. Edgar Thompson and Tom Scott, President and Vice-President of the Pennsylvania Railroad, respectively, Samuel Felton, former President of the Philadelphia, Wilmington and Baltimore Railroad, and Nathaniel Thayer of Baldwin Automotive Works formed the Pennsylvania Steel Company. In 1866, land was purchased near Harrisburg, Pennsylvania, and by 1867, the first rails using the Bessemer steel process were produced. Felton's son-in-law, Luther S. Bent, eventually was made Manager of what then became known as the Steelton plant. The company had originally targeted land in Lebanon to be closer to Cornwall, but was unable to purchase it. This same land later would serve as the site of American Iron and Steel in Lebanon. The company, as has been noted, purchased a large quantity of ore and iron from Lebanon County. They always had a close relationship with the North Lebanon furnaces, and George Dawson Coleman held a significant amount of stock in Pennsylvania Steel.

The Lebanon Daily News announced on June 14, 1901, a "Great Triple Sale, Cornwall Ore Hills, Cornwall & Lebanon RR and

Lebanon Furnaces controlling interest purchased by the Pennsylvania Steel Co, the Cornwall & Lebanon and Lebanon furnaces owned by the Colemans and also their allied interests ...The Lebanon furnaces are of the best, if not the very best, equipped furnaces in the United States". It was reported that Arthur Brock, a Director for Pennsylvania Steel, "perfected the deal", which involved much more than the North Lebanon furnaces. Pennsylvania Steel reached agreements with the George Dawson Coleman estate for their 15/96 shares of the Ore Banks, for the 15 1/8 shares of Anne Rogers, and the collective 16/96 shares belonging to the Grubb descendants. They also purchased 2/3 of the shares in the Cornwall and Lebanon Railroad. Altogether, Pennsylvania Steel paid $8,500,000.

Edgar C. Felton, the President of Pennsylvania Steel, his Vice-President and chief engineer, Frederick C. Wood, and Director Rund inspected the properties at the start of July. It was estimated at that time that there were at least 10,000,000 tons of ore left in the Ore Banks, but that estimate was raised after further study. They also acquired shares of the Cornwall and Lebanon railroad. The Lebanon Daily News reported that the purchase of the Cornwall and Lebanon "will have an important bearing on the construction of the Cornwall & Western Railroad". The Cornwall and Western Railroad had been incorporated in March 1901 to construct a twenty-five-mile line to ship ore to Steelton, connecting the Cornwall Ore Banks with the Pennsylvania Railroad. The primary investors were William C. Freeman, Edward C. Freeman, and Margaret Buckingham. Minor investors included B. H. Buckingham, R. Percy Alden, Sarah C. Derby, and others. The road was never completed.

Before the deal could be finalized, the members of the Coleman family involved with the North Lebanon property had to petition for permission to sell their holdings in the Ore Banks, given conditions in the will of George Dawson Coleman, which qualified the holdings. (Debbie Brown Coleman died in 1894, leaving her surviving children in full possession of all iron-related assets that had been the property of George Dawson Coleman.) On June 29, 1901, Goblin and McCurdy, attorneys for Horace Brock, Bertram Dawson Coleman, Edward Coleman, and the trustees under the will of George Dawson Coleman, with all children and grandchildren above age, filed a petition to allow the sale of 15/96 interest in the Ore Hills to Pennsylvania Steel. The shares were "non-divisible and must be petitioned since so many parties in it". The value of the Ore Bank shares was $2,025,000. The value of the furnaces added an additional $1,000,000. Bertram Dawson Coleman would remain in charge of the furnaces. On a personal note, Quincy Bent, the son of Luther Bent and a Vice-President with Pennsylvania Steel, married Deborah Brock, daughter of Horace and Debbie Brock and brother of John Penn Brock, on April 24, 1905.

General J. P. S. Goblin represented the Grubb descendants in the sale. This included Charles B. Grubb, Daisy E. B. Grubb under the will of Clement B. Grubb, and William D. Smith, guardian of Lillie G. Beall. Lillie, Daisy, and Jeanine G. Smith were the surviving daughters of Clement B. Grubb. Pennsylvania Steel bought their 8/96 shares of the Cornwall Ore Banks for a total of $1,200,000. C. Ross Grubb sold his 8/96 shares separately. The value of the shares was based on a valuation of all Ore Banks shares at $14,400,000.

The combined purchases left Pennsylvania Steel with 325 of 768 shares in the ore banks. Lackawanna held 275 shares. Of the remaining shares, 120 shares were still owned by Coleman descendants. Grubb descendants still held 40 shares, and 8 shares, purchased from the Grubbs, were held by the Pennsylvania Furnace Company, which operated the Sheridan Furnace. Based on the amount of the sales, each 1/96 share in the ore bank was estimated at a value of $135,000. While the Big Hill was mostly used up at this point, it was anticipated that underground mining would be accelerated to retrieve the underground ore. It was not exactly known how much ore could be mined underground. The iron content of the current ore being mined was diminished significantly, but its low phosphorus content was desirable. According to the industry publication, Iron Age, it was believed that retrieval costs would not exceed twenty-five to thirty cents per ton, and since Lackawanna owned the Cornwall Railroad and one-third of the Cornwall and Lebanon, with Pennsylvania owning the other two-thirds, there would be no appreciable cost of transportation. The Cornwall Ore Banks were still considered an extremely valuable property despite having slipped from the largest producing iron ore mine in 1893 to the twelfth in 1900.

The Lebanon furnace heights at this time were 100 feet. They had a compound condensing blowing engine capable of blowing 30,000 cubic feet of air pressure. They had four hot blast stoves, multiple Babcock and Wilcox boilers, a pig casting machine that poured the molten iron into ready-to-ship casts, and roasters. Pennsylvania Steel added a Sement-Solvay by-product coking facility. The furnaces could produce 400 tons of iron per day. In 1905, the Pennsylvania Steel Company built a concentrator just south and east of the North Lebanon furnaces. The concentrator used a wet mill equipped with Grondal magnetic separation. The concentrate was nodulized in three 7 x 100-foot kilns. A Wilfley table was added to recover nonmagnetic pyrite and chalcopyrite concentrates (which also allowed for the capture of waste minerals such as gold and silver). Pennsylvania Steel added over thirty new homes for its workers.

The Coleman families never engaged in large-scale steel production, content to supply iron ore and pig iron to support the large steel manufacturers (American Iron and Steel did, though, manufacture both iron and steel finished products). At the dawn of the 20th century, gone were the family-run furnaces. Iron making in Lebanon County was now directed by corporate interests. Following the sale of the North Lebanon Furnaces to Pennsylvania Steel, Bertram Dawson Coleman stayed on as manager of the furnaces, and Horace Brock's son, John Penn Brock, held a management position. William C. Freeman left the Cornwall Iron Company, which no longer ran their furnaces, leasing them instead to Lackawanna. Freeman took over at Robesonia, remaining active in the business until he died in 1903. Changes were also required at the mines. At the Cornwall Ore Banks board meeting on May 12, 1902, Freeman proposed, "The mines at Cornwall examined by three different experts (also familiar with mines at Mesaba) recommend use of steam shovels". While Freeman was no longer part of the Cornwall Iron Company, he still held shares in the Ore Banks. The composition of board members looked nothing like a decade before. Present were Edgar C. Felton, President of Pennsylvania Steel, attorney in fact for Archibald Rogers, who in turn was attorney in fact for Robert H. Coleman, trustee for Anne C. Rogers, and B. H. Buckingham, Margaret Freeman Buckingham's husband, Vice-President of the Lackawanna Iron and Steel Company.

For the most part, the Cornwall Ore Bank Company continued to operate smoothly and provided the necessary guidance and reporting required to keep the partners informed and protected in their interests. J. Taylor Boyd retired as General Superintendent in 1902 but remained as Treasurer. His replacement, Harrison Souder, came on board in 1905. In Souder's first ten years, he oversaw production of over four million tons of ore mined, representing over four million dollars in revenue and over two million dollars in profit, with a portion of these years occurring during a deep recession in which production was reduced. Issues, though, continued with Robesonia. In 1911, Souder reported that Robesonia was still accounting for the cost of mining at twenty cents per ton, which was the cost established in 1864.

Chapter 14. American Iron and Steel

It was announced in May 1899 that the Lebanon Iron Company would merge with the National Bolt, Nut and Rivet Works of Reading. After selling his interest in Pennsylvania Bolt and Nut, Charles W. Wilhelm started the National Bolt, Nut and Rivet Works. The new company was in need of a rolling mill, and rather than build one, they combined with the Lebanon Iron Company. The combined company, capitalized at $700,000 with over 300 employees, chose to operate under the Lebanon Iron Company's charter. Wilhelm was elected President, J. M. Shenk Vice-President, Abraham Hess Secretary, and Wilhelm's uncle, W. S. Davis Treasurer. Thomas Evans was made General Manager.

As the year progressed, negotiations began with J. H. Sternbergh and Son of Reading and the Pennsylvania Bolt and Nut of Lebanon regarding a combination. William Warren Gibbs was brought in as a "promoter". Gibbs, together with Peter A. B. Widener, was instrumental in the creation of United Gas Improvement. Gibbs also created the Electric Storage Battery Company, predecessor to Exide. The proposed combination would bring together the newly merged National Bolt, Nut and Rivet Works and Lebanon Iron Company with the Sternbergh works, Pennsylvania Bolt and Nut, and the East Lebanon Iron Company. In July, Pennsylvania Bolt and Nut purchased the land between themselves and the East Lebanon Iron Company for over $30,000. The two most significant companies in the merger were Sternbergh's Reading Works and the Pennsylvania Bolt ad Nut Company, which was advertised as the largest such works in the country. The Reading Works brought numerous patents to the combination, such as the "Harvey Grip Bolt" and "Ideal Nut", a nut that innovatively locked itself.

The new company, the American Iron and Steel Manufacturing Company, was incorporated on August 21, 1899. This brought together five operating plants, two in Reading and three in Lebanon. The plants were large, occupying many blocks of very specialized and diverse operations. The company produced hundreds of products, each in a range of different specifications. This was a different type of organization than Lebanon had seen before, with multiple layers of management. Sales extended beyond regional borders to national and even international horizons.

The initial officers were Arthur Brock, President, J. H. Sternbergh, Chairman of the Executive Committee, Horace Brock, Treasurer, and W. W. Gibbs, Secretary. James Lord was named General Manager, and Sternbergh's son Herbert was made Assistant Manager. The Executive Committee consisted of the elder Sternbergh, Horace Brock, James Lord, H. H. Light, the purchasing agent, and Charles W. Wilhelm. The Board of Directors consisted of J. H. Sternbergh, Horace Brock, H. M. M. Richards, who had been the Chief Clerk for Sternbergh and Son, replacing James Lord when Lord left to form Pennsylvania Bolt and Nut, John W. Brock, Arthur and Horace Brock's brother, C. W. Wilhelm, Arthur Brock, W. W. Gibbs, James Lord, H. H. Light, H. M. Sternbergh and H. J. Hayden, who had served as the General Manager for the National Bolt, Nut and Rivet Works.

The first annual report, published in 1901, noted there were 2,449 employees at the Lebanon plants and another 1,638 in Reading, for a total of 4,087. Sales of over $6,000,000 were reported with profits of $1,000,000 and dividends paid of $591,568, 12% on common stock. There were 31 puddling furnaces, 20 heating furnaces, and 15 pairs of rolling stands, including 8, 9, 10, 12, 16, and 18-inch stands. The company also employed Bessemer and open-hearth furnaces to remove carbon and other impurities from pig iron in steel production. The operations were spread over a combined 115 acres in multiple buildings, each with its own specialized machinery, bounded on the south side by the Quittapahilla Creek and on the north side by the Philadelphia and Reading railroad tracks.

A shift in leadership and control occurred at the annual meeting in February 1901. In a surprise move, Sternbergh had purchased the 100,000 shares of W. W. Gibbs[1] for $1,000,000 and, as a result, became the majority owner and ascended to the Presidency. Arthur Brock became Vice-President, and James Lord was made General Manager of the Lebanon plants, while Herbert Sternbergh was put in charge of the Reading plants, which were shortly reduced with the closing of the North Reading plant.[2] H. M. M. Richards was appointed Treasurer, and C. M. Hallman, who had been the Chief Clerk at the National Bolt and Nut, was appointed Secretary. Thomas Evans, W. H. Wallace, of New York, and Hallman were added to the Board of Directors. Rumors circulated that U. S. Steel was interested in "assimilating" American Iron and Steel, but any moves in this direction never materialized.

The 1902 Directory of the Iron and Steel Works of the United States and Canada listed The American Iron and Steel Company as having capital stock of $20,000,000 with $3,000,000 preferred at 5%, with par at $50 per share. The company's general offices were in Lebanon. At that time, they operated four plants, one in Reading and three in Lebanon. The Lebanon Central Works contained nine puddling furnaces, one gas furnace, six coal heaters, used fuel manufactured from gas and bituminous coal, and had an annual capacity of 50,000 gross tons. The total annual capacity of four rolling mills was 129,000 gross tons of finished rolled and forged products.

The moving of machinery to Lebanon and expanding the capacity there caused interest in the local paper, "With three such powerful companies moving forward to foster their interest here, the possibilities of this city as a steel centre can only be conjectured". The company made improvements to its fuel sources, equipment, and processes, all part of solidifying and streamlining the operations of five previously independent and competitive plants into one efficient corporation. This created a need for carpenters and mechanics, which took time to hire. During these efforts, the company suffered a large loss. At the end of June, a new rolling mill was demolished, wrecked by an electrical storm. The damage occurred at 4:30 in the morning. Fortunately, there were only 20 men in the plant.

On the heels of modernization, concerns were raised by the workers regarding wages. By the late 1890s, unions were making headway across multiple industries, and in Lebanon, there was a concentrated effort to unionize the workers at American Iron and Steel. In April 1902, the anthracite coal fields in Pennsylvania were hit by a widespread strike, and in that same month, a demand was put forward by the American Iron and Steel puddlers to increase the pay at the puddling furnaces, which would have a ripple effect across all operations. The puddlers and the finishing department workers requested an increase of fifty cents per ton, from $4.00 to $4.50. The owners felt the wages already set were reasonable and offered an increase to $4.25 instead, but the workers declined the offer. Between August 1900 and the start of 1902, hourly wages per ton, based on the price of bar iron, rose from $3.00 to $4.00.

Wage disputes had been an issue in Lebanon and Reading for over a decade. In 1891, the Amalgamated Association of Iron and Steel Workers of the United States, an American labor organization formed in 1876 to represent workers, published a scale of wages requesting companies to sign on. All the companies that merged into the American Iron and Steel Manufacturing Company had initially refused to endorse the published wage scale and had shut down their operations. Community tensions were heightened, and eventually, new wages were adopted, and operations resumed. Puddling wages were always a sticking point between the companies and the workers. Puddlers were paid $3.50 per ton in 1892, but with the Great Depression of 1893, wages fell to $2.50. It was not until 1895 that wages rose to $3.00.

A strike was declared on May 5th, 1902, in both the Lebanon and Reading operations. American Iron and Steel was adamant that they would not raise wages higher than the proposed $4.25, and the workers would not accept less than $4.50. The company advertised in Pittsburgh papers for replacements to "take the places vacated by our former employees ... union men need not apply". When the ad failed to produce fresh workers, the company decided to bring in a group of black workers, many from Birmingham, Alabama, a major area for iron and steel manufacture.

Replacement workers started work on August 26th. They had arrived at the Lebanon station from Reading, Pennsylvania, and were taken to the plant (housing was provided inside the plant). When they arrived, men and boys of the community jumped on the platform of the car, opened the door, and started harassing the replacement workers. Taunts of "Baa. Baa Blacksheep" and worse were shouted. The crowds followed the replacements to the plant, throwing stones and shouting further abuse. Once the workers were inside the company fence, the crowd continued to throw stones and other objects, and shots were fired.

A committee of striking employees called on General Manager Lord, demanding that the strike-breakers be removed. Lord denied the demand, and when the committee reported back to the striking workers, additional workers still in the plant (who had not gone on strike), 1,800 in all, were told to come out at 9 o'clock. Almost all left, each carrying a small American flag. Only foremen and a few blacksmiths stayed. This more than doubled the ranks of the striking workers. The first group of workers to strike numbered about 800. The company formed a Coal and Iron Police force, but there were daily attacks on workers who had decided to remain working, as well as shots fired at the non-union "scabs".

At the end of August, Sternbergh and Lord published their position in the Lebanon Daily News, stating they could not afford to pay the requested increase because costs were higher in eastern Pennsylvania than in the west, especially in Pittsburgh. They also claimed the strike was instigated from the outside, specifically referring to the Federation of Labor and the Amalgamated. Lord summed up his position on August 30th in the Lebanon Daily News, "We extremely regret that we have been so unjustly treated by our late employees of the puddling and rolling mills. We appreciated their ability to do good work. They were, as a class, men of excellent character and good citizens in a community. But when they want to assume our privileges and seek to destroy our business rather than co-operate to our mutual advantage to make it successful, they leave us no alternative to our present action except a weak submission to the decrees of a labor union".

On September 2nd, Charles Trump, a former employee of American Iron and Steel, replied on behalf of the strikers, noting the strike did not result from outside influences, but was solely a decision of the employees. He further pointed out it would be difficult to find locations in the United States where puddlers made less than $4.50, including nearby Lancaster. There was still a hope a peaceful resolution could be reached, but neither side was willing to compromise.

The company filed at least one lawsuit against strikers. The Lebanon Daily News reported on September 13th of the hearing in which American Iron and Steel Superintendent John Cullany accused George Stine, Granville Conner, and Wesley Moyer of causing a riot. Fellow machinists, Michael Glennon and G. Wolf, who had chosen to return to work, were accosted at Fourth and Weidman Streets by Stine, Conner, Moyer, and others. The crowd threw stones and shouted slurs (including the popular slur "Bah-bah-bah" alluding to "black sheep) at Glennon and Wolf, who had returned to work on September 8th after having gone out with the other strikers on August 28th. Deputy Horace E. Sternburgh accompanied Glennon and others as they left work. The crowd grew as they reached Glennon's home, and Sternburgh pulled out a revolver and waved it in the air. The Chief of Police, who had been following the crowd, attempted to pull Sternburgh from the crowd, but not before Sternburgh was hit with a brick and fell to the ground. He was eventually taken to the police station for safety.

The next day at 6:00 pm, when the workers left the plant, the entire police force was sent to 4th and Lehman Streets, and there were no further incidents. The activities prompted Sheriff Coppenhaver and Mayor Abraham Hess (who had been involved with the Lebanon Iron Company and still held ties with the company) to issue the following proclamation, "Inasmuch as the congregating of people anywhere in the vicinity of the American Iron and Steel Manufacturing Company plant at this time is likely to result in unlawful disturbances, which the police and officers will suppress. Therefore, it is directed that such gatherings be discontinued with a view of preventing a recurrence of violations of the law, such as that of last Monday evening. It is earnestly hoped that they will refrain from congregating in the vicinity of the works".

On Monday, September 22nd, around midnight, an attack was made on the plant. The strikers took up positions along the Quittapahllia Creek, which ran through the southern portion of the company property. During the tension, shots were fired on both sides. It is not clear which side fired first, but during the skirmish, William Hoffman, a 17-year-old messenger employed by the company, was shot in the temple and died within a half hour. Hoffman and a friend had gone to the site out of curiosity. Nearby homes received stray shots. Sallie E. Shay, who lived on Weidman Street, sued American Iron and Steel regarding the bullets fired into her house, claiming she was "frightened and shocked, thereby causing her to be permanently injured", but the suit was dismissed, the judge ruling American Iron and Steel could not be responsible.

Attacks continued the following day. Officers of the company, along with three detectives, barricaded themselves in the offices to defend the West Works plant. The attackers fired shots from revolvers and rifles, and even a small cannon. H. M. M. Richards, the Treasurer, along with several black replacement workers, was wounded. Fortunately for Richards, the shot entered his side, hitting a rib and was deflected outward through his flesh without injuring any major organs. The fighting only stopped with the arrival on Tuesday night of the Second Battalion of the Pennsylvania Twelfth Regiment under the command of Lieutenant Colonel C. M. Clement. The soldiers were surprised by the hostile greeting they received but proceeded to take control of the crowds and put an end to the fighting.

During the time the soldiers were encamped in Lebanon, there were no further serious incidents. The company continued to employ the replacement workers while they discussed possible resolutions. The strikers also continued to hold meetings. They posted a meeting announcement in the Lebanon Daily News on the 28th with a bold caption, "MILL MEN, READ THIS". A meeting was scheduled for that night at 8:00 pm at Miller's Hall on Cumberland Street. Clement was lavishly entertained in the evenings at various homes in Lebanon, including an evening with the H. H. Light family[3].

It was reported that on October 1st, five companies of the 12th Regiment returned to Shenandoah. On September 30th at 10:15 at night, two of the companies escorted 300 of the replacement workers to the train station and sent them to Pittsburgh. Talks resumed between the company and the workers to resolve the strike. T. H. Flynn of the American Federation of Labor helped bring negotiations to a close. After six months of struggle, the company agreed to the $4.50 increase for the puddlers, but a refiners wage was set at $4.25. All striking employees were welcomed back to work on Monday, October 20th. There was only one charge brought against an individual, John Arms of Avon, Pennsylvania (Avon borders the city of Lebanon on its northwest border), for firing a shot into the American Iron and Steel plant. It was a relief on all sides to return to normal operations after the long months of hardship.

As if the community, the company and the workers had not suffered enough, on November 13th in the afternoon there was an explosion "in the scrap-puddle furnace No. 3 at the West Works ... caused the death of four workmen, and about 40 others were more or less seriously injured ... worst that ever occurred in Lebanon ... in an instant the entire place was black with death-dealing debris. The wreck and ruin of the nine immediate puddle furnaces was complete. Thousands ... were attracted to the scene and weeping women and children ... ambulances ... office ... converted into a hospital ... some have eyes burned out, others hands blown off. Many of the injured cannot live".

Despite the events of the year, the company reported a positive financial state in their annual report, "... notwithstanding the interruption to our work in the rolling mill departments for nearly six months ending October 20 last, by an unreasoning strike of workmen". The company, clearly, though, still regarded the strike as unjustified. American Iron and Steel resumed the improvements they had started before the strike, which placed a burden on the financial resources of the company. In 1903, C. W. Wilhelm brought a suit against American Iron and Steel to prevent dividends from being paid on common stock, of which Sternbergh held the majority shares. Wilhelm had sold all his common stock and held only preferred. When it became clear he could not win his suit, he sold his stock to the Brocks and James Lord. In 1907, Sternbergh also sold stock to the Brocks and other associates but remained active on the board. A full reorganization of the company followed. Arthur Brock was made Chairman of the Board, James Lord became President, and Horace Brock's son, John Penn Brock, was introduced as Vice-President. Edward Coleman and William C. Freeman, Jr. were added to the board and the Executive Committee.

In 1909, two days before Christmas, after falling ill with pneumonia, Arthur Brock died shortly after noon at his home on Spruce Street in Philadelphia. It was reported he was "of a quiet and retired disposition son of John Penn Brock coal operator residing near Ashland, Civil Engineer in the employ of the Pennsylvania and Reading Railroad ... the ability to adapt himself to almost any kind of industrial and manufacturing activity ... possessed the capacity and energy for great work". Arthur's brother, John, and Bertram Dawson Coleman were brought onto the board of American Iron and Steel.

The company approved plans in 1913 for the erection of a large steel mill in Lebanon, which poured its first heat from Furnace No. 4 at 8:00 pm on Saturday, August 7, 1915. Four 50-ton Basic

Open-Hearth furnaces were added using pulverized coal. The company also built soaking pits, a dolomite furnace, a billet mill, and two 20-ton electric refining furnaces. The improvements cost $2,000,000. They had about 4,000 employees working at an annual payroll of $2,500,000. The total estimated value of all assets was $7,000,000. The company had a capacity of 160,000 tons per year, producing a wide range of products, including bolts, nuts, rods, and similar pieces, with annual sales ranging from $6,000,000 to $7,500,000. American Iron and Steel was a modern corporation. The company attended international exhibitions between 1876 and 1904 in Philadelphia, Chicago, New Orleans, Paris, Brussels, and St. Louis, winning first prizes at all. They established separate departments for sales, purchasing, accounting, engineering, and factory operations. They had separate superintendents for factories, mills, and furnaces, including the steel plant. There was one General Sales Agent in charge of the New England states, New York, the Pacific Coast, and foreign business, and another in charge of all other states in the U. S. There were sales offices in Atlanta, Boston, Chicago, New York, Philadelphia, and San Francisco.

Chapter 15. Bethlehem Steel

The Bethlehem Steel Company was incorporated in 1899, exchanging the stock of the Bethlehem Iron Company for bonds in the new steel company. Large corporations were being formed across the nation in a variety of sectors, the largest being United States Steel in 1901. Charles Schwab, who had risen through the ranks at Carnegie Steel, the centerpiece of United States Steel, became the company's first President. Working with E. E. Harriman to negotiate a merger with Bethlehem, Schwab had purchased Bethlehem Steel for $7,500,000. When the Harriman plans for a merger fell through, Schwab suggested that United States Steel purchase the company, but they were not interested. Schwab, feeling compromised owning a competitor of U. S. Steel, convinced J. P. Morgan to purchase Bethlehem for the price Schwab had paid, which Morgan did, only to have it re-purchased by Schwab as he put together a new shipbuilding company. The shipbuilding venture failed, and this and other events conspired against Schwab to the point that he resigned from United States Steel in 1903, presumably to retire. By 1904, though, with the Bethlehem Steel Corporation newly chartered in New Jersey, Schwab took over the reins of the company and for two decades created a steel company that competed head-to-head with his previous employer. In 1904, Bethlehem Steel had nearly 10,000 workers and by 1916 had 60,000.

Schwab started an aggressive expansion program in 1908 to acquire companies and erect new plants. Only a year later, Bethlehem Steel closed orders of $28,696,517 versus $14,458,998 the previous year. The expansion came at a cost, though. At the end of 1909, the total funded debt was $28,070,267. In 1912, with the expansion nearing completion, earnings reached $5,114,440 with a surplus of $2,063,640. Bethlehem Steel also purchased the Tofo Iron Mines in

Chile, estimated to contain over one million tons of iron ore, which provided ore with 67% iron, and in 1914, purchased the Fore River Shipbuilding Company of Quincy, Massachusetts, and the Titusville Forge Company in Pennsylvania. The buildup placed Bethlehem Steel in the best position among American steel companies to fill orders for shells, guns, and other material needed during World War I. At the end of 1915, Bethlehem Steel generated earnings of $17,762,813, paid its preferred dividend, and paid $112 dividend per share on its common stock. This set up a second wave of expansion.

Bethlehem Steel purchased Pennsylvania Steel and Maryland Steel in 1916 for $31,960,800. Eugene Grace had become Schwab's right-hand man at Bethlehem Steel and was spearheading an aggressive acquisition drive. Regarding Lebanon and Cornwall, he was looking to purchase all ore mining and iron and steel manufacturing in the area. Bethlehem did not want to share control with any other owner. With the purchase of Pennsylvania Steel, they acquired 832 of the Cornwall Ore Bank's 1,536 shares. The next largest block of 250 shares was owned by Lackawanna. They would purchase Lackawanna Iron and Steel outright in 1922, but at this time, they wished to purchase all holdings Lackawanna held in Lebanon and Cornwall, which included their 1/6 interest in the Cornwall Iron Company's holdings. In December 1917, Bethlehem Steel's auditor, F. A. Shirk, wrote to William Freeman (son of William Freeman, Sr.), "In the matter of the stock certificates now outstanding in the name of the Lackawanna Steel Company, I will take this matter up with Lackawanna, and endeavor to have them have the certificates transferred to us ... We understand from the Lackawanna Steel Company that all dividends on the six hundred sixty-seven shares held by them, which have been sold to us, will be paid direct to us in the future". Freeman was concerned about protecting the Cornwall Iron Company, which was in partnership with Lackawanna, regarding the transfer of agreements from

Lackawanna Iron and Steel to Bethlehem Steel. He elaborated on his concerns to Theodore C. Camp, "It appears that the Colebrook Furnaces and the Lackawanna's Ore Shares are pledged under the Lackawanna's issue of bonds maturing in 1950, and they will have to be withdrawn as security ... my opinion is that Bethlehem are going to hold up the matter of a formal transfer until the 40,000 tons of pig iron which we know is being sold at a loss of three dollars per ton, is cleared up". Bethlehem Steel Company paid Lackawanna a total of $4,502.25 per share on its 667 shares. The outstanding stock certificates were finalized on the last day of 1917.

In July of 1917, Freeman was looking for assurances that the furnaces would continue to operate after the sales, keeping the employees working, "He [Mr. Buck] assures me that it is their purpose to keep everyone of the furnaces going [including North Cornwall] and that assurance has been borne out by the blowing in of the second Bird Coleman furnace on Thursday last". Freeman wore two hats, representing the Cornwall Iron Company while also holding the Chairmanship of Robesonia. As late as November 1918, he expressed his concern, "I have given considerable thought ... Bethlehem Steel Company ... may be compelled to enter into a policy of retrenchment [due to the end of World War I] ... Moreover, I foresee the rapid approach of a conflict of interest in the mining operations of the Bethlehem Steel Company and the Robesonia Company. It is essential this agreement be consummated before the other matter begins to take shape". The final transfer of the Cornwall Iron Company and the Cornwall Railroad stock occurred on December 21, 1918, for $1,333,300. The proceeds were split with Isabel C. Freeman receiving $362,900, Margaret Buckingham $529,500, J. P. C. Alden $186,500, Anne Tucker $46,000, Richard, Roger, and James Derby $45,500 each, and Laura Buck $47,900. As a group, they were the surviving Coleman descendants still holding an ownership stake in the mines and furnaces.

Edward Freeman died May 5, 1912. He suffered a paralyzing stroke at 2:30 in the afternoon. He and a group of associates, which included Thomas Evans, had driven to nearby Fairview Farms. Freeman had gotten out of the car to unlock a door but stood fumbling with the keys. It is believed this was the moment the stroke occurred. He was taken to his home in Cornwall, and by ten minutes after four o'clock, he was dead. The farm had been in the family for generations and had stocked award-winning cattle as well as operated a dairy farm. After Robert H. Coleman's demise, Edward's brother, William, had bought up most of his cousin's land in the Cornwall area that had not previously been sold, including the farmland. When William died, Edward ended up with the farm. Edward left the farm to his sister, Margaret Buckingham. Edward's estate was estimated to be between $5,000,000 and $10,000,000. He left $200,000 to his nephew, William C. Freeman, Jr., and smaller sums to other individuals and charities, but the residue of his estate was split between his two surviving sisters, Margaret Buckingham and Isabel, who was unmarried.

Jack P. C. Alden had inherited his father's interest. Percy had died in 1909 after years as an invalid as a result of a stroke. Sarah Derby, who had died two years prior, left her shares to her four children. These interests involved shares in the ore banks as well as the assets owned by the Cornwall Iron Company.

Mary Ida Warren Alden died tragically in Washington, D. C., on May 28, 1899. She and Percy had been separated for a couple of years at the time, and Percy had registered his official address in Cornwall since Pennsylvania's divorce law was more liberal than New York's. She had suffered from a "nervous disorder" for years and had been staying at the Normandie Hotel for the past two winters.

The Washington Evening Star reported, "Yesterday afternoon from the result of burns accidentally received April 14. Mrs. Alden was a sufferer from an acute nervous disease, and came here several weeks ago to secure the benefits of the climate. A candle was kept in her room because she disliked a dark apartment, and the electric light gave too brilliant a glare. In some way Mrs. Alden, who was in her bedroom with the attendant nurse, brought the candle flame in contact with her nightdress, which immediately ignited. Her breast, neck, shoulders and arms were badly burned, and the victim was rendered unconscious. Dr. J. Taber Johnson was called, and at first it was thought the sufferer could not recover. The family physician, Dr. Frederick Paterson of New York, was summoned, and Dr. Presley M. Rixey of the navy was called into consultation. Mr. Alden arrived the day after the accident, Mrs. Alden survived the burns, and it was believed she was on the road to recovery, but a few days ago aseptic fever set in and attacked her lungs, resulting in pneumonia, which terminated fatally, as stated, at 5 o'clock yesterday afternoon. Mr. Alden and Mr. Lloyd Warren, a brother of the unfortunate woman, were at the bedside when death occurred, and will take the remains to Troy, N.Y., for burial". Other reports signified that Mary Ida had doused herself with benzine and then set herself on fire while sitting at her dressing table. A maid managed to douse the flames, but the damage was too extensive. Suggestions were made that the family tried to portray the fire as an accident. Percy stayed by her bed for the final days of her life. When her will was read, she had left $1,000 to Percy, which he refused to accept.

Sarah Derby had died in March 1907, while she and her husband, Dr. Richard Derby, were in Spain. Derby, the son of Elias Haskett Derby III, was a renowned Ophthalmologist with the New York Eye and Ear Infirmary (while at Harvard in 1864, Dr. Derby's roommate was Robert Lincoln, and he was close friends with John Hay, who would later serve as an aide to President Lincoln). He was the first surgeon to lose a suit for malpractice and took the loss extremely hard. He ended his life in July 1907 at Litchfield, Connecticut, where he was being treated for nervous exhaustion.

The Cornwall Ore Banks Company was no longer needed since Bethlehem Steel either owned all the shares in the company or was finalizing the purchase of all shares they did not own. At the November 15, 1916, board meeting of the Ore Banks, James Coleman Drayton, "gave notice of his intention to present at the next general or special meeting of this company, a resolution providing for the dissolution and termination of the company". Drayton's presence on the board followed an interesting journey beginning with his joining the Peace household as a young boy. Rosalie Parrant Coleman had left her shares in the Ore Banks to two of her friends, Ronald deReuter and Camile Besson, and Drayton, her nephew. Also present at the meeting were C. A. Buck, President Eugene Grace, F. A. Shick and W. A. Mitchel, all representing Bethlehem Steel, C. H. McCullough, Jr., for Lackawanna Iron and Steel, John J. Howard from Berkshire Iron Works (holding previous Grubb shares), Secretary William C. Freeman, Treasurer J. Taylor Boyd, General Superintendent Harrison Souder, and President Edgar Felton. C. A. Buck was elected as the new President. Eugene Grace, "outlined the ideas of Bethlehem Steel Company as to the future operations of the Cornwall Ore Bank and Mine Hills ..." and added, "The Bethlehem Steel Company has directed the General Superintendent to get the mine into shape for a yearly output of 1,500,000 tons of ore".

On November 28, 1916, the Lebanon Daily News reported, "Mysterious Visit of Steel Magnate, Schwab at the American Iron and Steel plant, sets tongues wagging – Mr. Schwab made the journey in his palatial private car, 'Loretto', accompanied by Eugene Grace, arrived around 10:00 (express from Bethlehem at 8:15 am) met by President Lord, Vice President J. P. Brock, Comptroller Reitzel, Horace Brock and others, inspection of newly built mill, left at 12:30 for Reading - additional American Iron and Steel plants. Lord, J. P. Brock, Reitzel and others went along including Bertram Dawson Coleman, Mr. Schwab had been a guest of the Lebanon Chamber of Commerce weeks before, already had acquired the North Lebanon furnace via the Pennsylvania Steel and Maryland Steel a short time ago - Schwab had at that time toured North Lebanon Furnaces". Negotiations between Bethlehem Steel and American Iron and Steel progressed rapidly. By the middle of February 1917, American Iron and Steel was ready for dissolution.

On the 27th at 2:30 pm, the plants and interests were sold to Bethlehem Steel, with total assets of $10,836,686.69. All stock was transferred. Present were the Executive Committee, John Brock, William C. Freeman, Horace Brock, and Edward R. Coleman, and other directors Edward Bailey, J. Harvey Sternbergh, Thomas Evans, James Lord, President, and Frank S. Reitzel, Comptroller. A formal announcement followed, "All of the property and business as a going concern of American Iron and Steel Manufacturing Company of Lebanon, Pennsylvania have this day been acquired by Penn Mary Steel Company, a subsidiary of Bethlehem Steel Company and such property and business will hereafter be operated under lease by Bethlehem Steel Company, which has taken over all contracts, has acquired all current accounts and is prepared to meet our outstanding obligations of such company when due. The Executive Treasurer, Accounting, Sales, and Purchasing Departments will have headquarters in South Bethlehem, Pennsylvania. Very Truly Yours, Bethlehem Steel Company by E G Grace, President, American Iron and Steel Company by James Lord, President".

On Tuesday evening, February 27th, the superintendents, clerical staff, and mechanical department heads organized a farewell tribute banquet for James Lord. Bertram Dawson Coleman served as the toast master, and William C. Freeman gave a "most inspiring speech". Forty-eight directors and other prominent officials attended. Two dozen department heads, clerks, and stenographers were transferred to Bethlehem, Pennsylvania. The headline in the next day's Lebanon Daily News would read, "American Iron and Steel Co. Fades Into Memory and Bethlehem Takes Charge", but on this night, the achievements of American Iron and Steel Manufacturing Company were fondly celebrated.

William C. Freeman, in his formal petition to allow the sale of shares to proceed, summed up the history, "Lackawanna Iron and Steel bought Robert H. Coleman's shares and introduced a new element into the ownership. This was followed by the sale of other interests to the Pennsylvania Steel Company, which shares were afterwards bought by Bethlehem, so that it has come down to the Bethlehem Steel Company owns 1082/1536 interest in that mine ... the price of ore used to be based on the percentage price of the selling value of the pig iron, but now the price is determined and fixed by the holder of the majority". The summation was to the point. The family's ownership, after 175 years, was ending.

Sadly, Horace Brock died at 7:30 am on August 4, 1917, from pneumonia at the Orthopedic Hospital in Philadelphia. His memorial read, "Mr. Brock was a true gentleman, a master in his special line of activity, generous in his hospitalities, kind in disposition, and largely imbued with philanthropic impulses that fruited in many public, as also in many unheralded, generosities". He had served as an officer and given generous support to the Good Samaritan Hospital in Lebanon, as well as on the board of the First National Bank of Lebanon. He and his brother Arthur, in addition to their participation in American Iron and Steel, had had numerous other investments, including mining operations in the West and the Poughkeepsie Bridge Company.

Bethlehem Steel had been most interested in the Cornwall Ore Banks and American Iron and Steel. The iron furnaces, while advanced at one point, had outlived their efficiency and were no longer modern. The Cornwall Anthracite furnaces were torn down in 1898, only four years after Lackawanna Iron and Steel took over ownership. The Bird Coleman Furnaces were torn down in 1922, and a year later, the North Cornwall furnace was dismantled. The Colebrook coke ovens and furnaces were demolished in 1924 after lying idle for a few years. The North Lebanon furnaces were torn down in 1929. In 1927, Bethlehem Steel purchased the Robesonia Iron Company, which still possessed mining rights at the Cornwall Ore Banks, and promptly dismantled their furnaces. Many furnace workers were moved to other positions within Bethlehem Steel's operations. The Coleman Dynasty in Lebanon County had come to a close.

Chapter 16. After the Iron

Bertram Dawson Coleman died in 1933, only two months after his brother Edward died. At the time of his death, he had been inactive in the iron and steel business for over a decade but still retained an interest in the First National Bank of Lebanon and coal mining operations in Pennsylvania. He formed a coal mining partnership with John Heisley Weaver in 1909. The company owned mines in Indiana and Cambria Counties of Pennsylvania and created numerous subsidiaries, including the Ebensburg Coal Company, the Heisley Coal Company, the Monroe Coal Mining Company, and a short-line coal carrier, the Cambria and Indiana Railroad. The two partners split in 1922, with Coleman receiving the Nanty-Glo and Ebensburg mines. He sold his 40% of the railroad to Weaver.

The youngest child of George Dawson and Debbie Coleman, Anne, was the last family member to marry at the Homestead. Her fiancée, Dr. Joachim Carvallo, made the trip from France to Mt. Lebanon to marry Anne. The two had met in France, where Anne was furthering her education, and Dr. Carvallo was engaged in research. The couple settled in France, where they bought and restored a 16th-century chateau in the Loire Valley, Villandry, for which they won recognition for their restoration.

Once Anne married in 1899, Edward and Fanny Coleman were the last members of the family to reside at Mt. Lebanon, sharing the Homestead between them. Debbie Brock, Horace Brock's widow, died in 1932. Sarah Brock shuttered up her house after her husband, Arthur Brock, died in 1909, and Pauline Biddle Brock, widow of John Penn Brock, spent the winters in Philadelphia, but still visited "Brookwood", as the Mt. Lebanon mansion was known, in the summers.

Mt. Lebanon, the family estate, at one time held five grand mansions within its roughly 100 acres. The Homestead, completed in 1853, was the sole remaining mansion to grace the grounds for almost twenty years until its eventual demolition. It was reported to contain thirty-six rooms and four stories. The second mansion was built in 1878 as a wedding present for George and Debbie Coleman's daughter, Debbie, when she married Horace Brock. The house was designed by prominent Harrisburg architect Luther M. Simon, who incorporated the original home that George Dawson and his brother Robert lived in when they were building the North Lebanon Furnaces. In 1882, Debbie Coleman deeded twenty-two acres to her daughter and son-in-law, Sarah and Arthur Brock. Bertram Dawson purchased land on the family estate from his mother and built a stone home with a corner turret in 1890. After his wife, Anne Churchill Coleman, died in 1915, he could not bring himself to stay there when in Lebanon; instead, he stayed at the Homestead. The final mansion to be built was for John Penn and Pauline Biddle Brock. John Penn Brock, son of Horace and Debbie Brock, purchased the land in 1908 from his uncle, Bertram Dawson, for $1,465.63. His cousin, John Penn Brock Sinkler, designed the house which was completed in 1909. John Penn Brock remained a Vice-President with Bethlehem Steel acting as General Manager of the Lebanon and Reading plants until his untimely death in 1928 while in Rome. He was survived by his wife Pauline Biddle Brock, descended from Nicholas Biddle, and four children.

Each mansion employed its own number of servants, many of whom spent their careers devoted to the family. In the 1900 Census, there were seven servants listed as living in the Arthur Brock mansion. There were separate Gate Houses, Carriage Houses, and other outbuildings devoted to each mansion, and each had its own spectacular gardens. They even had their own electrical power generator. When the family heirs deeded the estate to the city of

Lebanon, a condition was included that longtime servant, Oscar Muench, was provided residence in the Homestead Gate House for the remainder of his life.

Fanny Coleman died in 1935, signaling the end of the grand life in Mt. Lebanon. Pauline Brock sold her home to the City of Lebanon in 1936 for $25,000. The descendants of Bertram Dawson Coleman and Horace Brock donated the property they had inherited to the City of Lebanon as Coleman Memorial Park. Additionally, Sarah Brock donated her property as the Arthur Brock Extension to Coleman Memorial Park. The final three acres, located at the north-west corner of the park, were given to the city by J. H. Edmonds and his wife, Nellie. Edmonds had been Assistant General Manager for the Lebanon plants of Bethlehem Steel, having started in 1907 with American Iron and Steel. When John Penn Brock died in 1928, Edmond was promoted to General Manager.

In the Coleman Memorial gift, the deed included a clause, "The donors, without attempting, in any way to impose any obligation upon the said City of Lebanon, Pennsylvania, expressly stipulate that the use of the said real estate and any of the buildings, which are now erected thereon, for the purpose of maintaining a museum or other use or object incident to the purpose of this gift or grant, especially a museum for the preservation of colonial handicraft arts and a historical museum and library, and the use of the buildings to foster music, the drama, and handicrafts, are to be understood clearly within the purposes of the gift". There were no extra funds to create or maintain any sort of museum, and the gift was given in the middle of the Great Depression.

Lebanon used the services of the Works Progress Administration to tear down the Arthur Brock mansion (Sarah Brock had expressed her wishes that the mansion be torn down) as well as the Horace

Brock mansion. The city commissioned the John Penn Brock mansion to be torn down the year prior. Bertram Dawson's mansion was demolished in 1944. The last mansion to be razed was the Homestead in 1961. The big story at the time was the discovery of a hidden office and safe behind a false wall in the library, in which was discovered a century-old letter from President Lincoln to George Dawson Coleman appointing him to represent the country at the Exhibition of Industry of All Nations in London. Due to the Civil War, he never went.

Plans had been made to tear down the Homestead years before it was finally demolished. On April 12, 1953, the Sunday Patriot News reported, "The last of the five massive Coleman Mansions will be torn down stone by stone this summer, erasing the last monument to the memories of a past era. Its 36 rooms, rich with hand carved panel walls, enormous stained-glass windows and other fascinating structural details, will disappear from what is now Coleman Park, making way for more recreational space to benefit those of another age. The four other homes erected by the Colemans were razed years ago ... Morris Smith, groundskeeper and general handyman around the home since 1929 and now custodian of the park, knows every nook and corner of the old homestead ... he was making a 'normal day's wages' of about $3.00 it cost $15,000 annually to run the home. It took a ton of coal a day to heat the interior, augmented by roaring fires in the fireplaces that are in nearly every room. [at the end] eleven persons were employed in or about the house. Smith and four others worked about the grounds, while a butler and five girls worked inside tending to the housework".

Millions of dollars were inherited by the Coleman and Brock descendants. The Lebanon Daily News reported Jon June 18, 1966, the distribution of millions of dollars from trusts set up by Arthur and Horace Brock totaling, at that time, $3,500,000. Judge Thomas

Gates ruled in favor of the distributions, which awarded $2,093,564.62 from the will of Arthur Brock and $1,984,045.40 from the will of Horace Brock. One of the events that precipitated the request was the death of Debbie Brock Bent on March 14, 1965. Her son, Horace, received $942,022.27, and an equal amount was split between the four children of John Penn Brock. Joseph N. Dubarry IV was one of the trustees and a recipient of distributions from the Arthur Brock trust.

The Cornwall Charcoal Furnace, retired from operation on February 11, 1883, by 1901 was owned in parts by Edward Freeman, Isabel Freeman, and Margaret Buckingham with 4/18 of the property each, and Percy Alden and Sarah Derby with 3/18 each. On November 4, 1901, though, 1/6 of the property was transferred to Lackawanna Iron and Steel, forcing the ownership into 24 shares.

When Edward died[1], he left his portion to his sisters. Percy's shares passed to his sons and Sarah's to her children. Lackawanna's share transferred to Bethlehem Steel, who through a series of internal corporate shifts, ended up in the hands of Bethlehem-Cuba Iron Mines. Margaret received Isabel's shares upon Isabel's death in 1929, bought the shares of J. P. C. Alden and the Derby siblings in 1931, and purchased the shares held by the Iron Mines. Owning the furnace outright, she offered the furnace to the Commonwealth of Pennsylvania as a gift for the purpose of establishing a museum. She engaged Edgar Weimer at a cost of $30,000 to perform necessary repairs to the furnace, which took a year to complete. In 1931, the Pennsylvania legislature accepted the gift, and in 1932, Margaret officially turned over the furnace to the state. Fifty years later, the Cornwall Iron Furnace remains a part of the Pennsylvania Historic Museum Commission. In 1935, she added a $35,000 trust to assist with the upkeep.

Margaret Buckingham continued to live part of the year in the Cornwall mansion until she died in 1946. She left her nephew, William C. Freeman, as Executor of her estate. He offered the eighty-plus acres with the mansion to Cornwall Borough for a community park in early 1947, but the Borough declined the offer due to the estimated costs to create the park. The Borough's loss, though, opened an opportunity for the Methodist Church. Freeman understood his aunt's desires and her devotion to her faith as a Methodist, so it was natural that events would transpire with the Methodist Church, which resulted in the transfer of the Manor property, including the stables, the barns, and the grounds. Frank Campbell met with Church officials at 4:00 pm and provided a tour of the property on July 10, 1948. The purchase cost the church only $20,000. The transfer of title for the 4.44 acres wedged between Anthracite Road and what was then Route 322 occurred on February 15, 1949. The home, initially for retired ministers, officially opened on October 8th.

Anne Rogers died on March 2, 1934. The New York Times reported her estate to be worth over $3,000,000. This was divided among her six surviving children. Ellen Habersham Rogers married Kenneth Schley. Schley's father had co-founded the investment firm of Moore and Schley. The firm was rescued through J. P. Morgan's efforts in the Panic of 1907. Anne Pendleton Rogers married state Senator J. Griswold Webb. His uncle, Dr. William Seward Webb, married Eliza Vanderbilt. The couple founded Shelbourne Farms in Vermont. Edmund Pendleton Rogers was President of Fulton Trust, later Chase Bank. He married Frank Goodyear's daughter, Virginia. The couple's winter cottage at Jekyll Island still stands. Herman Livingston Rogers perhaps lived the most colorful life of Anne and Archibald's children. He and his wife, Katherine, befriended Wallis Simpson while they were all living in China. When the Duke of

Windsor, then the King of England, abdicated the throne to marry Simpson, a divorcee, Herman served as the duke's best man at the ceremony held at Herman's chateau in Cannes. The other surviving sons were William and Rae Habersham.

There were many inquiries sent to William C. Freeman, Jr. during his lifetime to purchase other land and properties he owned or managed under trust. One of the more desirable was Fairview Farms. Through a succession of land purchases and inheritance, the farm had finally passed from Edward Freeman to his sister, Margaret Buckingham. In 1950, Freeman responded to one such inquiry, "This farm ... is operated under lease by a competent and faithful employee of many years. Moreover, Mrs. Buckingham, in her will, specifically expressed the hope that Fairview Farm would not be sold". During the remainder of his life, Freeman refused all offers on the farm. The farm was sold by his widow, Alice, after he died, and today is a public golf course, named simply Fairview.

Freeman lived part of the year in Cornwall. His winter home was in Philadelphia at 1901 Rittenhouse Square. When he died in 1955, he was the last one alive of the Coleman descendants who had been active in the iron industry. He left an estate valued at over $1,600,000. His will provided gifts to many groups but also included sums for his employees. The largest amount to his employees, $5,000, was awarded to Frank Campbell. Freeman was on the board of American Iron and Steel at the time of the sale to Bethlehem. He was involved with the sales of shares of the Cornwall Ore Banks, and he was Chairman of the Robesonia Iron Company when it was purchased by Bethlehem. He watched the tearing down of the furnaces his family had built. He personally oversaw the sale of lands and property that had belonged to his father and his aunts and uncles.

The Coleman families provided significant support to the Lebanon and Cornwall communities. They helped fund the construction and improvements of numerous churches (most notably the Cornwall Methodist Church and St. Luke's Episcopal in Lebanon), supported educational institutions, created banks, organized and sustained the Good Samaritan Hospital, and contributed to many community programs. This support continued after the sale of their furnaces and their ore holdings. In 1927 various family members subscribed to a building and improvements bond issue for Cornwall Borough. Edward R. Coleman contributed $92,000, Fanny Coleman $30,000, William C. Freeman $26,000, and Margaret Buckingham $24,000. Their contributions represented over eighty percent of the entire bond issue. Sarah Brock, Fanny Coleman, William C. Freeman, Margaret Buckingham, and the grandchildren of George Dawson Coleman, representing the estates of those who had died, as well as themselves, contributed to the purchase of bonds for Cornwall Schools. Family members have donated paintings, photos, and family artifacts to both the Lebanon County Historical Society and the Cornwall Iron Furnace and continue to take an interest in ongoing talks and publications.

In June of 1972, Hurricane Agnes surged through Pennsylvania. One of the casualties left in her wake was the flooding of the No. 3 mine and the ore pit. Over a span of 234 years, approximately 106 million natural tons of iron ore were recovered. From the beginnings of surface mining to the construction of the underground mines (as deep as 1,200 feet), the ore bank had employed thousands and made a great deal of money for its owners. In addition to the iron ore, between 1908 and 1973, 67,000 ounces of gold and 443,000 ounces of silver were also recovered, as well as amounts of copper and cobalt. The copper, at one time, was crushed and sent to the Philadelphia

Mint. Cornwall was the largest producer of Cobalt in the United States during World War II. Agnes hastened the inevitable – Bethlehem Steel had known for years before 1972 that the mines were reaching the end of their viability. In 1957, it was estimated that the mines had a 15-year lifeline.

The mines were officially closed on June 30, 1973. Bethlehem Steel announced in September 1974 that they were reopening the concentrator and pelletizing plant, which would process outside ore and create pellets for Steelton and Bethlehem, but in 1977, they announced they would be closing down for good. By 1984, Bethlehem Steel was down to less than 500 employees as it started closing down operations in Lebanon. William Ecenbarger of the Chicago Tribune commented in 1987, "Lebanon, Pa., is a dog-eared town, about 90 miles west of Philadelphia. A mill town where the mill has become a millstone. Bethlehem Steel closed its Lebanon plant for good last year".

Remains from the concentrator and pelleting plant in Cornwall sit empty on the top of Big Hill. The Cornwall Grist Mill, the Cornwall Ore Banks Superintendent's home, and other buildings have been torn down, while others, such as the Cornwall Anthracite Furnace office, have been converted to single-family dwellings, and still others have been taken over by businesses. A limited number of small industrial businesses have taken over space in the old steel plant buildings in Lebanon. The Robert H. Coleman stable sits decaying, imprisoned inside a fence. The Homestead stable and two gatehouses are the only buildings standing in what was Mt. Lebanon but is now Coleman Memorial Park. The Lebanon County Historic Society houses a Coleman display, Cornwall Manor has restored many buildings in what was the Cornwall Mansion, and the Cornwall Iron Furnace allows visitors to walk through the cold-blast furnace and visualize the operations from start to end. There is still an interest in the Coleman Legacy among the Coleman descendants and local residents and as long as that remains true, the story lives on.[1]

Epilogue

It was a bright, sunny day on September 28, 2013. The Elizabeth Furnace mansion and the immediate property surrounding the mansion, 33 acres in Brickerville, Pennsylvania, were being auctioned as well as many Coleman family heirlooms. Guests and potential bidders parked at the Elizabeth Farms Tree Farm, which was not included in the auction, and were bused over to the mansion, where, if they were early enough, they were provided with a walk-through tour. They entered from the porch and, turning into the south parlor, looked straight ahead at a portrait of Ann Old Coleman. There were family portraits throughout the mansion, a few of which would be auctioned off, but most held privately by the family who had, for decades, kept the portraits in the home in keeping with Debbie Brown Coleman's wish that the mansion remain a retreat and museum for the family. On a wall in an upstairs bedroom hung the original lease agreement James Old and Robert Coleman signed in 1776 when Robert took over the operations of Elizabeth Furnace.

The auction was held at the rear of the mansion and attendees sat where, at one time, there existed a terrace of magnificent boxwoods. Anyone who was able to walk along the perimeter of the barracks where Hessian prisoners of war had been housed. The barracks still had the iron bars over the windows. The original three-room house, which James Huber, who built the first Elizabeth Furnace, lived in, was open for view, and the charcoal barn housed items that would be available for bid. People could also see where the remains of the second, enlarged furnace was located, which Baron Stiegel had built to replace the original Huber furnace.

It became clear with the bidding on Item # 1 that prices were going to be high. The $50 – $100 estimate on a brass, iron, and wood spring "Coleman" corporate seal went well over the estimate, selling for $3,100 to seventh-generation Craig Coleman. In fact, many of the family items and furniture were won by the family members present. Craig Coleman, along with his brother, Bruce, and cousin, William Dawson (Bill) Coleman, had inherited the property from their fathers, Bertram Dawson and Francis I. G. Coleman, grandsons of the first Bertram Dawson Coleman. There were discussions among the cousins regarding the value of the property and the possibility of selling. It was finally decided that the only resolution was to auction the property. If anyone feared that after 220 years a "stranger" would own the Elizabeth Mansion and furnace site, their fears were put to rest. Bruce and Craig Coleman paid $2,000,000 for the family treasure, which has been wholly owned by the family since 1794. The property has been rechristened Elizabeth Furnace Village and has been created as a luxury wedding venue.

The family retained the remaining land surrounding the mansion, known as Elizabeth Farms. Through similar discussions as those which preceded the auction of the mansion grounds, Elizabeth Farms went to auction on October 29, 2021. Over 340 acres were divided into three parcels of 190.5, 100 and 56.7 acres. The largest of the three was won by a local farmer from nearby Lititz for $3.42 million and the remaining two parcels by a group of three Lebanon County men for $2.95 million and $969,570.

Acknowledgements

This work has benefited greatly from a few researchers who started researching the Coleman family long before I started. The first obstacle that confronts anyone who investigates a family that spans multiple generations is getting the genealogy straight. It is challenging keeping track of all the Roberts, Edwards, Williams, Annes and Sarahs. Elaine Ainsworth and her mother, Martha Sorenson, contacted descendants and travelled all over to put together a comprehensive genealogy starting with Robert and Ann Coleman up through the generations, including descendants still living. I can't count all the times I have referenced their work. They also gathered numerous articles and other information on the family, as well as many photos. Elaine donated their research materials to the Cornwall Iron Furnace.

John and Margery Feitig's estate likewise donated their research to the Cornwall Iron Furnace. They made countless inquiries to libraries, historical societies, archives, and Coleman descendants, gathering copies of photos, articles, letters, and other material. Both Elaine and the Feitigs were in contact with William Powell, who was especially interested in the Mt. Lebanon branch of the family. I am also grateful to David N. Grubb for his genealogy of the Grubb families published in *The Grubb Family of Grubb's Landing, Delaware: Descendants of John Grubb (1652 – 1708) From Stoke Climsland, Cornwall.*

The Lancaster Historical Society has several Coleman family records, including deeds and personal letters, which were provided to them by William Coleman, a seventh-generation descendant of Robert Coleman. The Pennsylvania State Historical Archives housed an extremely large collection of business and family records and correspondence, which has provided a significant volume of information included in this work. The archives now reside at the Lebanon County Historical Society, where they had originally resided before being transferred to the state archives. Manuscript Group - 275 is the primary group I referenced. I do want to acknowledge Brett Reigh from the state archives. His friendly encouragement and interest in my efforts are deeply appreciated. He has also gone through, in his own time, the entire manuscript and provided very helpful feedback.

Mike Emery and Karen Viozzi at the Cornwall Iron Furnace, Site Manager and Assistant, respectively, have been invaluable help to me. In addition to their support, there is a group of volunteers at the furnace who have provided input. Bruce Chalbourne has been going through the Feitig materials and documenting his work. Mike Weber has been doing the same for a set of documents donated by Mike Trump, which include the records of Charlie Neil, who had been employed by Bethlehem Steel at the mines. Irv Muritz was critical in obtaining the Feitig materials for the furnace as well as seeing Elaine's research published and has developed an extensive Robert and Ann Coleman Family Outline listing numerous descendants along with a three-generation Coleman Family Tree. Irv also generously reviewed the manuscript and provided many helpful edits and suggestions. I am grateful to Mike Trump and Sue Wentzel for their research (edited by Kathy Donaldson) on the history of Cornwall. I have also benefited from resources generously shared by Michael and Jared Blouch. Finally, I owe a debt of thanks to my neighbor, Garret Church, who read through the manuscript and provided excellent feedback.

Much of the material for the Prologue came from the personal correspondence of Frank Campbell and William C. Freeman, Jr., which is in my possession. I was lucky enough to have purchased a filing cabinet full of letters and documents about the sale of the Alden property, Cornwall Manor, Fairview Farms, and other properties, as well as personal letters of the Freeman family.

Unless otherwise noted, the images are courtesy of the Cornwall Iron Furnace. I have tried to select some images that have not been included in previously published books but have made an exception for photos that made sense to duplicate in this book. Overall, it was my goal to present a reasonable selection to provide the reader with a visual depiction of the people and places discussed in the narrative.

Finally, I would like to thank my wife, Lisa. To my knowledge we are the only couple to be married at the Alden Villa. I am sure she wishes she had a dollar for every time the word "Coleman" came out of my mouth. She has gone on numerous trips with me to Hyde Park, New York, Long Island, South Carolina, and many other places, so I could tour a home or do some research. She accompanied me to lectures, not all of which were enjoyable, and gone along to visits to archives. She suffered embarrassment when we were asked to leave private property while exploring a previous Coleman property. She also suggested the title for this book.

Coleman Genealogy

This genealogy lists the primary family members mentioned in this book. For a more complete genealogy, refer to "From the Mists Over Furnace Hills: The Story of Robert and Ann Old Coleman and Their Descendants, The First Two Hundred Years of the Coleman Family" by Elaine Ainsworth, published by the Friends of the Cornwall Iron Furnace, Cornwall, PA.

<u>Generation 1</u>

Robert Coleman (1748 – 1825) m. 1773 Ann Old (1755 – 1844)

G2 1.1 - Margaret (1774 – 1853) m. 1806 Joseph Hemphill (1770 – 1842)

G2 1.2 - William (1776 – 1837)

G2 1.3 - Elizabeth (1778 – 1858) m. 1796 Charles Hall (1767 – 1825)

> G3 1.3.1 - Robert Coleman (1797 – 1844) m. 1824 Sarah Ann Watts (1804 – 1886)

> G4 1.3.1.1 - Julia Watts (1824 – 1905) m. 1846 John Penn Brock (1823 – 1881)

> G5 1.3.1.1.1 - Arthur Brock

> G5 1.3.1.1.2 - Horace Brock

> G3 1.3.2 - Louisa (1808 – 1884) m. 1828 Francis William Rawle (1795 – 1881)

> G4 1.3.2.1 - James (1842 – 1912) m. 1871 Charlette Parker (1849 – 1909)

> G4 1.3.2.2 - Charles (1827 – 1914)

> G4 1.3.2.4 - Norman (1829 – 1917)

> G4 1.3.2.5 - William (1806 – 1844)

G3 1.3.3 - Harriet (- 1810) m. 1818 William Norris

G2 1.4 - Thomas (1780 – 1782)

G2 1.5 - Peter (1782 – 1782)

G2 1.6 - James (1784 – 1831) m. 1822 Harriet Dawson (1802 – 1865)

G3 1.6.1 - Robert (1823 – 1878) m. Rosalie Parrant

G3 1.6.2 - George Dawson (1825 – 1878) m. Deborah Brown (1832 – 1894)

G4 1.6.2.1 - Debbie Norris (1858 – 1932) m. 1878 Horace Brock (1854 – 1917)

G5 1.6.2.1.1 -. John Penn Brock (1879 – 1928) m. 1905 Pauline Biddle (1880 – 1968)

G5 1.6.2.1.2 - Deborah (1884 – 1965) m. 1910 Quincy Bent (1879 – 1955)

G4 1.6.2.2 - Sarah (1859 – 1945) m. 1879 Arthur Brock (1850 – 1909)

G4 1.6.2.3 - James (1860 – 1874)

G4 1.6.2.4 - Frances (Fanny) (1861 – 1935)

G4 1.6.2.5 - Harriet (1863 – 1931) m. 1884 Harry Sheaf Glover (1858 – 1912)

G4 1.6.2.6 - Bertram Dawson (1865 – 1933) m. 1889 Anne Churchill (1869 – 1915)

G4 1.6.2.7 - Edward Rion (1867 – 1933)

G41.6.2.8 - Anna (1875 – 1940) m. 1899 Joachim Leon Carvallo (- 1936)

G3 1.6.3 - Anna (1826 – 1876) m. Charles Collins Parker (1823 – 1848), m. 1853 Edward Peace (1811 – 1879)

G3 1.6.4 - Sarah Hand (1828 – 1852) m. 1851 Henry Edward Drayton (1823 – 1862)

G4 1.6.4.1 - James Coleman Drayton (1852 – 1934) m. 1879 Charlotte Augusta Astor (1858 – 1920)

G3 1.6.5 - Harriet (1830 – 1901) m. 1850 William Heyward Drayton (1817 – 1892)

G2 1.7 - Stephen Chambers (1786 – 1816)

G2 1.8 - Robert (1788 – 1811)

G2 1.9 - George (1790 – 1821)

G2 1.10 - Edward (1792 – 1841) m. 1816 Mary Jane Ross (1797 – 1825), m. 1831 Anne Catherine Griffiths

G2 1.11 - Thomas Bird (1794 – 1836) m. 1817 Hannah Cassatt (1796 – 1830)

G3 1.11.1 - Anne Caroline (1817 – 1894) m. 1842 Bradford Alden (1811 – 1870)

G4 1.11.1.1 - Robert Percy (1848 – 1909) m. 1878 Mary Ida Warren (1852 – 1899)

G4 1.11.1.2 - Sarah Alden (1850 – 1907) m. Richard Derby (1844 – 1907)

G5 1.11.1.2.1 - Richard (1881 – 1963) m. 1913 Ethel Roosevelt (1891 -)

G5 1.11.1.2.2 - Roger Alden

G5 1.11.1.2.3 - James Lloyd

G5 1.11.1.2.4 - Anne Caroline

G3 1.11.2 - Margaret Cassatt (1819 – 1894) m. 1845 William Grisby Freeman (1815 – 1866)

G4 1.11.2.1 - William Coleman (1847 – 1903) m. 1880 Elizabeth P. Brown (- 1881)

G5 1.11.2.1.1 - William Coleman (1881 – 1955)

G4 1.11.2.2 - Isabel Coleman (- 1929)

G4 1.11.2.3 - Anne Coleman (1853 – 1887)

G4 1.11.2.4 - Edward Coleman (1856 – 1912)

G4 1.11.2.5 - Margaret Coleman (1857 – 1946) m. 1894 Benjamin Buckingham (1848 – 1906)

G3 1.11.3 - Sarah Hand (1822 – 1893)

G3 1.11.4 - Robert William (1823 – 1864)

G3 1.11.5 - Isabella (1825 – 1849)

G3 1.11.6 - William (1826 – 1861) m. 1855 Sue Ellen Habersham (1836 – 1892)

G4 1.11.6.1 - Robert Habersham (1856 – 1930) m. 1879 Lillie Clark (1853 – 1880), m. 1884 Edith Johnston (1858 – 1903)

G4 1.11.6.2 - Anne Caroline (1858 – 1934) m. 1880 Archibald Rogers (1852 – 1928)

G2 1.12 - Anne Caroline (1796 – 1819)

G2 2 1.13 - Harriet (1799 – 1810)

G2 1.14 - Sarah Hand (1802 – 1825)

Cornwall Ore Bank Ownership

"There, now, you have the story of Cornwall's ownership, and you had better paste it in your hat, for you may never get it straight again. I am sure I won't" – concluding remark by "Sinbad", author of an article published on March 24, 1886 in the Lancaster Intelligencer covering a history of the Cornwall Ore Banks ownership.

From	To	Date	Shares
Charles II	William Penn	1681	
William Penn	John, Thomas, Richard Penn	5/8/1732	
John, Thomas, Richard Penn	Joseph Turner	11/28/1737	
Joseph Turner	William Allen	11/29/1737	
William Allen	Peter Grubb	11/30/1737	
Peter Grubb	Curtis Grubb	1754	2/3
Peter Grubb	Peter Grubb	1754	1/3
Curtis Grubb	Peter Grubb, Jr	6/28/1783	1/6
Peter Grubb, Jr	Robert Coleman	5/9/1786	1/6
Robert Coleman	Peter Grubb, Jr	5/9/1786	
Peter Grubb, Jr	George Ege	5/1/1788	
George Ege Estate	G. D. B. Keim, et. Al	1837	
G. D. B. Keim, et. Al	James McCrea	1840	
James McCrea	Jas. Dundas	1844	
Jas. Dundas	H. P. Robeson	1845	
H. P. Robeson (Estate)	White, Ferguson & Co	1860	
White Ferguson & Co	Robesonia Iron Co, Ltd	3/7/1885	
Robesonia Iron Co, Ltd	Robesonia Iron Co	9/14/1923	
Robesonia Iron Co	Bethlehem-Cuba Iron Mines Co	8/15/1927	
Peter Grubb	Burd Grubb	1786	1/6
Peter Grubb	Henry Bates Grubb	1786	1/6
Burd Grubb	Henry Bates Grubb	5/4/1798	1/6
Henry Bates Grubb	Robert Coleman	5/12/1798	1/6
Henry Bates Grubb	Edward B. Grubb	6/13/1836	8/96
Henry Bates Grubb	Clement B. Grubb	6/13/1836	8/96
Edward B. Grubb	Henry B. Grubb	1867	2/96

Henry B. Grubb	Bethlehem Steel Co	5/1/1921	2/96
Edward B. Grubb	Charles Ross Grubb	1867	2/96
Charles Ross Grubb	Pennsylvania Steel Co	7/11/1901	2/96
Pennsylvania Steel Co	Bethlehem Steel Co	5/1/1921	2/96
Edward B. Grubb	Euphemia P. de Cerkez	1867	2/96
Euphemia P. de Cerkez	Pennsylvania Steel Co	1859	2/96
Pennsylvania Steel Co	Bethlehem Steel Co	5/1/1921	2/96
Edward B. Grubb	E. Burd Grubb	1867	2/96
E. Burd Grubb	Berkshire Iron Works		1/96
Berkshire Iron Works	E. J. Lavino & Co		1/96
E. J. Lavino & Co	Bethlehem Steel Co		1/96
E. Burd Grubb	Lebanon Blast Furnace Co		
	Richard Norris Estate		1/96
Richard Norris Estate	Bethlehem Steel Co		1/96
Clement B. Grubb	Charles B. and Daisy E. B. Grubb	1889	1 1/2 / 96
Clement B. Grubb	Daisy E. B. Grubb	1889	3 1/2 / 96
Clement B. Grubb	Mary L. G. Beale and Charles B. Grubb	1889	1 1/2 / 96
Clement B. Grubb	E. Jenny G. Smith and Daisy E. B. Grubb	1889	1 1/2 / 96
Charles B. and Daisy E. B. Grubb	Pennsylvania Steel Co	7/29/1902	1 1/2 / 96
Pennsylvania Steel Co	Bethlehem Steel Co	8/1/1918	1 1/2 / 96
Daisy E. B. Grubb	Pennsylvania Steel Co	7/29/1902	3 1/2 / 96
Pennsylvania Steel Co	Bethlehem Steel Co	8/1/1918	3 1/2 / 96
Mary L. G. Beale and Charles B. Grubb	Pennsylvania Steel Co	7/29/1902	1 1/2 / 96
Pennsylvania Steel Co	Bethlehem Steel Co	8/1/1918	1 1/2 / 96
E. Jenny G. Smith and Daisy E. B. Grubb portion	Pennsylvania Steel Co	7/29/1902	1 1/2 / 96
Pennsylvania Steel Co	Bethlehem Steel Co	8/1/1918	1 1/2 / 96
Curtis Grubb	Robert Coleman	9/12/1798	2/3

Robert Coleman	James Coleman	1825	20/96
Robert Coleman	Edward Coleman	1825	20/96
Robert Coleman	William Coleman	1825	20/96
Robert Coleman	Thomas Bird Coleman	1825	20/96
William Coleman	Thomas Bird Coleman	4/23/1828	20/96
Edward Coleman	James Coleman	4/23/1828	10/96
Edward Coleman	Thomas Bird Coleman	4/23/1828	10/96
James Coleman Heirs	Robert Coleman	1831	15/96
Robert Coleman	Rosalie Parrant Coleman	1878	15/96
Rosalie Parrant Coleman	James Coleman Drayton	1915	5/96
Rosalie Parrant Coleman	Ronald George de Reuter	1915	5/96
Rosalie Parrant Coleman	Camille Besson	1915	5/96
James Coleman Drayton	Bethlehem Steel Co	5/1/1921	5/96
Ronald George de Reuter	Bethlehem Steel Co	5/1/1921	5/96
Camille Besson	Bethlehem Steel Co	5/1/1921	5/96
James Coleman Heirs	George Dawson Coleman	1831	15/96
George Dawson Coleman	Heirs of George Dawson Coleman	1878	15/96
Heirs of George Dawson Coleman	Pennsylvania Steel Co	7/1/1901	15/96
Pennsylvania Steel Co	Bethlehem Steel Co	8/1/1918	15/96
Thomas Bird Coleman Heirs	Robert W. Coleman	1836	50/96
Robert W. Coleman	William Coleman	1836	25/96
William Coleman	Robert H. Coleman	1861	12 1/2 / 96
William Coleman	Anne Coleman Rogers	1861	12 1/2 / 96
Robert W. Coleman	Robert H. Coleman	1864	3 1/8 / 96
Robert W. Coleman	Anne Coleman Rogers	1864	3 1/8 / 96
Robert W. Coleman	Anne C. Alden	1864	6 1/4 / 96
Robert W. Coleman	Margaret C. Freeman	1864	6 1/4 / 96
Robert W. Coleman	Sarah H. Coleman	1864	6 1/4 / 96
Robert H. Coleman	Lackawanna Iron & Steel Co	6/1/1894	15 5/8 / 96

Lackawanna Iron & Steel Co	Bethlehem Steel Co	8/31/1917	15 5/8 / 96
Anne Coleman Rogers	Pennsylvania Steel Co	8/1/1902	15 5/8 / 96
Pennsylvania Steel Co	Bethlehem Steel Co	8/1/1918	15 5/8 / 96
Anne C. Alden	R. Percy Alden	1896	3 1/8 / 96
Anne C. Alden	Sarah H. A. Derby	1896	3 1/8 / 96
R. Percy Alden	Pennsylvania Steel Co	7/19/1906	3 1/8 /96
Sarah H. A. Derby	Pennsylvania Steel Co	8/22/1906	3 1/8 / 96
Pennsylvania Steel Co	Bethlehem Steel Co	8/1/1918	3 1/8 / 96
Pennsylvania Steel Co	Bethlehem Steel Co	8/1/1918	3 1/8 / 96
Sarah H. Coleman	William C. Freeman	1893	1 9/16 / 96
Sarah H. Coleman	Edward C. Freeman	1893	1 9/16 / 96
Sarah H. Coleman	Isabel C. Freeman	1893	1 9/16 / 96
Sarah H. Coleman	Margaret C. Buckingham	1893	1 9/16 / 96
Sarah H. Coleman Estate	Bethlehem Steel Co	1/8/1919	3 1/8 /96
Edward C. Freeman	Isabel C. Freeman	1912	25/32 / 96
Edward C. Freeman	Margaret C. Buckingham	1912	25/32 / 96
Isabel C. Freeman	Bethlehem Steel Co	1/8/1919	25/32 / 96
Margaret C. Buckingham	Bethlehem Steel Co	1/8/1919	25/32 / 96
Margaret C. Freeman	William C. Freeman	1894	1 9/16 / 96
Margaret C. Freeman	Edward C. Freeman	1894	1 9/16 / 96
Margaret C. Freeman	Isabel C. Freeman	1894	1 9/16 / 96
Margaret C. Freeman	Margaret C. Buckingham	1894	1 9/16 / 96
Margaret C. Freeman Estate	Bethlehem Steel Co	1/9/1919	4 11/16 / 96
William C. Freeman	William C. Freeman, Jr	1903	3 1/8 / 96
William C. Freeman, Jr	Pennsylvania Steel Co	12/2/1909	3 1/8 / 96
Pennsylvania Steel Co	Bethlehem Steel Co	8/1/1909	3 1/8 / 96

* The children of James Coleman inherited equal shares
in their father's holdings, as was the case for Thomas Bird

Coleman's children. In both cases, the sons purchased their sisters' shares.

Images

Figures 1. Robert Coleman and Ann Old Coleman by Jacob Eichholtz, c. 1820, Board of Trustees, National Gallery of Art, Washington, D. C.

Fig 2. Cornwall Plantation, c. 1803. Note, slag heap in center and ore pit on right (showing very little surface mining). Insert, Cornwall Ore Banks, 1873 (Elizabeth Opening upper right).

Figure 3. Cornwall Ore Banks Miners.

Figure 4. Martic Ironworks early 1800s, unknown painter, Landis Valley Village and Farm Museum, PHMC

Figure 5. Coleman Sisters by Sully (left) – Margaret, Isabel and Sarah. Board of Trustees, National Gallery of Art, Washington, D. C. Anna and Harriet Coleman (right) 1846 by Sully (privately owned).

Figure 6. Believed to be R. W. Coleman in front of Paymaster's
Office (left). William Coleman (right).

Figure 7. Sue Ellen Habersham, 17 years old (left). Anne Caroline Coleman, 1879 (right).

Figure 8. Mrs. Bradford Ripley Alden and her Children, 1852.
Robert Walter Weir, Detroit Institute of Arts.

Figure 9. North Lebanon Furnaces Drawing 1850s and George Dawson Coleman.

Figure 10. From top left and clockwise. Bird Coleman Furnace, North Cornwall Furnace, Colebrook after 1894 and North Lebanon workers during WWI.

Figure 11. Clockwise from top left. Elizabeth Furnace mansion, The Homestead, John Penn Brock rear and Bertram Dawson Coleman's mansion.

Figure 12. Clockwise from top left. Cornwall Manor, W. C. Freeman's home, proposed mansion for R. H. Coleman and Alden Villa.

Figure 13. The Faustian Players of Mt. Lebanon. Family
performance of Faust, the individuals are:

Top Row: Left to Right: (1) Charles Edward Ingersoll (2) Harriet
Coleman who married Henry Sheaf Glover (3) William Hunt (4)
William S. Carter (5) Marian Rawle who married first Thomas
Paton and second Giuseppi Bastinelli and (6) Fanny Coleman

Second Row (1) Alice Gibson who married Robert Coleman Hall
Brock (2) Henrietta (Rita) S. Sturgis who married Charles Ingersoll
(3) Julia Rush Biddle

Third Row: (1) Sidney W. Keith who married Mary C.
Catherwood (2) Christine W. Biddle (3) Robert Coleman Drayton
who married Henrietta Meigs (4) Mamie Thayer (5) Alexander
Krumbhaar (6) Thomas Robins who married Marie Ringgold
Naglee

Fourth Row: (1) B. Dawson Coleman (2) Linton Landreth (3)
Ringgold Lardner (4) William Elbert

Fifth Row: Heyward Drayton

Figure 14. Colemans and Freemans, 1879. Coleman and Freeman family members taken in Lancaster, PA after having driven from Cornwall "Four-in-Hand", July 29. 1879, pictured from left to right: Top Row, Uncle John Rae Habersham, Miss Edwards (visitor),

Robert H Coleman, William C Freeman, Middle Row Anne C Freeman, Sophie Montgomery (visitor), Lillie Clarke (first wife of Robert H Coleman, died 1880, Edith E Johnstone (second wife of RHC), Anne C Coleman, Bottom Row Edward C Freeman, Margaret C Freeman, Arthur Elliot (visitor)

Figure 15. Artemus Wilhelm

Figure 16. Rogers Family at Crumwold Hall, Hyde Park, NY.

Figure 17. Arthur Brock (left) and Horace Brock (right). American Iron and Steel Central Works, Lebanon PA (bottom).

Figure 18. Demolition of Bird Coleman Furnaces, 1922.

Figure 19. Margaret Buckingham (left) and Cornwall Iron Furnace, c. 1900 (right)

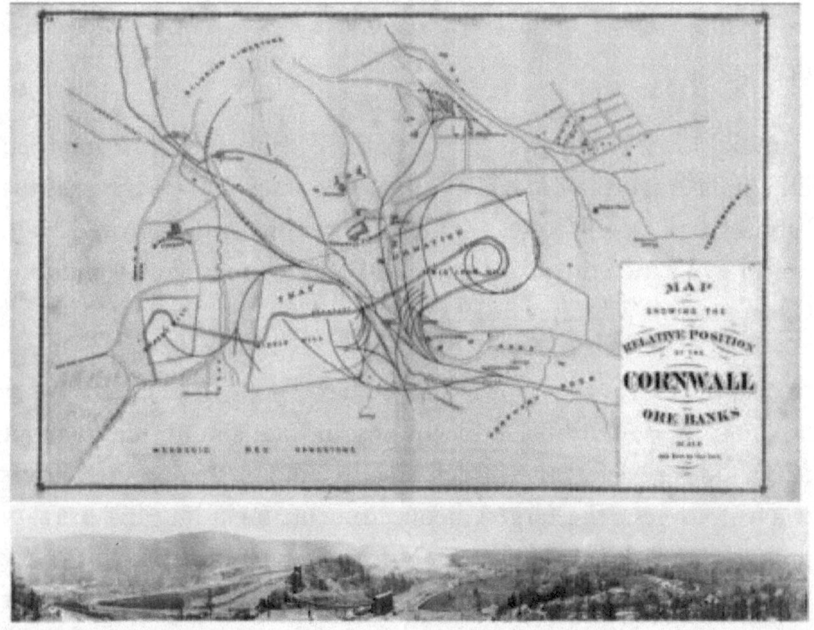

Figure 20. The vantage point is from the southern end of the ore pit between the Middle Hill and the Big Hill. The tall building in the center of the photo is still standing and is currently part of PRL Industries. To the left, or the west, are the Bird Coleman Furnaces and to the right is the Cornwall Mansion. The North Cornwall Furnace is in the center of the photo just north of the ore pit. A portion of the Cornwall Furnace is visible along the bottom right edge of the photo. The map marks off the areas of the Ore Pit which were mined and shows the numerous rails in the mines as well connecting the mines to the furnaces. Of particular note, is the spiral rail in the center of the Big Hill. The spiral railroad which would round the Big Hill to Number 4 mine is shown on the right side of the map.

Notes

<u>Prologue</u>

[1]James Lloyd Derby was married three times. He first married Ethelinda Augusta Morgan in 1914. His second marriage to Tersa Fabbri Clark Gesell, a great-granddaughter of Cornelius Vanderbilt, was in 1935 and ended in divorce in 1941. He married Gwendoline Constance McWhinney in 1943.

[2]In addition to the Cornwall property, Jack Alden left other holdings to each of his Derby cousins, in total amounting to about $200,000 for each. His will left smaller amounts to other relatives and employees. The largest bequeathment, including his primary property and all contents at 15 Sunset Avenue in Bronxville, New York, and his personal belongings, went to Dr. James Alexander Polson with the note, "who has long been my intimate friend". Polson passed away on October 3, 1950, and it is unknown what happened with the property following his death. Polson was survived by his wife and daughter. Homes at 11 Sunset Avenue and 17 Sunset Avenue have been recently listed at between $1,000,000 and $1,5000,000. It appears that 15 Sunset Avenue may have been absorbed by 17 Sunset Avenue.

<u>Chapter 1</u>

[1]How fair these negotiations were certainly can be debated. The Native Americans were paid, "20 brass kettles, 100 Stroudwater match coats of two yards each, 100 duffels, ditto 100 blankets, 100 yards of half-tick, 60 linen shirts, 20 hats, 6 made coats, 12 pairs shoes and buckles, 30 pairs stockings, 300 pounds gunpowder, 600 pounds lead, 20 fine guns, 12 gun locks, 50 tomahawks, 50 planting hoes, 125 knives, 60 pairs scissors, 100 tobacco tongs, 24 looking

glasses, 40 tobacco boxes, 1000 flints, 5 pounds paints, 24 dozen gartering, 6 dozen ribbons, 12 dozen rugs, 200 awl blades, 100 pounds of tobacco, 400 tobacco pipes, 200 gallons rum and 50 pounds money". The souvenir program published for Lebanon's 1940 Bicentennial celebration included a Historical Annals of Lebanon County and rather simple mindedly commented on the 1732 purchase, "The Indians gave up the land of their own free will, and for it received brass kettles, blankets, guns, shirts, flints, tobacco, rum, and many trinkets in which their simple hearts delighted".

[2]Records have been found with both Curtis Grubb and Curtis, Jr. spelled Curttis.

Chapter 2

[1]Wright, *The First Wall Street*

[2]Robert Coleman's brother William's will left 30 pounds each for the children of his sister Rebecca and for his sisters Ann, Mary, Suzannah, Faith, and Elizabeth. Most published accounts of Robert Coleman's life state that he had only four sisters (from his father's second marriage).

Coleman's ancestors, originally from England, were granted land in Ireland by Charles I in 1610 and for generations had done quite well, but harder times caught up with the family and by the time of Robert's birth much of the family wealth was gone, not so far gone, though, that Robert and his brother William were prevented from receiving a decent education.

[3]A report published by Joseph Livingston Delafield (The Pennsylvania Magazine of History and Biography, January 1912, The Historical Society of Pennsylvania), a descendant of the first Robert Coleman through the line of his son Edward, suggests that

Old did not approve of the union and that the couple eloped – an odd family story which goes against historical record. An announcement was published about the wedding conducted by the Rev. Thomas Barton at the Reading Furnace on October 4, 1773.

Chapter 3

[1]There is no record that I found in which a descendant of the Coleman families acknowledged the use of enslaved people on their plantations or in their furnaces and forges. Oral history exists that indicates there was an enslaved persons' graveyard on the property of Cornwall Manor, but no graves or headstones have ever been discovered.

[2]Samuel Rex owned a store a few miles north of Elizabeth Furnace and a slightly farther number of miles east of Cornwall Furnace. Both the Grubbs and the Colemans would often pay for their supplies in iron, which Rex would then take to Philadelphia and sell on the open market.

[3]Generally, during this period, steel was produced at a forge. Since Speedwell forge was owned by Old, it could have been that the steel was made at the forge but credited to Elizabeth Furnace. Robert Coleman did explicitly include the cost of puddling in his cost breakdown of making iron. The puddling process of stirring the molten iron was used to produce steel. The process often included two skilled workers, which may explain the cost Coleman listed.

[4]One of the cannons made at Cornwall, seemingly a poor cast, was found buried on the property and is now on display in the interpretation center at the Cornwall Iron Furnace, Pennsylvania State Museum.

[5]Peter III and Coleman had done business before in 1780. In 1779, Peter III had purchased much of Campbelltown, Pennsylvania, from Patrick Campbell, who had inherited the land when Patrick's brother John died. Peter III sold the land to Coleman at a profit.

[6]In the Coleman genealogy Elaine Ainsworth prepared, Peter Coleman is listed as dying young (in the same year as his birth, 1782). This is confusing because there was a portrait of Peter Coleman painted by Jacob Eichholtz c. 1810. This was one of nine profile portraits executed by Eichholtz of Coleman family members in 1810. There is no death record for Peter Coleman in the 1800s, and no burial site is known. A possible explanation that could make sense is that the portrait is of Robert, Jr., who died in 1811.

There is also a story regarding George. In the privately printed *Is This Your Son, George?*, the author claims to be descended from George, who in the official Coleman records is listed as unmarried when he died. The author claims George Coleman, who died in 1821, had married a domestic servant and fathered a son, William, in 1820. This marriage was purported to have been suppressed by the Coleman family. (It would be interesting, as a "wild" speculation, if the elopement Delafield (Chapter 2, Note 3) reported of Robert and Ann Coleman was that of George.) There are no formal records to support this proposal, but there was a Coleman family in Lebanon who named four of their children with the middle name "Dawson". This family is descended from William Coleman, born in 1820.

Chapter 4

[1]Mary Cassatt, born in 1844, was related to the York Cassatts. When Mary's family moved from western Pennsylvania in 1848, they purchased the Lancaster mansion, Hardwicke, previously owned by William Coleman. Hannah Cassat Coleman's father, David, was the

brother of Dennis Cassat, Mary Cassat's grandfather. The brothers married sisters from a family that their parents were close to, the Simpsons.

[2]In 1833, Buchanan purchased a home and property from Robert Coleman's sons William and Edward and Robert's widow, Ann Old Coleman, for $8,000. The Coleman family had multiple homes adjacent to each other off King Street in Lancaster. (*Bosom Friends*)

<u>Chapter 5</u>

[1]Despite the detail of the properties being partitioned, it was discovered in 1858 that there existed property in York County, Pennsylvania, of approximately 33 acres, which was still held in common by all living descendants of Robert Coleman. His grandson, also Robert Coleman, son of James Coleman, sued for partition of the land against all living primary descendants of the original Robert Coleman.

[2]An interesting association with these proceedings is that future descendants from both sides of the suit later married. Scott Huston, who descended from Isabella Lukens, married Meredith DuBarry, daughter of Joseph N DuBarry V. Joseph N DuBarry, III, married Ella Brock, the daughter of Arthur Brock and Sarah Coleman Brock. Their romance was described in the Lebanon Daily News on September 21, 1915, as "one of the oldest romances that society has known for many a day, one which the partners for life danced into each other's affections in many a brilliant ballroom".

[3]The Sully portrait of Anna and Harriet is in the possession of the Coleman family.

[4]Caroline Willing was from a wealthy Philadelphia family. Her grandfather, Thomas Willing, was a business partner with Robert Morris, involved in exports and imports. While initially not in favor of the war for independence, he eventually supported the cause, contributing five thousand pounds of his own funds. He served as the first President of the First Bank of the United States. Her father, Richard Willing, continued in the family business. He became the President of the Mutual Assurance Company of Philadelphia. Her niece, Ava Lowle Willing, was the first wife of John Jacob Astor IV, who famously died on the RMS Titanic in 1912. Their marriage had been an unhappy one. Ava had been described by some as cold and calculating - there were reports of her even calling her husband "stupid" in public. They were divorced in 1909. She married Thomas Lister, the 4th Baron Ribblesdale, in 1919.

[5]While Charlette Parker Rawle is the correct spelling for her name, internet searches often refer to her as Charlotte.

Chapter 6

[1]Robert Walter Weir named one of his sons Julian Alden Weir, a significant American Impressionist and one of the founders of the American Society of Artists and "The Ten". The younger Weir went by J. Alden Weir, honoring his godmother, Anne Alden, who sponsored his studies at the Ecole des Beaux-Arts in Paris. Robert Percy Alden, along with Elliot Roosevelt, Charles McKim, Stanford White, and others, attended Weir's bachelor dinner and marriage to Weir's first wife, Anna, in 1883. Alden and Weir remained close friends throughout their lives, and Alden left $2,5000 to one of Weir's daughters in his will.

Chapter 7

[1]There is an anecdote relayed by "Red" McDaniels in *Cornwall: The People and Culture of an Industrial Camelot 1890 – 1980* in which he describes the "dirt" from the North Lebanon Concentrator, "You talk about dirt from the concentrator! You couldn't sweep it off. You had to shovel the dirt off the pavement; that's how black it was. It all depended on the way the winds were blowing. If it was going towards your home, you had to put paper in your window sills so the dirt wouldn't come in your bedroom or any other room. ... It was real thick and dusty as heck".

When the hot-blast furnaces were first introduced, they used Anthracite coal as the fuel source. The Lebanon County furnaces were slow to introduce the use of coke. Iron heated with Anthracite produced a higher quality product than with coke, but as further experimentation continued, coke was introduced as a fuel source, often in combination with Anthracite.

[2]There is a statement made in *The Colemans: Lebanon's 'Royal Family'* regarding a Coleman family reunion held in 1994, "the ceremony [dedication of a Gazebo installed at Coleman Memorial Park in honor of Harriet Dawson Coleman Glover] witnessed a simple shaking of hands by Roger Alden Derby, of the Thomas Bird Coleman line, and LeRoy Glover Holman, of the G. Dawson Coleman line, thus ending a century-old feud between the two branches of the family". This is a statement of fiction. While it is true there were hard feelings between Robert W. Coleman and George Dawson Coleman resulting from the disputes over the amount of ore taken out of the Ore Banks, there were many accounts of harmony between the two branches. Robert Percy Alden attended weddings of George Dawson Coleman's children, and Anne C. Coleman wrote to her brother, Robert H. Coleman, that their mother was

entertaining the Brocks. In a letter from 1875, John Rae Habersham, Robert H. Coleman's uncle, writes that the Coleman cousins, Hattie and Sada (presumably Harriet and Sarah, George Dawson Coleman's daughters), rode down from North Lebanon in a "four-in-hand". Finally, the Brocks and Bertram Dawson Coleman, along with Bertram's brother, Edward, sat on the board of American Iron and Steel together with William C. Freeman, Jr.

[3]John Bezis-Selfa comments in *Forging America* on the prospects of iron workers in the late 1700s and early 1800s, but his observations still had value when discussing iron workers in the late 1800s. He notes, "Many ironworkers could never become truly independent, and they knew it. An increasing number of unskilled workers would never be their own bosses. Most tradesmen would always be employees; they had to redefine what they understood to be the appropriate relationship between manhood, industry, and independence to fit their lives. This kept them within the iron industry and proud of their craft".

Chapter 8

[1]Debbie Coleman, George Dawson Coleman's wife, began the North Lebanon Furnaces Sabbath School in 1856 for the furnace's workers and their families. This program expanded, and Debbie and George Dawson Coleman enrolled Harrisburg architect Luther M. Simon to design a chapel which would sit at the eastern end of the Mt. Lebanon estate. A cornerstone celebration took place on Sunday, August 28, 1870, and the completed chapel was dedicated on September 7, 1871. Originally, Christ Church was non-denominational, but by 1872, a request was made to be organized as a Presbyterian church.

[2]President Grant was a guest of George Dawson and Debbie Coleman at the Homestead, and the Colemans were guests at the White House on multiple occasions, including dinner at the White House when Grant's daughter, Nellie, married. Grant wrote a letter of introduction for Coleman, declaring Coleman "a warm personal friend of mine" and appointing Coleman as Commissioner of the United States for the Vienna Exposition of 1873. Grant's children and the Coleman children were also on friendly terms and exchanged letters and gifts. Grant gave appointments to individuals suggested by Coleman. Grant had to decline a request, stating, "I cannot very well appoint Biddle to Peru. Lebanon, PA has several foreign appointments while a number of states have none". Coleman was even rumored to have been considered for Secretary of the Interior, which elicited a satirical response regarding Coleman from Whitelaw Reid, "almost unknown except to a few Pennsylvanians!".

[3]The Colemans enjoyed creative family gatherings at Mt. Lebanon. There is a photo of the family and close friends dressed for a performance of Faust given by the "First and Only Appearance of the Talent's Company Lebanon Amateur Drawing Room". Invitations were sent announcing the performance in the "Garden". The character of Martha was played by Miss C. Biddle, and the chorus included Miss Julia Biddle, Miss Fanny Coleman, Miss Harriet Coleman, Mr. William Heyward Drayton, and Mr. Bertram Dawson Coleman.

They also held intimate "carnivals", setting up "booths" run by family members. This included such offerings as "Best Cakes" sponsored by Mrs. Arthur Brock, Music lessons on a second-hand banjo by Prof. Drayton, ice cream from Mr. and Mrs. Horace Brock, "SODA! SODA! SODA! The delicious beverage can be had fresh daily at the Famous Fountain of F Brown", photos at the gallery of Messrs.

A and H Brock and Miss Coleman whose work of ART were the admiration of all visitors at the "salon".

They also published funny poems among themselves. Samples included,

> "It is said that Julia Biddle's dress/From over the sea did come/And Worth promised it should harmonize/With bugle, fife and drum/But we think our Julia's beauty/Is not in her silk and lace/And we all should love her dearly/Though she had an ugly face"

> "Heyward Drayton the railroad king/Is making money in the ring/If in chorus he can't sing/He can lots of people bring"

> "Charles Brock is his name/Repartee made his fame/If you go to test his power/You will rue the evil hour"

> "Oh! Oh! Our own clever Harriet/Who drives the spike team and chute chariot/I suppose that you thought/Though you all of us caught/You'd go free, but your wit could not carry it"

Chapter 9

[1]There seems to have been a strain of mental illness that also manifested itself in his son's severe headaches and depression. Richard Derby, Jr., married Theodore Roosevelt's daughter Ethel. Derby grew up just a short distance from the Roosevelt home, Sagamore, in Oyster Bay. Ethel's brother, Kermit, met Derby while Dr. Derby was attending another of her brothers, Quentin. Kermit and Derby formed a fast friendship and, within weeks, introduced Derby to Ethel. The Roosevelt sons and Derby at one point invested

in a coffeehouse in New York City. Ethel announced the "wonderful engagement" to family and friends, and after they were married, Theodore Roosevelt confided in his daughter that he expected her and Derby to be the "happiest married couple" aside from his own with Ethel's mother. Derby had a personal income of $12,000 to $14,000 a year in addition to his medical practice.

Derby was descended from the Derby shipping empire, which originated in Salem, Massachusetts. Elias Haskett Derby, son of Captain Richard Derby, became one of Salem's leading patriots during the Revolutionary War as well as one of the more successful privateers, building a sizable fortune. One of his ships, Fame, a brigantine, carried sixteen guns and sailed with a hundred men. Following the war, Elias built up a sizable number of ships and spearheaded a very lucrative Asian trade with China, India, and other locations in East India. In 1787, his ship, the Grand Turk, returned to Salem with 500 chests of tea, 75 boxes of china, and assortments of clothing. He became America's first millionaire and ranks 72nd in the list of all-time richest Americans when the fortunes are set in current dollars.

[2]Robert H. Coleman and Lillie shared pet names. She was "Dove" and he was "Bird". In one love letter Lillie writes, "My dearest Bird, please accept the promised candy which I have just made for you and with it the compliment that you have entirely monopolized my thoughts since we parted and believe me I have been escorted by no gentleman before this Winter, who afforded me a more delightful time than your own self at the German last evening".

[3]According to Robert Powell, Thomas Ustick Walter was the architect who designed William C. Freeman, Sr.'s home in Cornwall. There are plans by Walter for the North Cornwall Manager's home,

but none have been discovered for Freeman's home. Walter did, though, do work on the family home in Washington D. C.

Walter was the architect chosen through a competition in 1850 to add an extension to the U. S. Capital building. From that point until his retirement in 1865, he was regarded as one of America's leading architects. He also founded the American Institute of Architects. Due to losses suffered in the 1870s, he was forced to return to work. He was unable to secure the major commissions he had previously enjoyed, but became second-in-command to John McArthur, Jr. on the building of the Philadelphia City Hall. McArthur was the lead architect for the Cornwall Manor Stable and the renovations to Sue Ellen Coleman's cottage. Both Walter and Powell were associated with MacArthur.

Freeman's mansion was razed in 1945.

[4]Lillie Coleman was laid to rest in a vault underneath the sanctuary of St. Luke's Episcopal Church in Lebanon, Pennsylvania. The Coleman families were generous supporters of the church. When Robert H. Coleman married Edith Johnstone, Lillie's casket was removed and interred at Laurel Hill Cemetery in Philadelphia, Pennsylvania.

[5]On a separate note, John Feitig had discovered a photo of what he believed may have been Robert H. Coleman's first mansion. The mansion pictured does not seem to match the construction records, and the architectural style does not resemble any of Powell's other buildings, and especially those executed around the same period. So, it seems that the elusive search for a photo of the first mansion remains unresolved.

Chapter 10

[1]Richard E. Noble put forward the theory that Robert Coleman was encouraged by Artemus Wilhelm to pursue an aggressive and risky path. Noble intimates that Wilhelm contributed to Robert's eventual reckless behavior. There really isn't any hard evidence for this suggestion. Wilhelm successfully watched over and protected the Coleman interests for decades. In fact, Wilhelm warned the other family of Robert's recklessness and questionable decisions. The full context of the letter Wilhelm wrote to Robert while he was still in college at Trinity was that he could spend the interest, but never touch the principal, advice that Robert clearly did not follow as he built his empire. Further, this advice was directly related to his spending while at college.

[2]The Lebanon Daily News was mostly biased in favor of Robert H. Coleman over William C. Freeman when covering the various disputes between the cousins. For example, when the paper reported on the "Railroad War" they stated, "The sympathy of the entire community is with him [Coleman], and condemnations of Mr. Freeman were severe". Coleman was at that time the largest employer in the county.

Chapter 11

[1]Aaron Wilhelm, originally from Easton, Pennsylvania, started the Wilhelm Paint Company with his brother, W. H. Wilhelm. He had one son, Charles W. Wilhelm. I have not been able to establish any blood relationship with Artemus Wilhelm, but after leaving the employ of the Coleman family in Cornwall, Artemus Wilhelm did write Robert H. Coleman a letter from York on Wilhelm Paint Company stationery.

[2]Hoffer would be found guilty of embezzling over 109,000 dollars from the First National Bank of Lebanon in 1896. He signed his confession on November 22nd of that year. He stole the money over six years to cover real estate losses he incurred related to an investment in the Modoc gold mine in Colorado.

<u>Chapter 12</u>

[1]The Robert H. Coleman stables, along with a farmhouse and farmland, passed to William C. Freeman, Jr.'s daughter, Isabel, and eventually to her children. Isabel married Theodore Clattenburg, an architect, and they had three children. Freeman's home and stables were sold to Thomas S. Quinn. Quinn descendants have since torn the stables down, but the mansion, as of the writing of this book, still stands.

[2]Archibald Rogers practiced reforestation on his estate and maintained a progressive agricultural program. This influenced Franklin Delano Roosevelt, who greatly admired his neighbor. Roosevelt held an emotional attachment to the family and the estate. When Roosevelt was Secretary of the Navy, he managed to secure a hull from a retired battleship, which became the base of the Rogers swimming pool. After Anne Rogers passed away, Roosevelt used Crumwold to house his Secret Service agents and even held some of his fireside chats there.

<u>Chapter 13</u>

[1]After leaving the employ of the Cornwall Iron Company, Andrew Brady moved to Emporium, Pennsylvania, where he purchased the Emporium Iron Furnace from the estate of E. H. Harriman. He later became involved with mining interests in the southwest United

States and Mexico. He retired from business in 1934 and lived in Williamsport, Pennsylvania until his death in 1949 at the age of 92.

Chapter 14

[1]W. W. Gibbs joined a new tube concern in Youngstown, Ohio, capitalized at $35,000,000. E. R. Chapman, Moore, and Schley of New York brokered the deal. Kenneth Schley married Anne Rogers, daughter of Anne and Archibald Rogers. Gibbs did not invest in companies for the long term but preferred to make short-term gains. By 1901, he was starting to show signs of financial strain, and by 1910, he was fairly wiped out. He died in 1925, basically penniless, in a North Philadelphia sanatorium.

[2]Charles Wilhelm purchased the property and converted it to a paint manufactory.

[3]H. H. Light left the board of American Iron and Steel in 1910, which made room for Bertram Dawson Coleman. It didn't take long for Light to return to the industry, being an original investor in the Lebanon Steel Foundry in December 1911. The Lebanon Steel Foundry was created through the vision and partnership of Thomas S. Quinn and William H. Worrilow. Quinn had at one time worked for American Iron and Steel, originally hired by J. H. Sternberg to work at the Reading plant (and then later transferred to the Lebanon plant). Quinn was the one to first approach Light to invest in the new company. The relationship between the partners and Light continued to strengthen as Quinn married Light's daughter Barbara Joyce in 1914 and Worrilow married Pauline Light in 1917.

[3]From the 1916 publication, *The American Iron & Steel Manufacturing Company: Lebanon's Great Iron Works* by Captain H. M. M. Richards, Treasurer, "In its factories it now makes an

almost endless variety of articles in iron and steel, such as machine bolts, carriage bolts, cotter and key bolts, joint bolts, patch bolts, plow bolts, stud bolts, special bolts and forgings of every description, clevises, nuts, either hot-pressed, cold punched, chamfered and trimmed, finished case-hardened or semi-finished, castle nuts, rivets for boilers, structural work or any other character, spikes of every variety, turnbuckles, washers, bolt ends, lag bolts, hanger bolts, screw spikes, tie rods, hook bolts, air-brake pins, knuckle pins, draw-head bolts, and brake-shoe keys, every species of pole line material, such as cross-arm braces, pole steps, pole straps, guy clamps, guy rods and insulator pins, and, in short, every metal article similar in character to those already enumerated". Richards was descended from Matthias Richards and Maria Salome Muhlenberg, the youngest child of Henry Melchoir Muhlenberg and Anna Maria Weiser, the daughter of Conrad Weiser.

Chapter 16

[1]The Lebanon Valley Conservancy (TLVC.org) has published numerous Heritage Trail maps for Lebanon County, Pennsylvania, including Cornwall and Lebanon City. The maps include buildings and sites that are part of the story of the Coleman families and the iron industry in Lebanon County.

Chapter Index

References

Ainsworth, Elaine, *From the Mists Over Furnace Hills: The Story of Robert and Ann Old Coleman and Their Descendants*, Privately Printed, Ed. Irvin Muritz

Balcerski, Thomas J., *Bosom Friends: The Intimate World of James Buchanan & William Rufus King*, Oxford University Press, University of Oxford, UK, 2019

Barton, Michael, Bronner, Simon J., *Images of America: Steelton*, Arcadia Publishing, 2008

Beck, John, *Never Before in History: The story of Scranton*, Greater Scranton Chamber of Commerce, Windsor Publications, Northridge, California, 1986

Bergman, Franklin K., *Robert Coleman 1748 – 1825*, Privately Printed

Bezis-Selfa, John, *Forging America: Ironworkers, Adventurers, and the Industrious Revolution*, Cornell University Press, Ithaca, New York, 2004

Binning, Arthur Cecil, *British Regulation of the Colonial Iron Industry*, University of Pennsylvania, Thesis in History, Philadelphia, Pennsylvania, 1933

Binning, Arthur Cecil, *Pennsylvania Iron Manufacture in the Eighteenth Century*, Pennsylvania Historical Commission, Volume IV, Harrisburg, 1938

Bitner, Jack, *Mt. Gretna: A Coleman Legacy*, Lebanon County Historic Society, Lebanon, Pennsylvania, 1995, Third Printing

Boyer, Charles, Donley, Robert, *Images of America: Cornwall*, Arcadia Publishing, Charlestown, South Carolina, 2011

Carmean, Edna J., *Lebanon County, Pennsylvania: A History*, Lebanon County Historic Society, Lebanon, Pennsylvania, 1976

Caroli, Betty Boyd, *The Roosevelt Women*, Basic Books, New York, New York, 1998

Cope, Gilbert, "The Grubb Family of Pennsylvania and Delaware", Daily Local News, 1893

Cotter, Arundel, *The Story of Bethlehem Steel*, The Moody Magazine and Book Company, New York, New York, 1916

Cowles, Virginia, *The Astors*, Alfred A. Knopf, New York, New York, 1979

Crumrine, Boyd, *Pennsylvania State Reports, Vol. CXXV, Containing Cases Adjudged in the Supreme Court of Pennsylvania*, Appeal of the Cornwall & Lebanon R. Co., Banks & Brothers Law Publishers, New York, 1889

Cummings, Hildegard, Fusscas, Larkin, Susan G., *J. Alden Weir, A Place of His Own*, The William Benton Museum of Art, The University of Connecticut, Storrs, 1991

Dibert, James A., *Iron, Independence and Inheritance: The Story of Curtis and Peter Grubb*, Cornwall Iron Associates, Inc., Cornwall, Pennsylvania, 2000

Diffenbach, Susan, "Cornwall Iron Furnace: Pennsylvania Trail of History Guide", Stackpole Books, Pennsylvania Historical Museum Commission, Mechanicsburg, Pennsylvania, 2003

D'Invilliers, Edward V., *The Cornwall Ore Mines, Lebanon County, Penna.*, American Institute of Mining Engineers, Author's Edition, 1886

Dolin, Eric Jay, *When America First Met China: An Exotic History of Tea, Drugs, and Money in the Age of Sail*, Liveright Publishing Corporation, New York, New York, 2012

Flibbert, Joseph, et al, *Salem: Cornerstones of a Historic City*, Commonwealth Editions, Carlisle, Massachusetts, 1999

Folsom, Burton W., Jr., *Urban Capitalists: Entrepreneurs and City Growth in Pennsylvania's Lackawanna and Lehigh Regions, 1800 – 1920*, The Johns Hopkins University Press, Baltimore, Maryland, 1981

Foster, John J., *The Circle L Story: A History of the Lebanon Steel Foundry, Lebanon, Pennsylvania*, Lebanon County Historical Society, Volume XV, No. 3, 1978

Gersh, Harry, *A Chapter in Labor History: Pennsylvania Joint Board 1933 – 1958*, Pennsylvania Joint Board, ACWA

Grittinger, Henry C., "The Iron Industries of Lebanon County", Lebanon County Historical Society, Vol. II, No. 1, February 20, 1901

Grittinger, Henry C., "Cornwall Furnace and The Cornwall Ore Banks or Mine Hills", Lebanon County Historical Society, Vol. III, No. 1, June 17, 1904

Grubb, David N., The Grubb Family of Grubb's Landing, Delaware: Descendants of John Grubb (1652 – 1708) from Stoke Climsland, Cornwall, Privately Printed, 2008

Hensel, W. U., "Old Elizabeth: Some Account of 'Baron' Stiegel and His Operations at Elizabeth; and Reminiscences of the Iron Masters who Succeeded Him", New Era Printing Company, Lancaster, Pennsylvania, 1913

Hessen, Robert, *Steel Titan: The Life of Charles M. Schwab*, Oxford University Press, New York, New York, 1975

Johnstone, William Clarkson, *The Johnston(e)s of Coastal South Carolina*, Privately print for the Johnstone Reunion, June, 1971

Klein, Philip Shriver, *The Lost Love of a Bachelor President*, The Aurand Press, Lancaster, Pennsylvania, 1955

Krawczynski, Keith, *William Henry Drayton: South Carolina Revolutionary Patriot*, Louisiana State University Press, Baton Rouge, Louisiana, 2001

Longacre, Mrs. James M., *Forges and Furnaces in the Province of Pennsylvania*, The Pennsylvania Society of the Colonial Dames of America, 1914

Lowrie, Sarah Dickson, *Strawberry Mansion*, Printed for the Committee of 1926 of Pennsylvania, 1941

Matthews, Nancy Mowll, *Mary Cassatt a Life*, Yale University Press, New Haven, Connecticut, 1994

Miller, Frederick K., "The Rise of an Iron Community: An Economic History of Lebanon County, Pennsylvania from 1740 to 1865", Lebanon County Historical Society, Lebanon, Pennsylvania, Vol. XII, No. 38, 1951

Noble, Richard E., *The Touch of Time: Robert Habersham Coleman 18956 – 1930*, Lebanon Historical Society, Volume 16, Number 1, Lebanon, Pennsylvania, 1983

Perfido Weiskopf Architects, Inc. / Noble Preservation Services, Inc., *Historic Structures Report, Cornwall Iron Furnace, Lebanon, PA*, prepared for The Pennsylvania Historic and Museum Commission, June 2008

Oblinger, Carl, *Cornwall: The People and Culture of an Industrial Camelot 1890 – 1980*, Pennsylvania Historical and Museum Commission, Harrisburg, Pennsylvania, 1984

Reutter, Mark, *Sparrows Point: Making Steel – The Rise and Ruin of American Industrial Might*, Summit Books, New York, New York, 1988

Rhinevault, Carney, Colonel Archibald Rogers and the Crumwold Estate, Privately Printed, 2003

Rhoads, Donald L., Jr., and Heilman, Robert H., *Railroads of Lebanon County: A Pictorial and Descriptive History*, Lebanon County Historical Society, Lebanon, Pennsylvania, 2000

Richards, Capt. H. M. M., "The American Iron & Steel Manufacturing Company: Lebanon's Great iron Works", Lebanon County Historical Society, Vol. VI, No. 17, Lebanon, Pennsylvania, 1916

Rinehart, Victoria E., *Portrait of Healing: Curing in the Woods*, North Country Books, Inc., Utica, New York, 2002

Rittner, Don, *The Legacy of Mount Ida: Troy New York's Historic Vista*, New Netherland Press, Schenectady, New York, 2016

Robesonia Iron Company, "One Hundred and Twenty-five years of Pig Iron Manufacture at Robesonia, Pennsylvania", Privately Printed, 1918

Roosevelt, Elliott, Ed., *F. D. R. His Personal Letters: Early Years*, Duell, Sloan and Pearce, New York, 1947

Rottenberg, Dan, *In the Kingdom of Coal: An American Family and the Rock That Changed the World*, Routledge, New York and London, 2003

Rudacille, Deborah, *Roots of Steel: Boom and Bust in an American Mill Town*, Pantheon Books, New York, New York, 2010

Ryan, Thomas R., Ed., *The Worlds of Jacob Eichholtz: Portrait Painter of the Early Republic*, Lancaster County Historical Society, Lancaster, Pennsylvania, 2003

Scott, Kenneth, Klaffky, Susan E., "A History of the Joseph Lloyd Manor House", Society for the Preservation of Long Island Antiquities, Setauket, Long Island, New York, 1976

Siegel, Irwin H., et al, *The Colemans: Lebanon's "Royal Family"*, Lebanon County Historical Society, 1996

Smith, Robert F., *Manufacturing Independence: Industrial Innovation in the American Revolution*, Westholme Publishing, LLC, Yardley, Pennsylvania, 2016

Stein, Susan R., Ed., *The Architecture of Richard Morris Hunt*, University of Chicago Press, Chicago, Illinois, 1986

Stoddard, Brooke C., *Steel: From Mine to Mill, The Metal That Made America*, Zenith Press, Minneapolis, Minnesota, 2015

Swank, James M., *Introduction to a History of Ironmaking and Coal Mining in Pennsylvania*, Privately Printed, 1878

Temin, Peter, *Iron and Steel in Nineteenth-Century America: An Economic Inquiry*, The M. I. T. Press, Massachusetts Institute of Technology, Cambridge, Massachusetts, 1964

Torchia, Robert Wilson, Chotner, Deborah, Miles, Ellen G., *American Paintings of the Nineteenth Century, Part II*, National Gallery of Art, Washington, D. C., Oxford University Press, New York, New York, 1998

Trump, Michael A., Wentzel, L. Susan, *The Communities of Cornwall Across Time: An Historic Tour, Bird Coleman, Cornwall Center, Minersvillage*, The Friends of Cornwall Iron Furnace and The Cornwall Historical Alliance, 2013

Trump, Michael A., Wentzel, L. Susan, *The Communities of Cornwall Across Time: An Historic Tour, Cornwall Manor, Grubb, Coleman, Freeman, Buckingham Estate*, The Friends of Cornwall Iron Furnace, 2015

Updike, John, *Buchanan Dying: A Play*, Stackpole Books, Mechanicsburg, Pennsylvania, 2000

Walsh, William David, *The Diffusion of Technological Change in the Pennsylvania Pig Iron Industry 1850 – 1870*, Arno Press, New York, New York, 1975

Weber, Michael, *Always More Production: The History of Mining Iron at Cornwall, Pennsylvania from 1737 until 1973*, 2021, unpublished

Wenger, Diane E., *A Country Storekeeper in Pennsylvania: Creating Economic Networks in Early America, 1790 – 1887*, The Pennsylvania State University Press, University Park, Pennsylvania, 2008

White, Samuel G., White Elizabeth, *Stanford White Architect*, Rizzoli International Publications, New York, New York, 2008

Wilhelm, A., *Muniments of Title of the Cornwall Estate*, Privately Printed for R. W. Coleman Heirs, 1872

Willing, Peter, *Private Journal of Anna Maria Coleman Parker May 30 to July 19, 1848*, Privately Printed, 2016

Wright, Robert E., *The First Wall Street: Chestnut Street, Philadelphia, & The Birth of American Finance*, University of Chicago Press, Chicago, Illinois, 2005

Zerr, Levi Hoffman, *The Cornwall Story: The Home That Faith Built*, The Story of the Methodist Church Home in Cornwall, Privately Printed, 1968

About the Author

The author grew up twenty miles north-east of Pittsburgh along the Allegheny River. As a young boy, he was fascinated by the steel mills which dotted the landscape up and down the "Three Rivers" for which Pittsburgh is famous. Later he spent over ten years working as a contractor for many steel and aluminum companies including Wheeling-Pittsburgh Steel, Dofasco Steel, Lukens Steel and Bethlehem Steel.

His interest in the history of Central Pennsylvania iron ore mining and iron manufacturing began when he purchased what had at one time been the Cornwall Company Store in Cornwall, Pennsylvania. He is a volunteer tour guide at the Cornwall Iron Furnace and a board member of the Friends of the Cornwall Iron Furnace.

About the Author

The author grew up twenty miles north-east of Pittsburgh along the Allegheny River. As a kid, he was fascinated by the steel mills which dotted the landscape up and down the "Three Rivers" for which Pittsburgh is famous. He spent over ten years working as a contractor for many steel and aluminum companies including Wheeling-Pittsburgh Steel, Dofasco Steel, Lukens Steel and Bethlehem Steel.

His interest in the history of Central Pennsylvania iron ore mining and iron making began when he purchased what had at one time been the Cornwall Company Store in Cornwall, Pennsylvania. He is a volunteer tour guide at the Cornwall Iron Furnace and a board member of the Friends of the Cornwall Iron Furnace. He resides on land once owned by one of the descendants of the once mighty iron empire.

9 7 9 8 9 8 5 7 9 9 8 1 1